*TWAYNE'S WORLD AUTHORS SERIES*
*A Survey of the World's Literature*


# GERMANY


Ulrich Weisstein, Indiana University
**EDITOR**




*Carl Zuckmayer*




TWAS 610

Carl Zuckmayer

*Courtesy of Wolfgang Isser*

# CARL ZUCKMAYER

## By SIEGFRIED MEWS

*University of North Carolina, Chapel Hill*

TWAYNE PUBLISHERS
A DIVISION OF G. K. HALL & CO., BOSTON

Published in 1981 by Twayne Publishers,
A Division of G. K. Hall & Co.
All Rights Reserved

Printed on permanent/durable acid-free paper and bound
in the United States of America

*First Printing*

**Library of Congress Cataloging in Publication Data**

Mews, Siegfried.
Carl Zuckmayer.

(Twayne's world authors series. Germany ; TWAS 610)
Bibliography: pp. 163–72
Includes index.
1. Zuckmayer, Carl, 1896–1977—Criticism and interpretation.
I. Series.
PT2653.U33Z77      832'.912      81–4859
ISBN 0–8057–6452–6      AACR2

# *Contents*

# About the Author

Siegfried Mews was born in Berlin, Germany, and studied History and English at the Universities of Halle in the German Democratic Republic and Hamburg in the Federal Republic of Germany. After the completion of his studies he was awarded an exchange scholarship to Southern Illinois University at Carbondale, where he taught German and resumed his studies in English (M.A., 1963). He received his Ph.D. in Comparative Literature from the University of Illinois at Urbana (1967) and has been employed as an Assistant, Associate, and Full Professor in the Department of Germanic Languages at the University of North Carolina at Chapel Hill since 1967. From 1968 to 1980 he served as Editor of the prestigious University of North Carolina Studies in the Germanic Languages and Literatures. His numerous publications in both domestic and foreign journals deal primarily with various aspects and authors of nineteenth and twentieth century German and comparative literature; apart from four books of explanatory, documentary, and interpretive texts on individual dramas by Bertolt Brecht and Carl Zuckmayer (published by Diesterweg), he edited two collections of essays: *Studies in German Literature of the Nineteenth and Twentieth Centuries. Festschrift for Frederic E. Coenen* (1970, 1972) and (with Herbert Knust) *Essays on Brecht: Theater and Politics* (1974, 1979).

# Preface

Although it would be virtually impossible to write a history of twentieth-century German literature without prominently mentioning the name of Carl Zuckmayer, the sad fact is that the writer in question is comparatively little known in the English-speaking countries in general and in the United States in particular. Hence there is a pronounced dearth of literature on Zuckmayer in English. Apart from several dissertations and a number of articles in scholarly journals, there is, at present, only one somewhat thorough introduction to that author's life and work available, Arnold Bauer's *Carl Zuckmayer* (1976). Significantly, Bauer's work is a translation of a book in German, originally published in 1970, and hence the author was unable to take into account the last decade or so of the writer's life. Moreover, the format of the series in which the original German version appeared did not lend itself to a thorough discussion of individual works. At any rate, Bauer's monograph may be productively supplemented by Zuckmayer's autobiography, published in the United States under the title *A Part of Myself* (1970), a work, incidentally, on which Bauer relies rather heavily.

In view of the lack of both substantial and easily accessible publications on Zuckmayer in English, this study seeks to redress, within the limitations imposed by the framework of the Twayne World Authors Series, the present state of affairs by providing an up-to-date, complete, and scholarly introduction to Zuckmayer's works. Since Zuckmayer's forte is the drama—surprisingly, the playwright occasionally expressed preference for his prose fiction—the plays will be discussed fairly extensively. At the same time, however, the prose fiction, poems, essays, autobiographical writings, and film-scripts will not be neglected altogether in order to counteract the tendency of Zuckmayer criticism to disregard the prose fiction and poems.

The works will be discussed in essentially chronological sequence. On account of the strong autobiographical strain in Zuckmayer's *oeuvre*, comparatively frequent reference is made to both the abridged English version of the autobiography *A Part of Myself* and the German original in *Werkausgabe in zehn Bänden 1920–1975* (1976). The use of the autobiography should not be construed as signifying uncritical acceptance of Zuckmayer's own interpretations; *A Part of Myself* is simply a major document that cannot be prudently ignored by anyone interested in the playwright.

A word about some matters of a technical nature is in order. All titles of plays, prose narratives, and other works by either Zuckmayer or other authors are given in English throughout—except when a character's name is involved (e.g., *Katharina Knie, Schinderhannes*). However, the index lists titles both in translation and in the German original. Likewise, all quotations are given in English. Unless specific reference is made to a published translation, the English rendition is mine. Zuckmayer's texts are quoted from the hitherto most complete edition of his works, the *Werkausgabe*. Since this edition is not all-inclusive, occasional reference is made to the *Gesammelte Werke* (1960) and other, separate editions of individual works. In order to facilitate access to bibliographical information, the following abbreviations have been used: *Gesammelte Werke (GW); A Part of Myself (PoM); Werkausgabe in zehn Bänden 1920–1975 (WA)*.

SIEGFRIED MEWS

*Chapel Hill, North Carolina*

# Acknowledgments

In a sense each author, however modest the scope of his work, benefits from the suggestions made and information provided by those who are familiar with the subject he is dealing with. The present book is no exception to the rule; there are a number of people who, in one way or another, contributed to this volume. Above all, I owe a debt of gratitude to the late Carl Zuckmayer who greatly facilitated my task by permitting me to spend some time in his private archives in Saas-Fee, Switzerland, in June 1973. Despite his ill health, the playwright and his wife, Alice Herdan-Zuckmayer, a writer in her own right, graciously welcomed me into their home and kindly and candidly responded to my queries. After my departure from Saas-Fee further communications had to be carried on by correspondence; Erika Heuberger, then Carl Zuckmayer's secretary, expeditiously answered my letters when the playwright was otherwise engaged.

Among the other persons to whom I am obliged for furnishing both published and unpublished materials, written and oral information or furthering my project in other ways, I should like to mention Harry Bergholz, University of North Carolina at Chapel Hill; Henry Glade, Manchester College in Indiana; Barbara Glauert, formerly of the S. Fischer Verlag; Jan Hans, Arbeitsstelle für Exilliteratur at the University of Hamburg; Walter Huder, Akademie der Künste in Berlin; Gerald P.R. Martin, Editor of the *Blätter der Carl-Zuckmayer-Gesellschaft* in Mainz; John M. Spalek, State University of New York at Albany; Ernst Schürer, Pennsylvania State University at University Park; the late Siegfried Sudhof, University of Bamberg; Ulrich Weisstein, Indiana University at Bloomington; and Harry Zohn, Brandeis University at Waltham, Massachusetts.

In the course of my research I either visited or received archival materials from several institutions such as the Deutsches Literaturarchiv in Marbach, the Leo Baeck Institute in New York City, the Manuscript Division of the Library of Congress, the Lilly Library at Indiana University at Bloomington, the Morris Library at Southern Illinois University at Carbondale, and the New York Public Library at Lincoln Center. Whenever I used any of these materials, mostly unpublished letters, I have properly acknowledged this fact in the notes.

Harcourt Brace Jovanovich has kindly granted permission to quote from the English translation of Carl Zuckmayer's *A Part of Myself: Portrait of an Epoch* (1970).

# Chronology

| | |
|---|---|
| 1896 | Carl Zuckmayer born on 27 December in Nackenheim, near Mainz. |
| 1900 | Family moves to Mainz. |
| 1903–1914 | Zuckmayer attends humanistic *Gymnasium* in Mainz. |
| 1914–1918 | Graduates from the *Gymnasium* and enlists as volunteer. Becomes lieutenant by the end of the war. |
| 1917 | First publication of poems in the weekly *Die Aktion*, edited by Franz Pfemfert. |
| 1918 | Member of the Workers' and Soldiers' Council in Mainz; member of the Revolutionary Students' Council at the University of Frankfurt on the Main. |
| 1918–1920 | Student at the Universities of Frankfurt and Heidelberg. Unsystematic study of a variety of disciplines. |
| 1919 | Contributes to the radical journal *Das Tribunal*, edited by Carlo Mierendorff. |
| 1920 | The play *Crossroads* opens in Berlin and folds after three performances. |
| 1922 | Travels to Norway. |
| 1922–1923 | Literary adviser *(Dramaturg)* for the municipal theaters in Kiel. Dismissed after a scandal resulting from the performance of Terence's *The Eunuch* in Zuckmayer's adaptation. |
| 1923 | First contacts with Bertolt Brecht in Munich. |
| 1924–1925 | Together with Brecht *Dramaturg* at Max Reinhardt's Deutsches Theater in Berlin. |
| 1925 | Premiere of *Pankraz Awakens* (one performance only). Marries the actress Alice Frank, born von Herdan. Premiere of *The Merry Vineyard* in Berlin. Awarded Kleist Prize for the play. |
| 1926 | First encounter with Gerhart Hauptmann. Acquires the Wiesmühl in Henndorf near Salzburg. Maintains residence in Berlin until 1933. Daughter Winnetou born. Publication of *The Tree*, a collection of poems. |
| 1927 | Premiere of *Schinderhannes* in Berlin. The collection *A Farmer from the Taunus and Other Stories*. |

1928 Premiere of *Katharina Knie* in Berlin.

1929 Premiere of the adaptation of Anderson and Stallings' *What Price Glory* under the title *Rivals* in Berlin. Receives Georg Büchner Prize and Dramatists' Prize of the Heidelberg Festival.

1930 Premiere of the play for children, *Cockadoo-Cockadoo*. Premiere of the film *The Blue Angel* in Berlin for which Zuckmayer wrote the script.

1931 Premiere of *The Captain of Köpenick* in Berlin. Premiere of Heinz Hilpert's and Zuckmayer's dramatization of Hemingway's *A Farewell to Arms* under the title *Kat* in Berlin.

1932 The prose narrative *The Monkey Wedding*.

1933 The serialization of *A Love Story* in *Berliner Illustrierte Zeitung* is suspended but resumed when Zuckmayer protests the action. Further performances of Zuckmayer's plays in Germany are prohibited.

1934 Premiere of *The Knave of Bergen* in Vienna. Premiere of *The Golden Toy*, Zuckmayer's adaptation of the Indian drama *Vasantasena*, in London. *A Love Story* and *The Knave of Bergen* are the last books by Zuckmayer to be published in the Third Reich. Residence in Austria.

1935– Frequent trips from Henndorf to London to work on screen-
1937 plays for films produced by Alexander Korda.

1936 The novel *Salwàre (The Moons Ride Over)* published in Vienna.

1938 Emigrates from Austria to Switzerland. Premiere of *Bellman* in Zurich. The prose narrative *Master of Life and Death* and the essay *Pro Domo* published in Stockholm.

1939 Deprived of German citizenship. Emigrates to the United States. Screenwriter in Hollywood.

1940 Conducts playwright class at the dramatic workshop of the New School for Social Research in New York. The autobiography *Second Wind* published in New York and London (1941).

1941 Rents Backwoods farm near Barnard, Vermont (until 1946). *Somewhere in France*, a collaborative effort with Fritz Kortner, performed in Washington, D.C.

1942 The essay "Appeal to the Living," prompted by the suicide of Stefan Zweig, published.

1945    The prose narrative *The Soul Brew* published in Stockholm.

1946    Official travels in Germany as a civilian employee of the United States War Department. Premiere of *The Devil's General* in Zurich.

1947    German premiere of *The Devil's General* (Hamburg and Frankfurt am Main). Zuckmayer participates in discussions about the play. Premiere of the German adaptation of John van Druten's *I Remember Mama* in Zurich.

1948    The prose narrative "The Walking Huts" and the essays *The Brothers Grimm* and "America is Different" are published. Receives Gutenberg Medal of the city of Mainz.

1949    Premiere of *Barbara Blomberg* in Constance.

1950    Premiere of *The Song of the Fiery Furnace* in Göttingen.

1951    Returns to United States. Resides alternately in Woodstock, Vermont, and Europe.

1952    Receives Goethe Prize of the city of Frankfurt. Is made honorary citizen of Nackenheim. Premiere of *Herbert Engelmann*, an adaptation of Gerhart Hauptmann's unfinished play, in Vienna. The prose narrative *Angela of Leuven* and the essay *The Long Walks* published.

1953    Premiere of *Ulla Winblad*, the second version of *Bellman*, in Göttingen.

1955    Premiere of *Cold Light* in Hamburg. Receives Great Cross of Merit of the Federal Republic.

1956    Receives honorary degree from Dartmouth College.

1957    Receives Literature Prize of the Rhenish Palatinate and honorary degree from the University of Bonn.

1958    Moves to Saas-Fee, Canton of Valais, Switzerland.

1959    The essay *An Approach to Schiller* and the prose narrative *Carnival Confession*.

1960    Receives Great Austrian State Prize. Collected Works in four volumes published by S. Fischer.

1961    Premiere of *The Clock Strikes One* in Vienna. Honorary citizen of Saas-Fee. *Dance of the Herons* published. Honorary citizen of Mainz.

1964    Premiere of *The Life of Horace A. W. Tabor* in Zurich.

1966    Autobiography *A Part of Myself*.

1967    Premiere of the one-act play *Dance of the Herons* in Zurich. Receives Order "Pour le mérite."

1969    *Memento*, an essay on the German resistance movement.

1970    *A Part of Myself* (English translation) published in New York and London.

1972    Receives Heinrich Heine Prize of the city of Düsseldorf. Founding of the Carl-Zuckmayer-Society.

1975    Premiere of *The Pied Piper* in Zurich.

1976    The ten-volume *Works* edition and *Appeal to the Living*, a collection of essays. Receives honorary degree from the University of Vermont.

1977    18 January, Zuckmayer dies at Visp, Canton of Valais, Switzerland. *Poems*.

1978    The early drama, *Pankraz Awakens*.

CHAPTER 1

# Literary Beginnings and Experiments

### I "A Look at the Rhine"

THE Rhineland, the great mill of nations, the wine-press of Europe! . . . all the whole mixed-up crowd that lived, brawled, drank, and sang . . . along the River Rhine! . . . the nations mixed like the waters from the springs and brooks and rivers that flow together in one great living stream. The Rhineland, that means: the West—That is natural nobility."[1]

These words are spoken by General Harras, the hero of one of Carl Zuckmayer's best-known dramas, *The Devil's General*. The drama itself was written during World War II when the playwright was living in Vermont, where he had found refuge after his flight from Nazi Germany and, later, Austria. Because these words were written in exile and because they are spoken by a character with whom the author strongly identified,[2] they belong among the dramatist's most convincing and sincere expressions of love for his home region—a declaration of love that transcends the specific purpose of refuting the absurd racial doctrines of the Nazis.

Like Dickens's London, Balzac's Paris, Fontane's Berlin, Joyce's Dublin, Kafka's Prague, Thomas Mann's Lübeck or, to leave the urban settings, Faulkner's Mississippi, Gotthelf's Emmental in Switzerland, Grass's Danzig and environs, Storm's Schleswig-Holstein, and Hauptmann's Silesia, the Rhine region, in which Zuckmayer spent his childhood and youth and to which he devoted an entire chapter of his autobiography,[3] provided vital impulses for his creative process. It is characteristic that, after Zuckmayer's reputation had been established, he took pains to point out that he was born and raised in the wine-growing area of Rhenish Hesse for which the ancient city of Mainz at the confluence of the rivers Rhine and

15

Main provided a focal point. According to Zuckmayer, this region is both fertile and austere. However, the austerity, one should hasten to add, is not necessarily reflected in the vivacious, life-affirming temperament of the region's inhabitants. Nevertheless, the landscape in which the writer grew up did not lend itself to romanticizing; it is, indeed, quite distinct from the "romantic" Rhine of popular songs and travel books (*PoM*, 98).

From the very beginning, Zuckmayer's native region plays a prominent role in his works. While in his first drama *Crossroads* (1920) the Rhine functions as the background for the shadowy happenings, the early short story, "The Vineyards near Nackenheim" provides a clearer indication of the artistic direction in which the writer was to proceed. It provides a realistic sketch of the small village in which Zuckmayer was born on 27 December 1896. In engaging in a kind of autobiographical writing and in focusing on a landscape and a people with whom he was intimately familiar, Zuckmayer, after a brief "experimental" phase, returned to his roots and employed strengths that were to sustain him in future years. In the masterful narrative "The Story of a Farmer from the Taunus," the main character derives his elemental force and unswerving determination from his native soil. Similarly, in such early poems as "The Land is Singing" and "The Fragrance of Wine," the praise of the land and its foremost product, wine, is couched in biblical language to indicate the poet's strong attachment to the region of his youth. Zuckmayer's first stage hit, the enormously successful comedy *The Merry Vineyard* (1925), was, in the truest sense of the word, "a love song to [his] homeland" (*PoM*, 297). Ironically, the play was resented by the playwright's fellow countrymen because they felt that he had carried authenticity too far in portraying the hometown folk. Zuckmayer's next drama, *Schinderhannes* (1927), again takes place in the vicinity of Mainz and in Mainz itself. In the prose narrative *Carnival Confession* (1959) the unraveling of a mysterious murder is set against the background of the famed Mainz Carnival.

The roots of the writer's attachment to his homeland reach deep. Not only does it provide the locale for several of his works but it genuinely and profoundly affects every aspect of his personality and every phase of his creativity. Far from indulging in narrow provincialism, regionalism, or nationalism, Zuckmayer combined the love for his homeland with openness toward the world at large. He felt it to be a special blessing "to be born by a stream and to grow up under the spell of a great river" because "rivers sustain the land and keep the earth in balance, . . . they connect the seas and make the network of communication within the continents. . . . It is along rivers that trade routes and languages meet. To be in the stream of things means to stand amid the fullness of life" (*PoM*, 99).

Such an attitude of openness enabled the writer to both preserve his ties with his native region and country and to adjust to an entirely different milieu—notably during his exile period in America. For *Heimat* ("home") is not merely to be conceived of as a geographic location determined by the accident of birth; an essential dimension of home is the intellectual and cultural climate that one must help shape. Thus Zuckmayer could talk about Germany in terms of its humanitarian mission rather than its political goals—a mission, needless to say, that was in complete contrast to that of the Nazis.[4] And he could cling to this idea of Germany while physically, emotionally, and intellectually coming to terms with his new home in the United States.

Even before the writer was forced into exile, first in Austria and then in America, the notion that it is man's inalienable right to have a home, a place where he belongs, is frequently to be encountered in Zuckmayer's work. The homeless cobbler Wilhelm Voigt in *The Captain of Köpenick* (1931), who is denied a place to live by the authorities, pleads despairingly: "But there must be *some* place a man belongs."[5] The same idea is expressed by old Knie, owner of a small circus in the play *Katharina Knie* (1928): "The main thing is that one knows where he belongs, with heart and lungs, liver and gall, and also with his head and his hands, and with his blood and toil, and pleasure and joy, and one's entire life."[6] Knie then continues to define the relationship between the place one belongs to and the outside world in quoting his grandfather: "Travel all over the world—but stay at home" (*WA*, 7:307). To some extent, these words can be applied to Zuckmayer's own life and works; while he traveled all over the world or, rather, lived far from home in the United States, the major works that originated during this period show the writer's emotional and intellectual involvement with the land of his birth. *The Devil's General* (1946), a sympathetic, non-accusatory portrayal of Nazi Germany during World War II, reflects the writer's deep concern about the fate and future of his homeland; the nostalgic tale *The Soul Brew* (1945) is an evocation of happy days in Henndorf near Salzburg before the *Anschluss* of 1938—"A Moment in Paradise."[7] Conversely, the author's serious efforts to come to grips with the phenomenon of the New World in works such as the essay "America is Different" (1948) and the dramas *Dance of the Herons* (1961) and *The Life of Horace A. W. Tabor* (1964)—both written after the playwright's permanent return to Europe—show that he had truly achieved the status of a citizen of the world. This status the playwright had once defined as "strong and loving determination [to opt] for the world."[8]

That Zuckmayer was able to combine "loyalty for the newly gained fatherland" with "continuing love and sympathy for the land of one's birth," as he put it in his essay on the Grimm brothers of fairy-tale renown,[9] must be attributed to the indelible stamp the Rhine region—both its landscape and its people—left upon the author's personality and work.

## II   *"I Had a Comrade"*

Zuckmayer claims: "I have not written a war book and have told no war stories. It seems to me impossible to communicate the experience, futile to attempt to reproduce the reality either in a transfigured, a heroic, or a critical way, or in the form of objective reportage" (*PoM*, 157). Although it is true that Zuckmayer never wrote anything even remotely resembling, for example, Erich Maria Remarque's *All Quiet on the Western Front*, World War I made a profound and lasting impression on him. In fact, apart from some youthful attempts at writing poetry and prose narratives,[10] it was the experience of World War I that stimulated the young writer's creativity. Barely eighteen years old at the outbreak of the war, Zuckmayer, together with most of his classmates at the Mainz *Gymnasium*, volunteered for the army. Initially, he had expressed his forebodings about the disastrous effects of war in poems such as "First" and "One Day" (*PoM*, 140–41). These poems were accepted for publication by the *Frankfurter Zeitung*. But almost immediately thereafter, when patriotic sentiments and national frenzy had seized large segments of the population, including the young poet himself, the poems were returned unpublished. The mood of euphoria and enthusiasm for Germany's just cause continued for some time. In a letter from the spring of 1915 the young volunteer expressed his hope for and belief in a general regeneration of Germany.[11] Soon, however, the initial enthusiasm waned; despite the fact that Zuckmayer unflinchingly carried out his duties as a common soldier and then as an officer, he gradually turned into an opponent of war. The poem "1917" (*WA*, 1:237–38) recaptures the dehumanizing effects of the prolonged slaughter that has turned human beings either into cynics or ferocious animals struggling for survival. But the poet himself did not yield to cynicism or despair. In two poems originally published under the title "Songs for Christmas" in the leftist magazine *Die Aktion* in 1917 (*WA*, 3:53–54) the prevailing mood is one of hope. Zuckmayer's basic optimism is also evident from two other poems written and published during the final phase of World War I.[12] The prose poem "Prelude"[13] concludes the first stage of the poet's artistic formulation of his war experiences. It is characteristic of Zuckmayer that in "Prelude" the despair resulting from the impending collapse of the old order, the Wilhelminian Empire, is mitigated by the vague hope for a new beginning, a new birth. Essentially, Zuckmayer's poetic utterances about the war are personal, subjective statements that lack specific references to concrete events. Only in the immediate post–World War I period, when the combatant had turned into a student at the universities of Frankfurt and Heidelberg (1918–1920), did Zuckmayer voice his disillusionment about the abortive German revolution that was not to accomplish the rejuvenation of Germany he had so fervently longed for.[14]

Zuckmayer's early poems provide but *one* clue to the impact of World War I. More revealing is the title of the chapter in his autobiography that is devoted to the years 1914–1918: "I Had a Comrade." The title is the first line of Ludwig Uhland's "Song of the Good Comrade," a text that originated during Germany's war of liberation against the Napoleonic armies from 1813 to 1815. Seen in the context of the song, the line evokes the spirit of comradeship and dedication to duty in the face of death. The extraordinary emphasis Zuckmayer places on loyalty and friendship emerges even more clearly when one considers the title of his autobiography in the original German. *Als wär's ein Stück von mir*, rendered into English by borrowing a phrase from Alexander Pope as *A Part of Myself*, is also a line from the "Song of the Good Comrade." In this line the speaker bemoans the irretrievable loss of his comrade whose memory will linger on forever. However, as the last stanza of the "Song" states, the loss of a good comrade does not result in insurmountable and incapacitating grief but rather in the will to fight and to live. Nietzsche, whom Zuckmayer quotes in this context, formulated such dedication to life rather more strongly: "*What doesn't kill me, makes me stronger*" (*PoM*, 158).

In the author's participation in World War I we may see, then, a factor that decisively shaped his notions concerning duty, loyalty, and friendship. That the writer adhered to these notions throughout his life is evidenced by two of his best-known plays, *The Captain of Köpenick* and *The Devil's General*. They reflect, to a considerable degree, the playwright's intimate knowledge of the military milieu but, more importantly, they also reveal his essentially positive attitude toward the soldier. Although in *The Captain of Köpenick*, for example, militarism or rather its external manifestation, the cult of the uniform, is at least implicitly condemned, the individual officers and soldiers appear in a comparatively positive light. Further, General Harras in *The Devil's General* seems to be, particularly in the beginning of the play, an extremely sympathetic character—despite his service for a regime about whose evil intentions he does not harbor any illusions.

While the two plays mentioned reflect the writer's experiences during World War I in a rather general way—the time of action in both plays either antedates or postdates the period from 1914 to 1918—in some prose narratives World War I provides the setting. Actually two wartime stories, the first and last pieces respectively in Zuckmayer's first collection of prose fiction, provide a kind of frame for the other narratives in the volume. As will be seen from our subsequent discussion of the early prose fiction, Zuckmayer did not write war stories in the traditional sense by either glorifying or condemning war and its assumed social and political causes. Thus, unlike Remarque, who dedicated his *All Quiet on the Western Front* to a generation destroyed by war, Zuckmayer conceived of himself and those of his comrades who had escaped the slaughter as having acquired a new lease on life and having gained "the freedom of thinking and of responsibility."[15] When life and freedom were threatened by the "chauvinist nihilism" of Hitler's followers in 1930, Zuckmayer raised his voice and, in the name of his fallen comrades, proclaimed his ideal of Germany as "the living heart of Europe that is open to all living things and through which run the connecting arteries of mutual understanding."[16]

## III   Crossroads

Although Zuckmayer briefly belonged to a Soldiers' Council and the Revolutionary Students' Council of the University of Frankfurt, he was not by any means a revolutionary in the strict sense of the word. Rather, he and many young men of his generation "who had escaped death in the war felt life as a powerful reality, a current carrying [them] forward. [They] were glad to throw the ballast of the past behind [themselves]. Away with it! A new age was dawning" (*PoM*, 183). Not politics but rather the theater, especially the Frankfurt Schauspielhaus with its performances in the expressionist style, captivated the budding dramatist's imagination. Zuckmayer himself participated in productions staged by lay actors, notably in those associated with the Heidelberg art historian Wilhelm Fraenger. Especially an evening devoted to the Swedish eighteenth-century poet and composer Carl Michael Bellman, "the Anacreon of Scandinavian rococo" (*PoM*, 202) provided materials for Zuckmayer's future dramatic production,[17] even while he was engaged in penning his first plays. Indicative of the mood of the postwar period is the plan for a drama on *Prometheus*, in which "the epilogue enjoined men to unite and overthrow all gods and altars, in order to establish their own kingdom of peace on earth" (*PoM*, 187). Characteristically, Zuckmayer did not write a drama on the *Spartacus* movement in post–World War I Germany that had been suggested to him. For the future playwright's enthusiasm for revolutionary action was tinged with "the horror of the unleashed masses" (*PoM*, 195). Moreover, Zuckmayer claims to have soon discovered that his "talents and . . . sensibility" did not point "toward the theater of political propaganda and proclamations" (*PoM*, 188) in the manner of Brecht and his followers.

Yet politics were all-pervasive. Zuckmayer's friendship with Carlo Mierendorff, to whose journal *Das Tribunal* he contributed, and Theodor Haubach stimulated the writer's continued interest in politics—a kind of politics, however, that was heavily "colored by the chiliastic faith in 'humanity' " (*PoM*, 209). Both Mierendorff and Haubach were actively engaged in the political realm; they eschewed radicalism in favor of joining the moderate Social Democratic party and ultimately perished in Nazi Germany. Zuckmayer, in memory of the "Season of Friendship" (*PoM*, 181–84) during his student days, later paid tribute to both men.[18]

A new phase in Zuckmayer's life and literary career began when he was called to Berlin where his drama *Crossroads* was being staged. The acceptance of his play by an important theatrical institution, the Staatliches Schauspielhaus, was attributable to a large extent to the efforts of Ludwig Berger, the author's fellow countryman from Mainz. Later, Zuckmayer was to extol Berger in addresses and essays—an indication both of his closeness to his home region and the importance he attributed to friendship. The premiere of *Crossroads*, a drama in four acts, on 10 December 1920, marked the twenty-three-year-old Zuckmayer's debut as a dramatist. Despite its historical setting, we may see in the drama a poetic expression of all the problems with which the author had to struggle during the postwar days in Frankfurt and Heidelberg. The play is infused with the awareness that the tide of human history is turning; after all the senseless slaughter of the immediate past there is hope that a new, just world without social privileges will be established.

The attempt to encompass too many problems in one drama may have contributed to its lack of cohesiveness. One of the reviewers of the play professed not to be able to reliably retell the plot, but then he continued that such retelling was entirely superfluous anyway. For, he argued, not what the characters did on stage was important but what erupted from within them, namely, their intense desire to be liberated from all forms of physical and spiritual oppression.[19] Not all critics took such a sanguine view of the lack of dramatic action in the conventional sense; the famous Alfred Kerr pronounced the play to be a hodgepodge of ethical, psychic, political, erotic, social, economic, religious, scientific, revolutionary, symbolic, and other assorted elements and caustically concluded: "All of this does not contain a single aspect of drama."[20]

In fact, the very difficulties in interpreting the play begin with its title. Although the literal translation of *Kreuzweg* as *Crossroads* is surely inadequate, even the more accurate rendering as *Ways of the Cross* does not solve all the problems. For it is not entirely clear whose way of the cross is depicted. Christa Kutter, a peasant's daughter, who is on stage at the play's beginning and at its end and who is also present in a significant number of scenes, would best seem to exemplify suffering and salvation.

The action, if the term is applicable here at all, centering around Christa—she is conceivably a female counterpart to Christ—begins with her encounter of the Brückenmann, the statue of a patron saint who has left his pedestal on the bridge leading across the Rhine. Despite the mentioning of the Rhine, a concrete geographical detail, Zuckmayer explicitly stated: "The play does not have any historical background" (*WA*, 7:7)—thus leaving the time and place of action purposefully vague. Vagueness and ambiguity are also one of the distinguishing traits of the encounter between Christa and the Brückenmann. It takes place at night when all contours become blurred and everything assumes a dreamlike quality. The Brückenmann has left his place on the bridge because of the general *Not* ("need," "want," "misery"). Actually, *Not* is a key concept of the play that encompasses both physical and spiritual suffering—none of which is ever clearly defined. Yet Christa seems predestined to alleviate the general suffering because of her purity and childlike innocence.

Christa's quest for a truly human being—"Is there no human being here?" she asks plaintively at the beginning and end of her encounter with Julle Rothendel, a creature resembling a demonic elemental spirit (*WA*, 7:14, 17)—comes to a temporary end when she is captured by Lenhart's servants. Lenhart vom Joch is, as his name indicates, a harsh lord and master whose peasants are suffering terribly under the yoke he has imposed on them. He is not only responsible for the material want in the appropriately named Spardorf, the village from which Christa hails, he also engages in the sexual exploitation, almost bordering on the sadistic, of the female population dependent on him. Christa, however, is spared the fate of becoming one of Lenhart's victims through the intercession of one of his concubines. The further stations of Christa's way of the cross are not depicted in terms of a logical progression toward a climax; rather, they reflect certain moods and states of the soul that elude precise analysis. To be sure, Christa's mystical task is vaguely defined after her return to her father's hut in act 2, scene 6—"to give love . . . and to suffer love"—but the inconsistencies abound. After Christa has promised her betrothed Heul (*heulen*, "to wail"), "I shall be your own" (*WA*, 7:51), she leaves him for the second time. Even her encounter with Hilario in a scene of great serenity (*WA*, 7:52–54), which holds the promise of a new dawn in general and personal fulfillment in particular, remains without further consequence. Despite her proclamation, "Love is alive" (*WA*, 7:70), she is ultimately responsible for Hilario's death. Christa undergoes her supreme test in act 3, scene 4 when she submits to the bestial advances of a creature named Spinnerich, so called because he both eats spiders (*Spinnen*) and is mentally retarded (*er spinnt*). In the end, Christa achieves peace and harmony in death. This death she depicts in language reminiscent of the ending of the second part of *Faust*. The play concludes on a note of optimism: Christa has presumably completed her mysterious mission and there is the implied hope that a regeneration will take place, that dawn will follow upon the night, and that all narrow, confining restrictions will be abolished.

Another major element of the plot, the peasants' uprising, seems to be more firmly rooted in historical reality—but only superficially so. What might have served as a vehicle for potent social criticism, the author turns into an abstract statement about unnatural oppressiveness that transcends the social realm. Just as Zuckmayer's preoccupation with love and sex foreshadows the unbridled zest for life in *The Merry Vineyard*, so the playwright's attitude of being "neither accuser nor judge"[21] provides an indication of his future stance.

Not surprisingly, the literary left resented the seeming desertion of the cause of revolution by a promising author who had belonged to their ranks: "At the crossroads between revolution and a literary career [Zuckmayer] opted for a career. He wrote a drama entitled *Crossroads* . . . that was penned by the cowardice of the bourgeois. . . . The revolution is misused as a romantic motif for poetry showing the hallmark of puberty."[22] True, the discontent and rebellious mood of the peasants in the play does not result in the formulation of concrete socioeconomic goals. Rather, individual peasants like Christian Kutter, Christa's father, adhere to somewhat mystical and vitalistic concepts that stress *Blut und Boden* ("blood and soil"), to use the slogan the Nazis were to popularize. Moreover, the peasants clearly lack leadership. The politically aware but anarchical Moder, whose name is derived from mold and decay, betrays the "peasants' savior" Hannes Böheim, whose message is faith, love, and patience. In the final analysis, the peasants take action only because their savior has been imprisoned by Lenhart. But the death of Lenhart and the seizure of his castle, the Joch, remain without tangible results and are overshadowed by Christa's death and transfiguration at the end of the play.

There can be little doubt that Zuckmayer's first drama is indebted to expressionism. Its central theme—the quest for man in the abstract—the dramatic structure in which the causal interrelationship between the individual scenes is missing, the lack of convincing psychological motivation, and the shadowy, ill-defined characters indicate that the playwright was following a contemporary trend. In addition, the employment of language that ranges from lyrics in various meters—some of which Zuckmayer subsequently included in his first collection of poetry—to ecstatic outcries consisting of one word or one short phrase is characteristic of expressionism.

Zuckmayer, incidentally, who later called the play "a muddled, chaotic affair, without a trace of theatrical technique" (*PoM*, 220), found the label "expressionism" unsatisfactory. He listed as "the influences at work . . . not so much the current German dramatists such as Unruh, Toller, Hasenclever, Kornfeld, Kaiser, and Sternheim [but rather] the gloriously eloquent plays of Paul Claudel, the secular 'prayers' of Francis Jammes, the animal paintings of Franz Marc . . . as well as . . . those mythic, earthy, lowly, universal characters created by Gerhart Hauptmann" (*PoM*, 220).

Both "mythic" and "earthy" characters are, indeed, to be found in Hauptmann's works, especially in the dramas *And Pippa Dances* and *The Sunken Bell* as well as in the novel *The Fool in Christ— Emanual Quint*. For example, in *And Pippa Dances* three characters—earthy old Huhn, young Hellriegel, and wise old Wann— endeavor to grasp and embrace what constitutes the modern myth with the help of elflike Pippa, the embodiment of imagination and beauty. In both their quest and their traits these characters resemble those of *Crossroads*. Further, it is also likely that elements of the peasants' uprising in Zuckmayer's play are derived from Hauptmann's drama *The Weavers* and his "tragedy" of the sixteenth-century peasants' war, *Florian Geyer*.[23] Next to Hauptmann Schiller with his Storm and Stress drama *The Robbers* should be mentioned—although his influence was presumably far less decisive.

But *Crossroads* is not merely derivative. To be sure, many critics praised Ludwig Berger's directing, the staging and acting rather than the play itself; but few failed to notice that *Crossroads* was the product of a genuinely talented playwright. It was Herbert Ihering in particular who discerned the direction that the writer was to take by emphasizing the "earthly" quality of the play: "The song of creative Earth resounds. The song of animals, of plants, of men is sung. God is not declamation, not a concept apart from that of man; God is not accusation, not approval. God is not something different. God is the elements, is animal, plant, man. God is creation. God is genesis."[24]

#### IV Pankraz Awakens

After the failure of *Crossroads*, published by the progressive Kurt Wolff in Munich in 1921, Zuckmayer embarked on another dramatic project, *The Anabaptists*. Although, as we may infer from a letter to his publisher,[25] he attempted to avoid the weaknesses of *Cross-*

*roads* and write a play that would also be understood by unsophisticated audiences, the drama *The Anabaptists*, which occupied Zuckmayer practically throughout the entire year of 1921, was never completed. "[It] was doomed by the subject matter," Zuckmayer wrote and continued: "But its wild prose scenes did have some trace of theatrical craft and language. Friends, actors and directors encouraged me, and I obstinately stuck [to] a task that seemed beyond my powers" (*PoM*, 229). We may gather from the early poem "The Anabaptists' Song of Assault" (*WA*, 3:34) that the play was not only rooted in the same period as *Crossroads*, the first half of the sixteenth century, but that it was similar to Zuckmayer's first drama in tone and mood by emphasizing the aspects of chiliasm and apocalypse rather than socioeconomic factors.

Berlin provided an exceedingly stimulating intellectual climate for the playwright. But "without money, without a job, without fame" (*PoM*, 227) Zuckmayer was forced to live in utterly reduced circumstances—an existence whose bohemianism provided but scant glamor. A turn for the better occurred when a Mainz acquaintance of Zuckmayer's offered him the position of *Dramaturg* ("literary adviser") at the municipal theaters in Kiel, a port city on the Baltic, for the 1922–1923 season. Before assuming his duties in Kiel Zuckmayer embarked on a voyage to Norway. It was to last several months and yielded the material for several short stories and poems.

In Kiel itself Zuckmayer enjoyed considerable freedom of expression and had ample opportunity to immerse himself in theatrical life. Dr. Kurt Elwenspoek, the general manager of the Kiel theaters, not only tolerated but actively supported Zuckmayer's innovative suggestions. Thus the moderns and their forerunners, dramas by Lenz, Büchner, Grabbe, Strindberg, Wedekind, Barlach, and Brecht (although Brecht's plays were not performed) were proposed for the program—hardly an orthodox theatrical fare for the stodgy, respectable audience of a provincial town with a strong, conservative naval tradition. Although Zuckmayer, in retrospect, may have exaggerated the importance of his Kiel theatrical experiments, we cannot but accept his and his friends' sincere, if youthfully exuberant goals that were still inspired by "chiliastic postwar ecstasy": "We enjoyed provocation and rebellion, and the sense of a mission. Starting from Kiel, we intended to renovate the theater, and starting from the theater, the world" (*PoM*, 255). The desired shock effect was achieved with devastating force when Zuckmayer adapted Terence's *The Eunuch*. As a consequence of the performance both the adaptor and his benefactor and protector, Elwenspoek, were summarily dismissed. The adaptation was replete with deliberate references to the phallus, an almost totally nude slave girl, and political parody couched in slang and aimed primarily at the revered old Field Marshal Hindenburg. In adapting contemporary events for a satirical purpose and in extolling the circus, carrousel, and country fair as sources for the revitalization of the theater,[26] Zuckmayer gradually began to abandon expressionism.

From Kiel the jobless playwright went to Munich, where he again was able to become affiliated with the theater—the Schauspielhaus under the direction of Hermine Körner. In the fall of 1923 Zuckmayer met Brecht, whose play *In the Jungle* had been performed at the Munich Residenztheater in the spring of the same year. Zuckmayer fell temporarily under Brecht's spell and wrote his second full-length play, *Kiktahan or The Backwoodsmen*, later performed under the title *Pankraz Awakens*. In one laconic sentence Zuckmayer draws attention to the creative impulses transmitted by Brecht: "Brecht thought it [*Kiktahan*] was good—it was the only play I wrote under his influence" (*PoM*, 273).

*Kiktahan* lacks the intensity and obscurity of *Crossroads*. Yet the play is not without complexity. A brief plot summary may provide an indication as to the problems facing the interpreter.[27] The settler Pankraz, a former pirate and uxoricide, lives in a log cabin in the Far West at the turn of the century. He feels an incestuous desire for his younger daughter Alit. Alit, after having spent a night with the Indian Teton, seems to respond to Pankraz's advances. But the ex-pirate's older daughter Judith, possibly motivated by jealousy, interferes. Later, when Alit joins Pankraz in a woodshed, the latter inexplicably kills her with an ax. Then Teton, the Indian, is murdered by a European outcast who pretends to be a priest. The false priest in turn is sentenced to die by a hastily assembled jury. Before he is hanged the condemned man assumes the responsibility for the murder of Alit for no obvious reasons. In the typescript version Pankraz is killed by the Negro Kongo; in the actual performance of the play, however, Pankraz apparently survived and began devoting his attentions to his older daughter.

At first glance, there seem to be no compelling similarities between *Kiktahan* and any of Brecht's works. Yet on closer scrutiny a remarkable number of parallels emerge between Zuckmayer's play and Brecht's *In the Jungle*, the first version of *In the Jungle of Cities*.

Exoticism and sensationalism such as murder, sex, and violence—
closely related to the depiction of an American milieu—the similarities between a number of scenes, and the theme of man's isolation
are aspects testifying to the kinship of the two plays in question.
Further, the occasionally aphoristic quality of the dialogue, the use
of songs and ballads, the vitalistic concept of the strong man, in part
derived from Kipling, and the predilection for the carefree and
antibourgeois life of adventurers in general and pirates in particular
relate *Kiktahan* to *In the Jungle*. The close affinity between the two
playwrights in Munich and during their common tenure at Max
Reinhardt's Deutsches Theater in Berlin (1924–1925) is also attested
to by their concept of the "natural cycle of becoming and passing
away" to which all living organisms are subject—a concept with
which Brecht's *Baal* and early poems are particularly strongly infused.[28]

When *Kiktahan*, now entitled *Pankraz Awakens*, was performed
by the experimental Junge Bühne in Berlin on 15 February 1925—
the planned production of Zuckmayer's play in the regular program
of the Deutsches Theater did not materialize—such perceptive critics as Herbert Ihering immediately noted Zuckmayer's dependence
on Brecht. At this time, Brecht was far from being universally recognized. In fact, the first Berlin performance of one of his plays, *In
the Jungle*, had only taken place on 29 October 1924. Hence not all
critics considered Brecht's influence on Zuckmayer a salutary one.[29]
But more to the point than the wholesale condemnation of the
younger dramatists by some reviewers was Ihering's sage observation about the difference between Zuckmayer and Brecht. While
Brecht, he noted, rarely succumbed to "exoticism as a romantic
evasion,"[30] Zuckmayer tended to engage in escapism. Without
doubt, Zuckmayer's escapist tendencies were enhanced by two literary models who were instrumental in shaping his view of the New
World in general and providing the pattern for the setting and some
characters and motifs in particular. These literary models were Karl
May, the most popular promulgator of fictional lore about the Wild
West in the German-speaking countries, and James Fenimore
Cooper.[31] Especially the influence of Karl May was to extend far
beyond Zuckmayer's experimental period that essentially came to
an end with the failure of *Pankraz Awakens*.

The playwright, who was nearly thirty years old and had yet to
achieve success and recognition, realized that "the piece was uneven
and murky, sketchy in plot, badly organized" (*PoM*, 279). Unlike

Brecht, he had "neither the gift nor the wish to inaugurate a new epoch in literature, a new theatrical style, a new artistic direction." Instead, he writes, "I wanted to reach out to nature, life, the truth without divorcing myself from the demands of the hour, the burning questions of my own time" (*PoM*, 279–80).

Zuckmayer's new orientation resulted in an artistic parting of the ways with Brecht, although personally amiable contacts between the two men continued. The new outlook on theater and life was partially shaped by Zuckmayer's participation in Max Reinhardt's rehearsals for Shaw's *Saint Joan*, a play that provided a new mode of presenting historical events on stage, and Pirandello's *Six Characters in Search of an Author*, a drama that likewise signified a departure from the traditional illusionist stage.

The playwright's "sense of theater" (*PoM*, 277), which he developed through enthusiastic participation in rehearsals and similar activities, is not totally absent in *Pankraz Awakens*, however. Although the play exhibits a certain affinity with *Crossroads*, especially in the depiction of the chaotic struggle in Pankraz's soul and his semiconscious striving for salvation, it also shows elements of realism that were largely missing in the former play. Above all, the raucous, boisterous drinking scenes and songs foreshadow the uninhibited enjoyment of life with which *The Merry Vineyard* is imbued. Again it was Herbert Ihering who predicted the course of Zuckmayer's future development in his review of *Pankraz Awakens* by designating him a prospective writer of comedies.[32]

## V  *Early Poetry and Prose Fiction*

Zuckmayer's new artistic orientation, his striving for "a new vitality in effects and in values" by means of "a kind of humane art that can never be outmoded as long as human beings think of themselves as what they are" (*PoM*, 279–80) is reflected to some extent in the poems and prose narratives from the early and middle twenties. For the most part, the poems originated before *The Merry Vineyard;* however, they were not published until after the play's hugely successful premiere. The early poems are essentially accessible in two collections. The slender volume entitled *The Tree* was published in 1926, while the collection "Leaves" did not appear until after World War II.[33]

Precisely because the poet shunned artistic experiments, there is some justification to his claim that he had found his unmistakable "own tone" (*PoM*, 280).[34] Above all, in *The Tree* life as a natural phenomenon is celebrated in its many manifestations, but particularly in that of animals—from small reptiles to horses and cattle. It is interesting to note that, in retrospect, Zuckmayer claimed his poetic independence by taking issue with his erstwhile companion, Bertolt Brecht.[35] In particular, he rejected the two following lines in Brecht's famous autobiographical poem "Of Poor B.B.": "In the grey light before morning the pine trees piss / And their vermin, the birds, raise their twitter and cheep."[36] Zuckmayer professed his inability to associate the life-giving morning dew in the forest with human excretion and to conceive of birds as vermin. To be sure, he does not indulge in a romantic or sentimental view of nature but bases his concept on scientific observation; in this instance on the fact that the birds of the forest do, indeed, perform a useful function by eating small parasites on trees. Hence they cannot be called "vermin" by any stretch of the imagination, Zuckmayer argues. Regardless of Brecht and Zuckmayer's differing poetic sensibilities and concepts of nature, two observations are in order. First, as Zuckmayer acknowledges, the nature imagery employed by Brecht is essentially that of the modern city-dweller who has an acute sense of impending social catastrophes and who is no longer capable of finding solace in nature. Conversely, the realm of the big city, a dominant topic in the poetry of German naturalism and expressionism, is conspicuously absent in *The Tree*. In fact, in the poem "Praise of the Sparrows" (*WA*, 3:23), the uncomplicated and contented existence of the sparrows is favorably contrasted to the hectic tempo of the modern industrial world.

Second, if Zuckmayer emphasizes the differences between his view of nature and that of Brecht, he does not take into account their similarities. It should be remembered that "Of Poor B.B." originated in 1922 but was not published until 1927 in *Manual of Piety*. Still, the poem constitutes a kind of "sum of all of [Brecht's] experiences in Augsburg and, at the same time, the prologue of a new phase in his life."[37] Among Brecht's earlier lyrics, however, there are several that decidedly show some correspondence to Zuckmayer's view of nature. Such poems as "Birth in the Tree,"[38] which originated in 1920, and "On the Death in the Forest,"[39] which is included in Brecht's first drama *Baal*, express the idea of new life springing from decaying corpses whose decomposition prepares the soil for the eternal natural cycle of death and rebirth. This idea is most conspicuously demonstrated in trees—which are rooted in the earth yet reaching toward sky and heaven. Even in Brecht's *Baal* and his "Grand Hymn of Thanksgiving,"[40] both of which run counter to the Christian ethic of salvation, Zuckmayer found the "choral heaven [that is] by no means to be understood merely as a physical phenomenon. Rather, it is a contrapuntal countervoice to death and nemesis" (*PoM*, 268). Significantly, the title poem of Zuckmayer's first published collection shows growth and decay, life and death of a tree, its origin in a swamp, its struggle for survival, and its eventual return to the swamps. The lack of the life-death antithesis points toward Zuckmayer's life-affirming views, which, ultimately, rest on a religious foundation. For Zuckmayer the divine order manifests itself in nature. Hence living in harmony with nature amounts to being in a state of divine grace. Yet the poet's use of unorthodox images that combined the profane and the sacred re-sulted in a charge of blasphemy—despite the religious ethic of many of his poems—of which he was eventually acquitted.[41]

It is not surprising that a poet who is concerned with the wide spectrum of natural phenomena and the origin of life should pay poetic tribute to his own origins—the region of Rhenish Hesse that provided him with sustenance and stimulated his creativity. We do find such praise, for instance, in "The Fragrance of Wine" (*WA*, 3:16–17) and even more so in "The Land is Singing" (*WA*, 3:43).

Here the home region is declared to be the poet's "beginning and end." Zuckmayer's almost mystical belief in the regenerative powers of the soil and of nature make it understandable that he, unlike Brecht, rarely addresses himself to man in his social milieu. As was mentioned earlier, there are only a few poems that resulted from the despair of the last phase of World War I and the ultimately illusory hope for social justice and spiritual regeneration in the im-mediate postwar era. Thus the collection *The Tree* concludes with an unabashedly optimistic poem that proclaims in nondidactic fash-ion "how beautiful life is" (*WA*, 3:48).

The eight stories in the collection *A Farmer from the Taunus and Other Stories* (1927) reflect Zuckmayer's essential affirmation of life. In "Story of a Pond" the small creatures inhabiting the pond fight for survival in the course of the seasons. The story does, indeed, demonstrate "the love of a young writer for all creatures" rather than exact "zoological knowledge" (*WA*, 4:35); but more importantly, the struggle and fight for survival, which Zuckmayer depicts in metaphors derived from war, are accepted as integral parts of life. Even in "A Few Lumps of Earth," one of the earliest artistic expressions of Zuckmayer's lifelong infatuation with the New World, the futile struggle of the protagonist for his piece of land does not result in tragedy. For George Black's corpse serves as refuge, nourishment, and place of procreation for insects and other small animals. Thus the natural cycle has been reestablished and life has emerged victorious—despite the sacrifice of an individual.

Zuckmayer's celebration of life is not devoid of aspects that might offend the squeamish reader, yet the writer never engages in the depiction of lurid details for the sake of either sensationalism or morbid curiosity. To be sure, such tales as "The Story of Bal, Governor of the Lapps" are full of seemingly gratuitous violence. In this particular instance, however, Zuckmayer was able to defend himself against the charge of having indulged in "excessive youthful imagination" by claiming to have retold an old legend that he had heard during his sojourn in Norway (cf. WA, 4:124). At any rate, in his best stories Zuckmayer clearly succeeds in formulating his life-affirming and humanitarian ethos despite his unadulterated view and unabashed depiction of such elemental facts as birth and death. In the two narratives "Story of a Birth" and "The Story of a Farmer from the Taunus," war serves merely as a somber background of annihilation and death against which the life-asserting forces, symbolized in each case by children conceived and born by men and women belonging to nations at war with each other, prevail. Particularly in the ending of the narrative about the farmer Zuckmayer succeeds in suggesting the close and wholesome symbiosis between man and nature. Just as the recently plowed soil, "the bare flesh of the earth" (WA, 4:160), receives the fertility-imparting rays of the sun in a quasi-sexual embrace, the farmer's wife receives her husband and his child by another woman—both husband and child have miraculously survived the chaotic end of the war—openly and unquestioningly.

It is hardly surprising that, because of Zuckmayer's new orientation, the political and social upheavals of the post–World War I period play a comparatively inconspicuous role in the collection of prose narratives. However, in "The Story of a Farmer from the Taunus" there is a sympathetic, if, as one Marxist critic argues, romanticized portrayal of the Soviet Union.[42] Yet there can be little doubt that Zuckmayer is ultimately not concerned with the portrayal of societal conditions but with the fate of his protagonist, Seuffert. An old and wise former rabbi, who has now joined the Cossacks in the Red Army, declares Seuffert to be a saintly man who carries "the seed of life that makes fertile the fields of mankind" (*WA*, 4:159). Indeed, Seuffert's single-minded, compulsive, and almost monomaniacal attempt to rescue his child in the face of enormous obstacles contributes to the aura of providential guidance that pervades the story. For Seuffert's "fate has been decreed; it is inescapable. He must endure the harrowing ordeal of violent combat; he must fight his way through the most extreme physical dangers, the most intense mental trials to which life can expose the individual . . ."[43] in order to reach his goal.

Once more the writer returned to the war in a short story. In "Angela of Leuven," strictly speaking, a piece from Zuckmayer's exile period,[44] the true love of two pure and innocent human beings, a girl from German-occupied Belgium and a German officer, overcomes all the obstacles the hatred and vindictiveness of those in the hinterland of the Western Front put in their way. Once again this story is an affirmation of Zuckmayer's belief in the sanctity of life and the possibility of reconciliation between individual members of nations at war because, significantly, it is a group of Belgian combat soldiers who rescue the lovers from the hands of an angry mob in "Angela." Despite Zuckmayer's general condemnation of war, he viewed the combat soldier—quite in contrast to the noncombatant in the military—in a predominantly positive light. On him, Zuckmayer believed, rested the hopes and future of the nation.

While the experiences Zuckmayer had undergone during World War I clearly provided a vital stimulus for his writing, there is one sketch in the present collection, entitled "The Vineyards near Nackenheim," which is indicative of the direction the writer was going to follow. The sketchy, but realistic depiction of the milieu, customs, dialect of his home town, and above all, the praise of the ubiquitous vineyards, are the ingredients that were also to be found in Zuckmayer's first major stage hit, the folk play *The Merry Vineyard*, in which *joie de vivre* asserts itself fully without the admixture of death and destruction.

## CHAPTER 2

# The Folk Plays and Adaptations

## I The Merry Vineyard

"SIC transit gloria expressionismi" ("thus vanishes the glory of expressionism"),[1] wrote Alfred Kerr in his review of *The Merry Vineyard*, whose premiere took place in Berlin on 22 December 1925. Unlike the abortive performances of *Crossroads* and *Pankraz Awakens*, the opening of Zuckmayer's third full-length play was an almost totally unmitigated success—both in terms of its reception by the critics and that accorded to it by the Berlin audience. Kerr's aphoristic formulation summarizes the play's significance in terms of literary history, and, at the same time, provides a partial explanation for its immediate popularity, which is attested to by the fact that the play ran for two and a half years in Berlin alone; in addition, the play was produced at most stages outside Berlin.

There was unanimity among the Berlin critics that *The Merry Vineyard* represented a wholesome departure from the feverish atmosphere, violent antibourgeois sentiments, and plots centering around wars and revolutions to be encountered in expressionist dramas.[2] The drama critic Paul Fechter who, in 1925, was responsible for awarding the prestigious Kleist Prize, noted in his citation that Zuckmayer had responded to one of the most urgent demands of the contemporary stage by achieving the "breakthrough to reality."[3]

Both the setting, Zuckmayer's home region of Rhenish Hesse, and the contemporary time of action (1921) point toward the playwright's realistic intent. He no longer indulged in the penchant for remote eras and faraway, exotic places that he had previously displayed but firmly rooted *The Merry Vineyard* in his native soil nd based his characters on the people he knew best. The employment of native dialect contributed to the authenticity of the milieu. Yet the realistic milieu depiction and character portrayal were not designed to revive the naturalism of yesteryear; rather, Zuckmayer availed himself of time-honored comedy traditions to induce laughter and create merriment.

The play begins in a startling way, the rather unconventional condition that the vineyard owner Gunderloch imposes upon the prospective bridegroom of his daughter Klärchen. Gunderloch demands that Knuzius, who in his student days belonged to a dueling fraternity, prove his virility by putting Klärchen in the family way before the marriage contract is drawn up. However, in Gunderloch's view the premarital sexual intercourse should not be exclusively dominated by the business of procreation and the task of producing the desired male offspring; the vineyard owner further stipulates that Klärchen must voluntarily participate and enjoy the affair. Zuckmayer here inverts the father-daughter relationship to be found in Friedrich Hebbel's domestic tragedy *Maria Magdalene* (1844). Hebbel's master carpenter Anton was ultimately responsible for the suicide of his pregnant and unwed daughter Klara (of which Klärchen is the diminutive). Klara took her own life out of a sense of extreme filial duty in order to spare her puritanical father public shame and embarrassment. Quite in contrast to master Anton, Gunderloch defies public opinion by ignoring conventional morality and dealing with the facts of life in terms of biological and physiological functions:

What do people want? Before they buy wine, they'll taste it [first]. . . .
And if someone buys a sow, he wants to know whether she'll farrow. For that we have the public mating sponsored by the community. But when someone gets married, when it is a matter of one's physical and spiritual well-being, then he is supposed to play blindman's bluff. (WA, 7:97)

Gunderloch's comparison with, and emphasis on, the animal sphere is not accidental in a play that exudes earthiness and reaches a climax of sorts in the third act when three unmarried couples engage more or less simultaneously in sexual intercourse offstage. The offstage frolicking signals the imminent resolution of all plot complications that had culminated in a tremendous brawl in the second act. The joyous occasion of Knuzius and Klärchen's engagement had turned into a free-for-all when the rendition of a popular song by Gunderloch and his guests was interrupted by freeloading and drunk veterans. But the widower Gunderloch, who emerges victorious and revitalized from the fighting, abandons his plans to retire and sell half of his vineyard to the highest bidder; instead he proposes to his housekeeper. Klärchen had been only temporarily impressed by the fine manners and elegant appearance of Knuzius; she now returns to her first love, the boatman Jochen Most, brother of Gunderloch's housekeeper. Even Knuzius is recompensed for the loss of Klärchen and her substantial inheritance by becoming engaged to the daughter of Eismayer, in whose inn the festivity took place. In addition, one of the wine salesmen, who is present because of the auction, and the daughter of another wine merchant become engaged. So the play actually ends with four happily united couples. Such a blissful ending induced the aforementioned Alfred Kerr to remark sardonically: "Really, four engagements. This young man [Zuckmayer] is more catholic than the Pope himself."[4] Thus moral conventions prevail, after all, and the sexual excesses, the Dionysian vitality exhibited by many of the characters, are legitimized retroactively by the impending matrimony for all those concerned.

Zuckmayer's "total affirmation of life as it is"[5] presents a stark contrast to the chiliastic or revolutionary orientation of many expressionist dramas. In rejuvenating a realistic mode of presentation, which had fallen somewhat into disrepute after the heyday of naturalism in the late nineteenth century, Zuckmayer resorted to the well-established subgenre of the *Volksstück* or folk play. With its uncomplicated plot and entertaining musical numbers, the folk play originally appealed to the lower classes among the city-dwellers. Above all, it had flourished in Vienna, where both Ferdinand Raimund (1790–1836) and Johann Nepomuk Nestroy (1801–1862) had achieved such a high degree of popularity that posthumously they were elevated to the status of Austrian classics. Much closer to Zuckmayer's home, Ernst Elias Niebergall had produced his folk play, *Datterich* [The Trembler] (1841), in Darmstadt dialect.

Apart from literary tradition, new developments in the socioeconomic realm fostered a return to the realism of the *Volksstück*. In the early twenties, after the hopes of the immediate postwar years for an all-encompassing regeneration of both individual man and society had been shattered, and the currency reform of November 1923 had prepared the way for a modest economic stabilization of the Weimar Republic, expressionism began to yield ground to the literature of *Neue Sachlichkeit* (new objectivism). It is indicative of the new matter-of-fact mood that Georg Kaiser, for example, who during and shortly after World War I had published such expressionist dramas as *The Citizens of Calais* (1914), *From Morn till Midnight* (1916), and the plays of his *Gas* trilogy (1917–1920), now turned out a play in the mode of the new objectivism. *Side by Side* (1923) is subtitled *Volksstück*—although one would hestitate to call the play a perfect example of the subgenre.

Conversely, Zuckmayer conformed rather well to the norms of the folk play—so well, in fact, that Brecht may have been obliquely referring to *The Merry Vineyard* in his "Notes on the Folk Play" (1940). In this essay Brecht castigates the run-of-the-mill popular play as "crude and humble. It is a mixture of earthy humour and sentimentality; homespun morality and cheap sex."[6] Actually, there is a considerable number of correspondences between *The Merry Vineyard* and Brecht's own *Volksstück, Puntila and Matti, His Hired Man,* which originated in Finland in 1940 and deals with both the master-servant relationship and the two souls in master Puntila's breast.[7] For example, in both plays we find the triangular situation in which a university-educated, upper-class dowry hunter intends to marry a rich heiress. But both young ladies prefer less well-educated, and less well-mannered but virile, members of the lower classes. Further, there are the abortive engagement parties at which alcohol flows freely. Above all, Zuckmayer's vineyard owner Gunderloch and Brecht's estate owner Puntila (the latter, alas, only in his drunk, euphoric state) express the same uninhibited Dionysian zest for life. However, despite these and other similarities in tone, atmosphere, frank language, and disregard of sexual taboos, there is one fundamental difference. Whereas in Zuckmayer's play all complications are resolved in a conventional happy end, Brecht's Matti leaves Puntila's estate because he realizes that the differences between master and servant are irreconcilable. Socioeconomic factors determine human relationships; hence Matti cannot marry his master's daughter. True equality among men, he states didactically, can only be achieved when there are neither masters nor servants.

Unlike Brecht, Zuckmayer was not primarily concerned with social or economic conditions. On the contrary, the sow that innkeeper Eismayer refers to throughout the play points toward a different intent: The sow is killed in the third act, shortly before the happy couples are photographed for posterity. Destined for the wedding feast, it will become part of the life-sustaining vegetative cycles of dying and giving birth. Man's animalistic nature reasserts itself in his being subject to this eternally recurring cycle. As Gunderloch states: "There is a bit of animal in each of us" (WA, 7:148). Conversely, in Brecht's play the slaughtered pig serves as an object of demonstration for social injustice. It will be eaten by master Puntila and his guests; the working folk, who created Puntila's wealth, have to be content with lesser fare.

Without a doubt, the fact that *The Merry Vineyard* is not primarily a problem play but an unpretentious, rather conventionally constructed comedy of the popular variety contributed to its becoming such a smashing hit with the Berlin audience. In his autobiography Zuckmayer has provided a vivid and detailed account of the play's origin, its rehearsals, and the premiere—whose success established him as a dramatist to be reckoned with. When both dramatists were still in Munich, Brecht had remarked to Zuckmayer that an aspiring playwright had to go to Berlin: "That was where the theatrical battles were being fought" *(PoM,* 273). Ironically, it was Zuckmayer who achieved sudden fame almost three years before Brecht's *The Threepenny Opera,* which opened on 31 August 1928, became a sensational hit in the same Theater am Schiffbauerdamm in which *The Merry Vineyard* had premiered.

The Berlin audience thoroughly enjoyed "the mood of unclouded gaiety" of a play that was so strongly reminiscent of "the landscape, the melody, and the whole world" of Zuckmayer's boyhood *(PoM,* 281). Even the somewhat freely rendered dialect did not prove to be an obstacle to the appreciation of the comedy. However, the reception in the provinces proved to be far more problematic.

Although Zuckmayer lacked the satirical and critical intent of Ödön von Horváth, another leading representative of the folk play during the twenties who was awarded the Kleist Prize on Zuckmayer's recommendation in 1931, the seemingly innocuous *The Merry Vineyard* proved to be unexpectedly controversial and came under attack from different quarters. Tumults frequently erupted during performances outside Berlin. To be sure, many of these theatrical scandals may be considered an indication of the growing mood of intolerance and polarization of public opinion during the latter half of the Weimar Republic. Yet one should not overlook the fact that the play's notoriety significantly contributed to making the hitherto fairly unknown Zuckmayer a household word. In Munich, for instance, a National Socialist city council member proclaimed *The Merry Vineyard* to be "an incredible obscenity that offends the Christian *Weltanschauung,* German morality, German women, disabled German veterans, and German officials in the most vulgar manner."[8] The play was briefly banned, and subsequently an expurgated version was presented on stage. In the same year (1926), conservative students in Halle disrupted the premiere by whistling, singing patriotic songs, and battling the police. These students, as well as their colleagues in other cities, objected in particular to the caricatured portrayal of Knuzius. In the third act Knuzius awakens from a night of excessive imbibing on a manure heap amid the laughter of the other characters. Confronted with the loss of the heiress Klärchen, he endeavors to save face by proposing to inn-keeper Eismayer's daughter and extolling the virtues held dear by the political right. He pompously declares that his marriage con-stitutes "not only the fulfillment of personal wishes" but will also contribute to the "regeneration of our people with regard to its virtue, military preparedness, cleanliness, devotion to duty, and racial purity" (*WA*, 7:150).

Zuckmayer thought that he had composed a "love song" to his homeland. But the "uproar against *The Merry Vineyard* proved worst of all" in Rhenish Hesse (*PoM*, 297). The playwright was accused of having become a homeless, rootless individual who be-fouled his own nest by maligning the people of his native region in general and some well-established families (whose names he had inadvertently used) in particular. A lengthy debate raged in the Mainz newspapers concerning the advisability of having the comedy performed in that city. When *The Merry Vineyard* was eventually produced in March 1926, vintners from the environs of Mainz, including those from Zuckmayer's birthplace, Nackenheim, dem-onstrated both against high taxes and the performance. Only after World War II was Nackenheim prepared to forgive its supposedly errant son.

In short, "there was an endless list of . . . groups who felt that the play was aimed at them: innkeepers, pig breeders, veterans' organizations, wine dealers, bureaucrats, even the Jews" (*PoM*, 295). The play continued to stir up divergent emotions. On the one hand, Jews felt offended because they seemed to discover undesir-able traits in two Jewish wine salesmen; on the other hand, the salesman Hahnesand was bedeviled during the Third Reich as the incarnation of "oriental licentiousness," a "Jewish brute" who lusts after blonde, Germanic maidens for the purpose of soiling their racial purity.[9]

Seen from the vantage point of the post–World War II period, *The Merry Vineyard* does not appear to be an entirely harmless trifle. Predictably, Marxist critics disapproved of Zuckmayer's fun-damentally conciliatory attitude and his failure to expose thoroughly the pre-Fascist mentality of Knuzius and his ilk.[10] Even non-Marxists

such as the contemporary Swiss playwright Friedrich Dürrenmatt
expressed similar reservations in pointing out that the ostensible
harmlessness of the comedy tended to detract from important developments such as the imminent advent of Nazism.[11]

At any rate, with *The Merry Vineyard* Zuckmayer had made his
mark in the theatrical and, in a wider sense, cultural-political scene
of the twenties. The very fact that the comedy aroused widespread
controversy attests to its topical significance. Thus it is not entirely
unjustified to consider the comedy the first part of Zuckmayer's
"German Trilogy,"[12] in which he comes to grips with important
phases of twentieth-century German history.

## II  Schinderhannes

After *The Merry Vineyard's* sensational success, the playwright
relates, he set out to prove that the widespread attention the comedy
had attracted "had not been due to sheer chance" and that his work
had not been "ephemeral" *(PoM,* 298). In a sense, Zuckmayer continued to employ his rediscovered strength by again locating his
new play in his native region, in Mainz and its environs. But this
time the playwright drew on legends and childhood memories about
Johann (Hans, Hannes) Wilhelm Bückler, who was called Schinderhannes not because he was an oppressor of the people *(Leute-
schinder)* but because he had been a knacker *(Schinder)* before he
became an outlaw.

The historical Bückler who, together with nineteen members of
his gang, was beheaded in Mainz in 1803, had little in common with
the Schinderhannes of legends and ballads. In the imagination of
the people Schinderhannes had been elevated to the stature of a
German Robin Hood who, motivated by a social conscience, took
from the rich to help the poor. Zuckmayer's childhood memories
lingered on and found their first expression in "The Mainz Popular
Ballad of Schinderhannes."[13] These hardly polished verses that, in
a fashion typical of the form, emphasize the gruesome aspects of
Schinderhannes's career but, atypically, employ ironic and parod-
istic elements, are a re-creation of those which Zuckmayer had heard
in his youth. During his brief tenure at the Kiel municipal theaters
from 1922 to 1923, he used the popular ballad as one of the means
for revitalizing the theater by having the singing of the ballad accompanied by the appropriate, crudely drawn posters.[14]

In the play itself Zuckmayer retained the element of popular balladry. In fact, the first scene opens with the "Song of Schinderhannes," which constitutes a kind of abbreviated version of the earlier Mainz ballad. It is sung by Julchen, daughter of a balladmonger, and recurs throughout the play. But apart from childhood memories and theater experiments, other stimuli, which attracted Zuckmayer's attention to the Schinderhannes legend, may be assumed.

There are, for example, the topical aspects of the play. The action takes place "during the time of Napoleon" (*WA*, 7:155). Yet Zuckmayer specified in his stage directions that the historical elements with regard to costumes, makeup, characters and their speech should be de-emphasized. Whereas such de-emphasis did not automatically turn the play into a drama of contemporary significance, one historical parallel tended to underscore its topicality. Both during Napoleon's reign and after World War I, from 1918 to 1930, Mainz and the left bank of the Rhine were occupied by the French. Particularly after World War I the political aspirations of the French were supported by a German separatist movement. Given this context, Zuckmayer might have presented Schinderhannes as a national hero, a fighter against foreign invaders. However, the playwright explicitly rejected two allegedly prominent traits of the historical Schinderhannes, that is, his enmity toward the French and his anti-Semitism. According to Zuckmayer, Schinderhannes fought the French because they represented authority and he merely robbed those Jews who happened to be wealthy.[15] At the same time, he did not endorse the cause of the separatists and thus displayed a conciliatory attitude toward the enemy whom he had fought in World War I[16]—an attitude that is also reflected in his post–World War II drama *The Song of the Fiery Furnace*.

Actually, Zuckmayer pokes gentle fun at the Prussian or German military, particularly in act 3, scene 1 of the first version (1927). This recruiting scene, later revised for a production in 1933, as well as the one set in the barrack square (act 3, scene 3), clearly foreshadows the military atmosphere that pervades *The Captain of Köpenick*.

In adapting the Schinderhannes materials for the stage, Zuckmayer had not only to take into account the legends and contemporary literature about the outlaw, he also invited comparison with the literary treatment of other famous criminals. Both Schiller's Karl Moor in the drama *The Robbers* (1781) and Friedrich Schwan in the narrative *The Criminal from Lost Honor* (1786) come into conflict with the established order because of injustices they had to suffer and seek to rectify by recourse to extralegal means. Likewise, Michael Kohlhaas in Kleist's novella by that name (1808), becomes a rebel because he cannot obtain justice by peaceful means. Even in the influential and popular "romantic tale" *Rinaldo Rinaldini* (1798) by Goethe's brother-in-law Christian August Vulpius, the outlaw is rejected by the representatives of society, the nobility and the church.

Zuckmayer's Schinderhannes, however, owes comparatively little to his literary ancestors. A closer look at the play itself will demonstrate that his concept of the outlaw corresponds more closely to the socially well-integrated, yet exuberant and life-affirming Gunderloch in *The Merry Vineyard* than to those noble criminals in literature who fight for a better world.

After the hero of the play is introduced in the initial song in the tap room of an inn, at which Schinderhannes stays under an assumed name, the social milieu is broadly developed. According to their social status, the guests sit at separate tables. The antagonism between the "better" people and their "ordinary" counterparts becomes evident in the discussion revolving around the exploits of Schinderhannes and his gang. On the one hand, a carter defends the "native bandits" against the slurs of a traveler and declares that "none of them has ever harmed a beggar or a poor man—only merchants, military officers, and rich Jews" (WA, 7:158). On the other hand, a greedy master tanner denounces those who sympathize with the outlaws: "Those are rebels who support Schinderhannes. The dishonest people who don't have any money and any morals" (WA, 7:159). The tanner's remarks are reminiscent of the Hessian Georg Büchner's Woyzeck who, in the shaving scene with the captain in the drama named after him, wistfully reflects on the interrelationship between money and morals from the perspective of the underprivileged and disadvantaged and thereby anticipates, by roughly one hundred years, Brecht's famed "Food is the first thing. Morals follow on" from the second-act finale of *The Threepenny Opera*.

But Zuckmayer does not pursue the serious exploration of social antagonisms; rather, in the case of the tanner poetic justice is achieved by means of a practical joke that adds a farcical element. The tanner belatedly discovers that the unidentified Schinderhannes has sold him the same hides that the outlaw had previously stolen from him. Although Schinderhannes shows that he is the poor man's friend by liberally treating all impecunious guests at the inn, he gives a clear indication that he is not primarily motivated by social compassion: "I was born a show-off. Even as a schoolboy I pretended to have butter on my bread by substituting chalk. But I prospered. Boasting makes you fat, if you know how to do it" (WA, 7:161). Schinderhannes exhibits the same lack of social awareness in a conversation with Julchen who has deserted her fiancé, the policeman Adam, and unhesitatingly joined Schinderhannes. In response to her question about the seriousness of his offenses, he simply replies: "I don't understand that. Only those who make the laws know about such things." And he continues to explain his role by using an analogy from nature: "Everything that has to grow will sprout" (WA, 7:169). The German verb *ausschlagen*, which is used in this context, denotes both growth and a violent striking out. It follows that the wild, unchecked growth, which Schinderhannes envisions for himself, must necessarily lead to conflict with the existing social order—an order upheld by the German police and the French army. The inevitable conflict arises, and Schinderhannes's limits become apparent when he is on the verge of becoming a true leader of the people against their oppressors. In the second act, he leads both his gang and a group of peasants and workers against a detachment of the French army that has been sent to restore internal stability. Before the attack Julchen had warned Schinderhannes, now intoxicated with his power, not to succumb to hubris: "You are lifting with your wrong shoulder, and you will fall to your knees" (WA, 7:200). Julchen's homely message does not only refer to the hopelessness of waging war with an adversary of superior strength, the Napoleonic army, it also alludes to the fact that Schinderhannes's social role—like that of many of Zuckmayer's heroes—must be ultimately interpreted in a metaphysical context. In the given social situation the presence of such an individual as Schinderhannes, even if he is not a social revolutionary, "creates a ferment which eventually lays bare the evils and faults of society's structure. . . ." He "fulfils his function, not in the conscious pursuit of a social ideal, but unconsciously, simply by succumbing to his own nature and to his fate. . . ."[17]

The wanted Schinderhannes seeks refuge in the German army that is mobilized on the right bank of the Rhine. But he is betrayed by former members of his gang and turned over to the French authorities as a "political criminal." Yet his defeat and impending execution in Mainz turn into a triumph of sorts. The life force, symbolized by the child that sprang from Schinderhannes and Julchen's union, asserts itself in the end. Life conquers death as expressed in the fourth stanza of Martin Luther's Easter choral (1524), which serves as the drama's motto and is sung by the sectarians in the play. The atmosphere of the final scenes in the fourth act is that of a festive occasion, albeit with an admixture of the macabre; even before his execution (not shown on stage) Schinderhannes is on the way of becoming a legend as balladmongers are hawking printed versions of his exploits. The condemned man himself anticipates death as his final triumph; he is jubilant about the crowd of fifteen thousand people who have come to witness his execution.

The play, which in the view of a critic writing in the 1970s combines "elements of the popular ballad, the coarse dialect comedy, the romantic ballad, and the drama of social criticism,"[18] elicited differing critical responses after its premiere in the Berlin Lessing-Theater on 14 October 1927. Whilst Felix Hollaender bemoaned the lack of both revolutionary determination and original poetic strength and did not think the play an improvement over *The Merry Vineyard*,[19] Alfred Kerr offered a more balanced appraisal of the dramatist who by now seemed to be irrevocably committed to the folk play. He praised Zuckmayer's strength (*das Volkstum*) and pointed out his weakness (*das Volkstümliche*).[20] In a sense, the artistic acclaim of future plays would depend on whether Zuckmayer succeeded in establishing the proper balance between genuine folkways and artificial folksiness.

### III   Katharina Knie

The subtitle of *Katharina Knie*, "The Tightrope Dancer," indicates the milieu in which the play takes place. Again the playwright drew on memories from his youth when the name Knie was indiscriminately applied to all circuses and troupes of acrobats and tightrope dancers who practiced their craft along the Rhine.[21] Again, the action takes place comparatively close to Zuckmayer's home, in a small, unidentified city of the Palatinate; again, the local dialect, that of the Rhenish Palatinate, provides additional local flavor.

But in his third folk play Zuckmayer is perhaps farthest removed from the portrayal of genuine folkways if we assume that the folk represented should include a comparatively broad spectrum of social types and characters, as is actually the case in both *The Merry Vineyard* and *Schinderhannes*. In contrast, in *Katharina Knie* we encounter primarily people from the tightrope dancers' troupe; a visible manifestation of the prevailing circus atmosphere are the caravans that provide a prominent feature of the setting throughout the four acts. Hence all encounters between the artists and the representatives of the nonartistic world take place in the tightrope dancers' domain.

The play begins with two incidents that establish the pervasive sentimental mood. The circus, directed by the patriarch of the enterprise, the elder Knie, has fallen upon hard times during the inflation year of 1923. After barely escaping from having his property seized because of nonpayment of the entertainment tax, old Knie suffers another indignity when the local police commissioner and the estate owner Rothacker appear to accuse the artists of having stolen oats from Rothacker. Incensed, the head of the troupe defends the honor of both his centuries-old profession and his family. Under no circumstances does he wish the members of his troupe to be confused with those shiftless gypsies who also happen to live in caravans.

But the threat of a conflict is defused when Katharina, Knie's only daughter, confesses that it was she who stole the oats in order to be able to feed her donkey. Rothacker withdraws his charges and, attracted by Katharina, returns later with the proposal to employ her on a probationary basis so that she might become proficient in the skills required for the administration of estates. Knie is extremely proud of not belonging to the disreputable, homeless "gypsies in the green caravan," who to the writer Tonio Kröger in Thomas Mann's novella by the same name (1903) represent the very antithesis of a bourgeois existence. On the contrary, in the opinion of Knie his economic independence, however threatened, his profession, and his family tradition make him entirely the social equal of a landowner like Rothacker. Ultimately, he is swayed by Rothacker's argument that agriculture will prosper regardless of economic conditions. Without much hesitation Katharina decides to go with Rothacker, but the second act ends with Knie's "fanatically" expressed conviction: "She'll return" (WA, 7:276).

Thus, it seems, the stage has been set for the external conflict between the two men who not only vie for Katharina's affection but also for her loyalty to diametrically opposite ways of life. At the same time, Katharina must resolve the central question of the play, which is repeatedly stated by the circus veteran Bibbo and paraphrased by others: "One has to know where one belongs" (WA, 7:262). Yet the external conflict never materializes. In the third act—it takes place one year after the first and second acts—Katharina does, indeed, come back. Contrary to Knie's assumption that she will rejoin the troupe, she has merely come to inform him of her impending marriage to Rothacker. Almost overcome by joy about her seemingly voluntary return, Knie performs daring feats on the tightrope and celebrates afterward with his troupe. The excitement proves too much for him, and he dies. Now that the circus has lost its director, Katharina unhesitatingly assumes the leadership and breaks completely with her previous existence by paying some of the troupe's debts with the engagement ring she received from Rothacker.

The critics did not favorably review the play, whose premiere took place in the Berlin Lessing–Theater on 21 December 1928. The drama seemed to present an overly sentimental, nostalgic view of a vanishing art and focused only peripherally on questions of contemporary significance. The third and fourth acts lacked dramatic tension, some critics charged, and suffered from overly long, though poetically inspired speeches, especially those by old Knie and the clown. Moreover, Rothacker and the way of life he represented did not effectively counterbalance Knie and his world. For example, when Rothacker might have claimed Katharina's affection and loyalty in the third act, he stayed discreetly in the background. Further, courageous as Katharina's decision to lead the troupe may be—she is the first woman character after whom Zuckmayer named one of his plays—it is rather dubious whether she will be any more successful than her father in reestablishing the circus's prosperity. Even after the inflation had been overcome and the people were willing to spend money again, the new technology, which had created such novel forms of entertainment as the cinema, proved to be strong competition.

Curiously, the negative reviews did not greatly detract from the play's popularity—an indication of the limited function of criticism in influencing public opinion. Admittedly, to a considerable degree the success of the play was attributable to Albert Bassermann, who played old Knie in Berlin and elsewhere. His performance was uniformly praised. In London, however, where *Katharina Knie* was produced under the title *Caravan* in 1932, one critic judged the play's folding to be "fully deserved" because it constituted merely "a great chunk of sentimentalism about circus life."[22] Harsh as this assessment may seem, it was shared by several German critics, who had expected Zuckmayer to proceed along lines that would combine the folk play with the contemporary play.[23]

## IV  The Captain of Köpenick

It is not entirely coincidental that *The Captain of Köpenick* was to become both Zuckmayer's masterpiece and his most popular play. In that play the author's considerable dramatic talents are brought to bear on a topic that was, at the time of the play's creation, highly relevant and, at the same time, possessed sufficient significance to transcend mere topicality.

After the completion of *Katharina Knie*, a play that drew crowds everywhere but was condemned by the critics, Zuckmayer was engaged in creating a modern Eulenspiegel with the aim of presenting for the Heidelberg Festival a contemporary version of the fifteenth-century prankster. However, "the discrepancy between the outlines of the old chap-book . . . and the modernity and living reality" (*PoM*, 311) proved an insurmountable obstacle, and the playwright was on the point of abandoning this major project when his actor-director friend and future collaborator, Fritz Kortner, suggested to him a new subject: *The Captain of Köpenick*.

The actual *Köpenickiade*, as the events in the small town of Köpenick became subsequently known, of the ex-convict and unemployed cobbler Wilhelm Voigt in 1906 had achieved considerable notoriety both in Germany and abroad. Voigt's stroke of genius, his purchase of a captain's uniform from a pawnbroker's shop, his impersonation of an officer who appeared with a small detachment of unsuspecting soldiers at the town hall of Köpenick (then outside the city limits of Berlin) and confiscated the city's cash box, was widely interpreted as an indictment of German-Prussian militarism in general and the devout reverence of the uniform in particular. Although writers of many persuasions, but particularly those of a satirical bent, immediately capitalized on the cobbler's exploits, none of these literary products achieved lasting fame.

In 1930 interest in the events of Köpenick was revived by the publication of Wilhelm Schäfer's novel *The Captain of Köpenick*—a work that Zuckmayer quite plausibly claims to have read only after he had completed his drama so as not to be influenced by it. As the playwright saw it, Wilhelm Voigt was a modern rogue who could hold up a mirror to Germany at the beginning of the 1930s. Although the story had happened more than twenty years ago, it was still highly pertinent in 1930. For, Zuckmayer writes, in this year

. . . the Nazis were entering the Reichstag as the second-strongest party and thrusting the nation into a new craze for uniforms. The story was an image, a farcical mirror image, of the evils and dangers that were growing in Germany, but also of the hope that they could be overcome as the shoemaker had overcome his difficulties by native wit and humane insight. (*PoM*, 312)

The play itself consists of three acts and twenty-one scenes; seventy-three major and minor characters appear and represent various segments of Wilhelminian society. There is careful attention to minute detail such as the nuances in the characters' speech and the realistic depiction of the milieu; both emphasize the picture-book quality of the play. Yet in their depiction of the fate of the captain's uniform and that of the protagonist Wilhelm Voigt, the scenes are skillfully interrelated to form an organic whole. The uniform assumes a life of its own; as the symbol of an oppressive order it is Voigt's antagonist until he conquers or, in Zuckmayer's words, "marries"[24] it. The very first scene of the play is dominated by the uniform, whose wearer, Captain von Schlettow, enjoys the adulation of those not privileged to belong to the army. As a narrow-minded but still sympathetic representative of a social system that attributes exaggerated importance to the military, he is unable to comprehend that essential human qualities are not determined by outward manifestations of authority. Von Schlettow's rigid mentality, however, pervades the entire social fabric, as Wilhelm Voigt is soon to experience. The ex-convict, who has been harshly dealt with by the authorities, wishes to become reintegrated into society; yet this reintegration is impossible to achieve because he cannot escape the maze of bureaucratic regulations that deny him the very means of existence. In fact, he is caught in a vicious circle; in order to be gainfully employed Voigt needs a residence permit, but he cannot be issued one without producing proof of his being employed. At the police station (act 1, scene 2) as well as at the shoe factory (act 1, scene 4) Voigt encounters functionaries who insist on strict application of rules and regulations in the face of Voigt's very real human needs. Thus he is driven to the desperate step of burglarizing a police station to obtain the necessary forms for forging his papers. As Voigt has learned, only when officially registered and certified can he expect to be treated like a human being by the authorities. The cobbler's attempt to obtain his papers by illegal means fails; at the end of the first act we learn that he again has disappeared behind the walls of a maximum security prison.

In the meantime, like Voigt, the uniform has begun its gradual descent. Although it was destined to provide new glamor for Captain von Schlettow, officer in an elite regiment, and enhance his stature, in the last scene of the first act (scene 7) it is purchased by a mere lieutenant of the reserves. It is of little consequence that the new owner of the uniform, Dr. Obermüller, also happens to have acquired an advanced academic degree. As the servile but jovial tailor Wormser states quite accurately: "A Doctor's degree is only a visiting card, but to be an officer in the reserves opens the door to everything" (222).[25] The enormous power of the uniform is further demonstrated by an ingenious invention on the part of the playwright. Before dealing with the actual historical event, the comedy of the impostor in a captain's uniform, he presents the tragedy of the genuine captain who, temporarily out of uniform, is not recognized as an officer, becomes involved in a brawl in a tavern, and, as a consequence, has to resign his commission.[26]

The second act begins ten years later. Wilhelm Voigt has been a model prisoner. Above all, he has eagerly accumulated the only kind of knowledge freely dispensed by the warden, an enthusiastic participant of the Franco-Prussian War: military lore and regulations. It is one of the many ironies of the play that the warden unwittingly predicts Voigt's further course of action by praising his mastery of military matters and his initiative: "Bravo, Voigt! Excellent! Excellent, Voigt! You have not merely paid careful attention here but you have learned something as well. On some future day you shall see just how useful that information will be. . . . Splendid, Voigt, splendid! . . . You're a born soldier despite your bowlegs"(228–29).

But after his release from prison Voigt, who has found temporary refuge with his brother-in-law, Hoprecht, again unsuccessfully attempts to assert his right for a place to live. Again he has become the victim of the insensitive bureaucracy that threatens him with eviction as a parole violator. Yet instead of succumbing to bleak despair, Voigt gains self-assurance and quiet determination in the pivotal scene of the play (act 2, scene 12), in his encounter with a poor, naive, and guileless girl. In comforting the girl, whose death is imminent, Voigt realizes more clearly than ever before the universal law governing all life: "It's like this—the earth is alive, and you can see that, because it always changes. And what's alive wants to rise up, get to the top, way up high, like a blade of grass, or a seed potato, or a child, eh?" (246). Applied to his own situation, this means that Voigt is determined to fight the Wilhelminian order that denies him the right to a decent existence. For, as he retorts to the petty state official Hoprecht, a firm believer in law and order: "First the human being, . . . then human law and order" (WA, 7:406).[27] Although he is neither a revolutionary nor an uncompromising nature, Voigt is no longer willing to be trampled on. The means, by which he hopes to escape his predicament, the captain's uniform, no longer fits the corpulent Dr. Obermüller. It has been stained at a ball and ends up in a pawnbroker's shop.

It is in the pawnbroker's shop where the captain of Köpenick is "born" as the result of the "marriage"[28] between the useless uniform and the unwanted, homeless cobbler. The entire third act is devoted to the preparation, execution, and resolution of the masterful prank—from the purchase of the uniform (scene 15), Voigt's mental preparation (scene 16), his "dress rehearsal" (scene 17), his occupation of the townhall in Köpenick (scenes 18 and 19), his exhaustion and dejection after the foray that did not yield the passport he so intensely desired (scene 20), and, finally, his surrender to the police (scene 21). The play ends on a conciliatory note. When Voigt sees himself in uniform for the first time (he put on the uniform in a public toilet without a mirror), he bursts out in uncontrollable laughter at the sight of the sorry spectacle he presents.

The ending is indicative of Zuckmayer's intent in at least two respects. First of all, the satire directed against the Wilhelminian military and bureaucratic establishment is blunted by the final reconciliation that tends to overshadow the fact that, although Voigt has triumphed over an ultimately inhuman sociopolitical system, the system itself will not change. Second, in the final analysis it is not men acting in a clearly definable context who are responsible for the injustices that are committed in the name of law and order but rather the irrational, almost magical powers emanating from the uniform. In this context, it is well to remember that the play begins with the creation of the uniform and ends with its final display on stage. As has been pointed out, not the wearer of the uniform, but the uniform itself is of supreme importance—a fact of which Voigt himself is fully cognizant and which he patiently explains to the chief of police at the end of the play: "Any child in Germany knows that to do what you want all you need is a uniform. I've known that all my life. . . . it wasn't really all that much. In fact a uniform can do it almost all by itself " (294).

Precisely the emphasis on the uniform resulted in adverse reactions from critics with leftist leanings. In his review of the Berlin premiere on 5 March 1931 Herbert Ihering noted that the play might be called *Uniformfieber* ("uniform craze") and that Zuckmayer lacked a clear *Weltanschauung*.[29] Ihering's line of reasoning was adopted by Marxist critics after World War II, especially by Paul Rilla, who wrote that the uniform triumphed over the satirical intent of the author,[30] and Wilfried Adling, who noticed that Zuckmayer indulged in idolatry of the uniform and neglected to pay sufficient attention to the societal forces that had created the fetish in the first place.[31] Conversely, conservative critics did not find the play to their liking either and accused it of being a caricature of Germany's glorious past, a stance that was also adopted by the Nazi propagandist Joseph Goebbels.[32]

Zuckmayer's conciliatory and subtle approach to a factual event that could have easily been turned into an aggressively satirical or a purely tendentious play is evident everywhere. For example, on the one hand, Voigt, unlike the two minor characters Kalle and Zeck, is not a criminal in the ordinary sense. He tells the chief of police: "My dear sir, I never in my life stole anything from my fellowman. I never ran up against anyone but the government" (295). On the other hand, he is not a rigid, rebellious nature bent on justice at all costs like the hero of Kleist's novella, *Michael Kohlhaas*. In fact, Voigt's chief goal is to be accepted by society, and only through the rejection on the part of the authorities is he driven to commit criminal acts. Thus Voigt may be considered a new type of criminal: a criminal who by the very nature of his crimes draws attention to the existing anomalies in society.[33] While the portrayal of Voigt as an intensely humane, helpless, and naive underdog cannot but evoke sympathy for him and resentment against the Wilhelminian order, there are no clearly recognizable villains in the play against whom this resentment can be directed. Despite their dogmatic and narrow-minded belief in preconceived notions about law and order and the place of the individual in society, such characters as Captain von Schlettow or the petty official Hoprecht are basically honest and well-intentioned people. They do, however, consciously or unconsciously adhere to the notion that "all the various manifestations of the system—uniforms, discipline, residence permits, prisons— . . . [are] direct emanations of a general principle in its purest and most abstract form."[34] Such "obsession with the abstract at the expense of the concrete,"[35] on the part of the system's representatives that Zuckmayer in his essay *Pro Domo* defined as a characteristically German attitude, points to the core of the playwright's critical intent. It is not primarily directed against specific social institutions or individuals functioning in a social context but rather against the underlying ideas and assumptions. In other words, like *Schinderhannes* the play discussed constitutes "metaphysical" theater rather than "littérature engagée." The detachment of the play from contemporary or historical reality is also enhanced by the fairy-tale elements with which the author endowed *The Captain of Köpenick*—the play is subtitled "A German Fairy Tale" and quotations from the Brothers Grimm appear at the beginning and the end (albeit not in all editions) as well as in a crucial scene (act 2, scene 12).

Although Zuckmayer claimed in retrospect that "friend and foe alike understood the play as the political act it was meant to be" *(PoM,* 315), it is more plausible that, in the politically explosive years before the collapse of the Weimar Republic, "history, impatient with all gentle jokes, seized *The Captain of Köpenick* by the scruff of the neck and made it, in spite of itself, a dangerous satire."[36] From the vantage point of the 1970s, it is safe to say that Zuckmayer's play has stood the test of time. Although in the sixties some leading German critics declared *The Captain of Köpenick* to be hopelessly outmoded and lacking in relevance, others have staunchly defended it and pointed out that—despite its historical costume—the drama does, indeed, mirror problems that are entirely familiar to the reader or spectator of today: the misplaced trust in authority, the miscarriage of justice, the disregard for essential human needs in the name of law and order, and the dialectic of appearance and reality. Above all, the play is splendid theatrical fare that has secured it a firm place in the theatrical repertoire. Thomas Mann called it "the best comedy in world literature since Gogol's *The Inspector General"* *(PoM,* 315)—a compliment that is particularly significant in view of the often lamented dearth of genuine comedies in German literature.

The play offers humor, wit, and compassion without succumbing to maudlin sentimentality of which, for example, *Katharina Knie* is not entirely free. Zuckmayer's realism in the depiction of a broad spectrum of Wilhelminian society—from the last refuge of the dis-

possessed, the flophouse, to the elegant surroundings of the privileged few—is heightened by his superb facility in endowing his
characters with the appropriate regional and social speech patterns.
The plight of the downtrodden Voigt resembles that of Büchner's
exploited Woyzeck. He is engaged in a seemingly hopeless struggle
with an enormous bureaucratic machinery that, like that of Kafka's
novels, eludes his, and the spectators', grasp. Voigt's plight, his
search for a home *(Heimat)* and decent living conditions, is intensified by the brilliant juxtaposition of boisterous scenes in which the
upper crust enjoy life and somberly moving ones taking place in the
milieu of the petty bourgeois.

Although the dialogue—conducted to a large extent in Berlin
dialect that can only be imperfectly recaptured in English—provides
a major source of wit and humor, there is also uproariously funny
slap-stick comedy, such as the prisoners' simulated attack on broom-
sticks in act 2, scene 8 on occasion of the reenactment of the battle
of Sedan (1870) or the first appearance on stage of the cobbler as
officer. Of the latter scene (act 3, scene 17) it has been said that
"Voigt's superb emergence from the lavatory in full uniform [is] no
doubt the best single entrance in the twentieth-century theatre."[37]

Perhaps it is the hallmark of a great play that it can accommodate
and even endure various interpretations by critics and theater directors. Thus is it entirely justified to consider *The Captain of
Köpenick*, because of its unquestionable topical relevance, the second part of Zuckmayer's "German Trilogy."[38] At the same time, the
play's longevity cannot be solely attributed to its being a vehicle for
grasping historical events more clearly. From a British perspective,
for example, the play's virtues consist in its eminent theatricality;
it exhibits "a dramatic spectrum which ranges from near Gogol to
Prussian Feydeau, taking in a Dickensian deathbed, a transvestite
ball and a hugely difficult final scene which raises Pirandello-like
questions of appearance and reality."[39]

## V  *The Adaptations and* The Blue Angel

Among the "pieces of craftsmanship, finger exercises, études"
*(PoM,* 311) preparatory to *The Captain of Köpenick* Zuckmayer lists
his adaptation of Maxwell Anderson and Laurence Stallings's war
play *What Price Glory*, which was first performed in New York City
in 1924 and published in 1926.[40] The hugely successful American
play reached Germany via the medium of film; in fact, Zuckmayer

professes to have been unaware of the play by Anderson and Stallings until he had seen the film—probably in 1927.[41] The German title of the film version, *Rivalen* [Rivals], was then adopted by Zuckmayer for his adaptation. It is easy to understand that Zuckmayer would feel a close affinity to a drama that depicted fighting men in World War I—a war that had exercised its profound and lasting effect upon the playwright and a topic he had dealt with in some of his early prose narratives.[42]

In addition, toward the end of the 1920s a veritable wave of war literature, often with a pacifist slant, swept not only through Berlin and Germany but throughout many of the countries that had participated in World War I. Above all, Erich Maria Remarque's *All Quiet on the Western Front* (1928) had great impact and rekindled the discussion about the war. Such earlier antiwar novels as Henri Barbusse's *Under Fire* (1916; German translation 1918) or John Dos Passos's *Three Soldiers* (1921; German translation 1922) were now followed by Ernest Hemingway's *A Farewell to Arms* (1929), to be discussed below, Ludwig Renn's *War* (1928), and Arnold Zweig's *The Case of Sergeant Grischa* (1927).

As a result of the tendency by writers from various countries to view the war in an unbiased fashion, and often from the perspective of the common soldier, the fighting man in the trenches, it became now possible to present former "enemies" on the German stages.[43] "The Other Side," in this instance the British side, could now be seen and heard in Berlin. For Robert Cedric Sheriff's war play *Journey's End*, after successful runs in London, Paris, and New York, also attracted full houses in Berlin, where it was performed under the title *Die andere Seite*.[44]

*Rivals* opened on 20 March 1929 in the Theater in der Königgrätzer Strasse and was billed as "freely adapted" from *What Price Glory*. Precisely what degree of license Zuckmayer took with the original was a matter of some debate among the critics. German reviewers who, in general, did not have access to the text of the original tended to assume that Zuckmayer had adhered fairly closely to his model. Curiously, the foreign correspondent of the *New York Times* took exception to the adaptation for this very reason. He wrote: ". . . Zuckmayer's work on the play was of the slightest. He has in nowise improved the plot—merely done some cutting and substituted German soldier oaths for the curses of the American Expeditionary Force."[45]

However, a close examination of both the original and the adaptation reveals that Zuckmayer "changed the spirit of the play, . . . altered the characters, language, and structure of the original."[46] At any rate, even if Zuckmayer had intended to follow the original closely, he would have encountered great difficulties for the simple reason that, by his own admission, his knowledge of English was rather inadequate at the time and he was dependent on the translations by others.[47]

Whereas *What Price Glory* may be said to be a "war play, not febrile and pitying, but virile, fertile, poetic and Rabelaisian all at once,"[48] without, however, exhibiting any explicit antiwar tendency, it is an overstatement to claim that "Zuckmayer made use of the Americans' plot as a vehicle for his own feelings against militarism."[49] Rather, the atmosphere of "war, wine and women"[50] evokes *The Merry Vineyard*, if we disregard the element of war. Indeed, Zuckmayer made the language of the original even more colorful, particularly by the addition of a prologue in pidgin English and provoked some raised eyebrows among critics because of an explicit seduction scene. Actually, only act 2 in both the original and the adaptation deals with the grim realities of trench warfare and is most likely to arouse antiwar sentiment. Acts 1 and 3 are largely devoted to the rivalry between Captain Flagg and First Sergeant Quirt who both vie for the favors of Charmaine, the only woman left in a French village immediately behind the front line. Incidentally, the adaptation acquired some fortuitous publicity because of the intense rivalry between the two male leads, Hans Albers and Fritz Kortner, who fought both on and off stage (see *WA*, 2:455).

Zuckmayer's criticism, directed against those noncombatant officers and administrators who populate the hinterland (*Etappe*) of the Western Front—a criticism also to be found, for instance, in "Angela of Leuven"[51]—cannot be construed as a wholesale condemnation of war. As Herbert Ihering observed, the "ideological foundation is so weak that the play could be used for either the fight against war or for its glorification."[52] The innovative staging—which included sound effects—by the proponent of the political theater during the Weimar Republic, Erwin Piscator, rather underscored the ambivalent impression. At the end of the play Captain Flagg and Sergeant Quirt march off together to the front once more. In the face of danger the former rivals become comrade-in-arms again. Thus comradeship, to which Zuckmayer attributed such great importance,[53] emerges as a positive value and war as the medium that generates comradeship. The lack of a clear antiwar tendency was one of the main reasons that several critics compared Zuckmayer's adaptation unfavorably to Remarque's *All Quiet on the Western Front*.

Despite the ambivalent message conveyed by *Rivals*, the sincerity of Zuckmayer's antiwar sentiments is beyond question. In 1930, for example, the playwright publicly protested against the ban on the further showing of the American film version of Remarque's novel. As a former front-line soldier he claimed his right to speak out against Hitler and his cohorts' attempts to silence opposition by pressuring the Republic's authorities to adopt censorship.[54]

A second adaptation Zuckmayer undertook upon the urging of Heinz Hilpert,[55] director of both *Pankraz Awakens* and *The Captain of Köpenick*, revolves like that of *What Price Glory* around the problem of war. In fact, the ending of Hemingway's *A Farewell to Arms* (1929)—the rejection of war by the novel's hero Frederic Henry, as indicated in the title—would seem to make the novel a more suitable vehicle for a dramatic antiwar statement than the previous adaptation. Without doubt, both Zuckmayer and Hilpert, who is listed as one of the adaptors, were aware of the political relevance an adaptation of the novel with its elements of both the topical play *(Zeitstück)* and the war play *(Kriegsstück)* might assume in the volatile atmosphere of the last years of the Weimar Republic. The adaptors used the German translation of *A Farewell to Arms* by Annemarie Horschitz, published by Ernst Rowohlt under the title *In einem anderen Land* [In Another Country] in 1930. The materials available in the Carl-Zuckmayer-Archives also suggest that Zuckmayer was familiar with Laurence Stallings's American dramatization of *A Farewell to Arms* which ran in New York City in the fall of 1930.

The playwright humbly claimed that, unlike the "German reinterpretation" of *What Price Glory*, the Hemingway adaptation constituted a more modest creative effort, a "purely dramaturgical work."[56] The premiere of *Kat* (the name is derived from that of Catherine Barkley, Hemingway's heroine) took place at the Deutsches Theater Berlin on 1 September 1931, where *The Captain of Köpenick* had opened only a few months before. The critics were divided as to the adaptors' success in recapturing the spirit, mood, and language of the novel. Apart from the obvious structural difficulties that arose from translating a piece of prose fiction into dramatic form,[57] much of the discussion centered on thematic aspects.

Although most critics acknowledged the antiwar tendency of both the novel and the adaptation, some tended to direct their attention to the love story between Catherine and Frederic Henry. One reviewer wrote: "Ernest Hemingway's war novel . . . is less a war novel than a bittersweet, tragic love idyll."[58] To be sure, the strong and acclaimed performance by Käthe Dorsch, who had previously played Julchen in *Schinderhannes* and had expressed considerable interest in the role of Catherine (*PoM*, 317), may have shifted the focus of the discussion from the political to the personal level. It is true, Zuckmayer and Hilpert essentially retained the characteristics of Hemingway's hero, "who rejects political and military slogans used to justify aggression, tyranny, and murder [and who] deserts from the army, discards his uniform, and makes his separate peace."[59] However, it seems to be overstating the case to claim that "in dramatizing *A Farewell to Arms* Zuckmayer permitted Hemingway's endorsement of individual freedom to come to life on the Berlin stage at a time when the cause of freedom was under attack as never before in German history."[60]

The resonance of *Kat*, especially when compared to that of *The Captain of Köpenick*, was simply not great enough to justify interpreting the adaptation as an effective political play. Further, despite his courageous public statements against the rising tide of Nazism, in his dramatic production Zuckmayer had turned away from overtly topical plays after the completion of *The Captain of Köpenick*. One of the reasons the playwright gave for his initial hesitance when asked by Hilpert to undertake the adaptation of *A Farewell to Arms* was that he was engaged in the writing of a new drama.[61] This drama was presumably *The Knave of Bergen*, although Zuckmayer indicated that he did not begin to work on the play until 1932 (*WA*, 8:8). That play was not performed until 1934 and demonstrates a new orientation on Zuckmayer's part. Ultimately, then, it is difficult to see in *Kat* more than an interlude, though not an insignificant one.

The humor, which had become one of Zuckmayer's hallmarks and with which he had also endowed his adaptation, particularly in the lovers' encounter with the Swiss customs officials, is quite evident in his play for children, *Cockadoo-Cockadoo*. The play opened on 30 January 1930; like *Rivals* Zuckmayer counted it among the "finger exercises" (*PoM*, 311) that preceded *The Captain of Köpenick*. *Cockadoo-Cockadoo*, in which the two leading roles were played by

children, was cheered by children and adults alike; even the stern
Alfred Kerr felt impelled to write a laudatory review in verse.[62]

But the adaptations and the play for children were not the only
"pieces of craftsmanship" (*PoM*, 311) that Zuckmayer turned out
before receiving the suggestion for *The Captain of Köpenick* from
his friend, the actor Fritz Kortner. There was also a piece of work
that, unlike many of Zuckmayer's dramas, achieved world fame.
This was *The Blue Angel*, a film based on Heinrich Mann's novel
*Small Town Tyrant* (*Professor Unrat*, 1905)[63] and starring Emil Jannings and Marlene Dietrich. In the novel the "tyrant," an elderly
teacher at a boys' school in the Baltic Sea port of Lübeck (a setting
both Thomas and Heinrich Mann used), becomes incensed when
he discovers that some of his charges visit a cabaret singer in a
disreputable tavern. But when he endeavors to catch his students
with the singer, he falls in love with her and eventually becomes
a public disgrace. In the end, he turns the tables on the respectable
burghers by opening a gambling casino in which, with the help of
the singer, he mercilessly fleeces them.

When the novel was published, it had not attracted too much
attention; it was considered an attack on the rigidly disciplinarian
Wilhelminian school system in the manner of Frank Wedekind's
*Spring's Awakening* or Thomas Mann's *Buddenbrooks*.[64] Only some
twenty-five years later the novel became world-famous through the
medium of the film. Precisely the fact that *The Blue Angel* achieved
such acclaim may have led to the contradictory claims that have
been made about the making of the movie in both a German and
an English version in 1929. Zuckmayer flatly states, "the scenario
and dialogue were entirely my own" (*PoM*, 311). This statement is
contradicted by Josef von Sternberg, the Viennese-born American
who came to Berlin to direct the first German sound film. Von
Sternberg asserts that he initiated the changes in the structure and
concept of the novel, notably the change of the title from *Professor
Unrat* to *The Blue Angel* (the name of the establishment in which
the singer appears), the change of the name of the singer from Rosa
Fröhlich to Lola (a derivation of Lulu, the elemental seductress in
two of Frank Wedekind's dramas), and a complete change in the
ending (the professor, utterly disgraced, now returns to his class-
room and dies there).[65] On another occasion von Sternberg dismissed Zuckmayer's contributions to *The Blue Angel* as "not worth
mentioning."[66]

Whatever the merits of von Sternberg's claims,[67] it should be noted that it is difficult to detect any features characteristic of Zuckmayer's work in either Heinrich Mann's *Professor Unrat*, with its biting attack on bourgeois society, or in *The Blue Angel*, with its individual tragedy of a man's downfall caused by his enslavement to a heartless and immoral female. Curiously, while Zuckmayer's fame in Germany certainly did not depend on his association with *The Blue Angel*, in the United States he was often identified as the scriptwriter of the film.[68]

## VI  *Prose Fiction*

Without doubt, Zuckmayer's fame rests on his plays, particularly those which were first performed during the Weimar Republic—from *The Merry Vineyard* to *The Captain of Köpenick*. Hence critics have paid comparatively little attention to Zuckmayer's prose fiction, and the playwright himself mentions these works only in passing in his autobiography *A Part of Myself*. But the prose narratives are by no means an insignificant part of the writer's total *oeuvre*. After the publication of his first collection, *A Farmer from the Taunus and Other Stories* (1927),[69] Zuckmayer considerably broadened his thematic range and refined his narrative skills. In the fragmentary *Sitting Bull: An Indian Novel* the writer had returned once more to the world of *Pankraz Awakens*, although such sensational aspects as incest, miscegenation, and blatant displays of masculinity appear muted. Only a few chapters were published individually in newspapers and magazines during the late twenties; the entire fragment appeared in the *Gesammelte Werke* of 1960[70] but not in the *Werkausgabe* of 1976. Zuckmayer's infatuation with America, the land of the Indian, persisted beyond *Sitting Bull*, yet presumably he never completed the novel because his newly found artistic creed, to be encountered in such works as "The Story of a Farmer from the Taunus" and *The Merry Vineyard*,[71] demanded a subject matter that was firmly rooted in Zuckmayer's realm of experience. Still, the very fact that the writer chose a historical figure as the hero of his narrative and that he planned to include historical events such as Custer's last stand in 1876 are indicative of a more pronounced realistic orientation than in *Pankraz Awakens*. Zuckmayer draws on a well-established tradition in European literature when he endows Sitting Bull with the traits of the noble savage and presents him as the leader of his people's fight against the villainous white men. At any rate, literary models such as James Fenimore Cooper and Karl May, together with the writer's own conception of man's symbiosis with nature, provided more vital stimuli than historical fact.[72]

Eventually the big city Berlin, which also provides the background for *The Captain of Köpenick*, began to assume some significance in Zuckmayer's prose fiction. *A Christmas Story* (1931) takes place in the milieu of the common people whose Berlin dialect Zuckmayer renders with great accuracy. The central event is not the demonstration of the jobless and hungry on the Christmas Eve of 1929 but rather the birth of a child in a tavern to a young woman from abroad. She and her youthful and impecunious companion arouse feelings of protectiveness, generosity, and compassion in the unsentimental and hardened taxi drivers and even in the authoritarian innkeeper. Thus, despite economic deprivation and hardship, the birth of a child imparts, in analogy to the biblical Christmas story, a glimmer of hope in a world of economic crisis.

In the short story *The Monkey Wedding* (1932)[73] contemporary Berlin again provides the setting. The narrative derives its title from the unconventional wedding gift—a rhesus monkey—the artist Robert Rottenbach presents to his friend, a successful lawyer, who marries a rich society girl. The artist and city-dweller Rottenbach, in several respects an alter ego of Zuckmayer, draws his strength from the elemental forces of nature and has not succumbed to the artificial refinements of city life. He and his group of friends, who have preserved their childhood memories and youthful sense of adventure as depicted by James Fenimore Cooper and Karl May, behave in a natural, unaffected, and humane fashion. They provide a stark contrast to the parvenu ostentation, crass materialism, and unenlightened self-interest of the Berlin bourgeoisie. Youthful enthusiasm, sincerity, and defiance of shallow social conventions—traits that, in the context of the short story, Zuckmayer associates with Karl May—are then the positive values that may counteract the debilitating influence of the big city. As in *A Christmas Story*, love and compassion emerge victorious. The occasionally boisterously humorous short story concludes on a tender note when an elderly lady, who lost her son, adopts the unwelcome wedding gift and provides a home for the lonely creature with almost human features, the monkey.

Neither of the two prose narratives that were published in the 1930s is politically or socially oriented; on the contrary, both stories implicitly state that innate human goodness will ultimately overcome the deprivations caused by the severe economic crisis. Yet the publication history of the following prose narrative, *A Love Story*, in 1933 indicates that even a nonpolitical stance was an insufficient legitimation in the eyes of the new masters. In August 1932 the *Völkischer Beobachter*, the organ of the Nazi party, had published a list of writers whose works would be suppressed once the Nazis assumed power.[74] Next to Bertolt Brecht, Lion Feuchtwanger, Klaus Mann, Zuckmayer also appeared on the list—a sinister foreshadowing of things to come. But, curiously, the Ullstein publishing company rather than the Nazis stopped further publication of the serialized *A Love Story* in the weekly *Berliner Illustrierte Zeitung* after the burning of the Reichstag on 27 February 1933. Only Zuckmayer's angry protestations led to the completion of the serialization and even to the book publication of the story in the following year—but now with a different publishing company.[75]

*A Love Story* is a historical tale that takes place in a soldierly milieu—a milieu that had left its indelible impression upon Zuckmayer during his service in World War I. This impression is reflected in such narratives as "Story of a Birth" and "Angela of Leuven."[76] The protagonist Fredersdorff, an officer in the army of Frederick II of Prussia, resolves the conflict between an officer's code of honor and his love for a woman with a tarnished reputation by resigning from the army but then committing suicide in the story's impressive, climactic, and unsentimental finale in which the battle-hardened veterans take leave from their commanding officer. The implicit criticism of the strict and unbending code of the Prussian army, which does not accommodate personal feelings and demands Fredersdorff's resignation, is blunted by the protagonist's ultimate realization that life without the army is not worth living. This realization had already been formulated by Captain von Schlettow in *The Captain of Köpenick*—although with less drastic results.

Fredersdorff's farewell from a world to which he belongs but that rejects him is, in a sense, indicative of Zuckmayer's own fate. *A Love Story* was the last of his prose works to be published in its entirety in Germany. Soon the writer found himself in involuntary exile in Austria and not until after the collapse of the Third Reich would he be able again to have his works published and performed in the country of his birth.

CHAPTER 3

# The Writer in Exile

## I The Knave of Bergen

AT THE beginning of 1933, the year in which Hitler came to power, Zuckmayer was one of the most successful German dramatists. Three of his plays—*Schinderhannes, Katharina Knie,* and *The Captain of Köpenick*—were running in Berlin, and the prose narrative *A Love Story* was being serialized in the pictorial magazine *Berliner Illustrierte Zeitung.* In addition, the playwright was working on a new drama, *The Knave of Bergen,* a play that promised the leading actors of Berlin splendid roles and, for this reason, was eagerly awaited by them. In retrospect Zuckmayer wrote: "Berlin could not offer a writer more. And more could not be taken from a man in the best working period of his life" (*PoM,* 323).

Although the advent of Hitler was to alter the cultural and intellectual climate very drastically and was eventually to affect Zuckmayer very seriously, the change occurred only gradually. For "the tyranny needed time to organize, to close its ranks, to fix on its strategy" (*PoM,* 323). In the beginning, it almost looked as if Zuckmayer's works might escape banishment and that the playwright himself might not be in grave danger. For a time, his works continued to be published in Berlin,[1] and when the writer left the city in the spring of 1933 to visit the Wiesmühl in Henndorf near Salzburg, the small estate he had acquired in 1926, he did not feel like an emigrant. But subsequent events, that is, the increasingly strict control the Nazis assumed over cultural and intellectual life, prevented him from permanently returning to Berlin—although he made a daring expedition to the German capital as late as 1936.

It is indicative of the changed cultural climate that *The Knave of Bergen* was Zuckmayer's first play that did not premiere in Berlin. To be sure, the Vienna Burgtheater, where the drama opened on 6 November 1934, was one of the most prominent stages in the

German-speaking countries. But politics, not choice, had dictated Zuckmayer's decision. Strictly speaking, *The Knave of Bergen* is not an exile play because it was begun before Hitler became German chancellor and because the play was published in Berlin in 1934. Still, as will be seen, there are elements that are attributable to the playwright's awareness of the new circumstances in which he found himself.[2]

At first glance, the play seems far removed from contemporary events. The stage directions state that "the action takes place during the time and in the space of [medieval] legends" (*WA*, 8:8). Further, Zuckmayer cites among his sources the *German Folk Legends from the Lower Rhine*. It is clear, then, that any semblance to actual historical occurrences—as in *The Captain of Köpenick*—has been avoided, and that the substance of the play has been derived from legend. The action, however, takes place in a recognizable setting near the Rhine in the vicinity of what is today the city of Düsseldorf.

After a picturesque and vivacious prologue, which occasionally resembles a medieval version of *The Merry Vineyard*, the central occurrence of the drama, the fateful encounter between the young and beautiful empress and the son of the executioner, takes place. The empress, married to a man many years her senior, visits the old executioner to ask for a cure for her affliction of childlessness. According to medieval superstition, the executioners were also healers—last but not least because of their jurisdiction over the blood of the condemned. The blood was believed to cure ills but could also serve as an aphrodisiac, as Zuckmayer has it in the execution scene of *Schinderhannes* (*WA*, 7:230–31). When the empress and Vincent, the executioner's son, meet, they fall in love without knowing each other's identity—the encounter that, according to the old executioner, was needed for the empress's fulfillment, has taken place. The innocence and purity of the two young people are emphasized in dreamlike scenes of great emotional intensity such as act 1, scene 3. At the same time, the impossibility of a permanent union had been foreshadowed by the minnesinger's song about the cold break of dawn that parts the lovers (*WA*, 8:25). The secret encounters between the empress and Vincent are made possible by the absence of the emperor, who is battling rebellious knights. Yet the lovers' plan to flee Germany is foiled by the return of the victorious emperor and by the watchfulness of a courtier.

A further turn for the worse in Vincent's fortunes occurs when his father falls mortally ill and the son must take over the duties of executioner. However, Vincent is spared shedding the blood of a young infanticide—Zuckmayer here avails himself of a literary motif that is also to be found in Goethe's *Faust*—because the emperor has granted a general pardon. A masked ball offers the lovers the last opportunity to see each other and dance with each other. But Vincent is recognized and, as a transgressor against the law that forbids him social intercourse, sentenced by the emperor to die.

The empress pleads for Vincent's life with the argument that she is pregnant and that no bloodshed should cloud the destiny of her as yet unborn child. An astute politician and a man governed by humanitarian instincts, the emperor pardons Vincent. For the prospect of a male heir—even if conceived out of wedlock—will strengthen his position within the realm. In addition, the emperor boldly ignores the delicate matter of adultery on the empress's part by declaring her inviolate: "She can never be degraded physically or spiritually by being touched by anyone of inferior position. However, whoever is touched by her will be ennobled. Hence he shall become a true member of the nobility and remain so" (*WA*, 8:91). With these words the emperor knights Vincent—who now is free of the curse of the blood shed by his father and free of his inferior social position as a virtual outcast.

The happenings at the masked ball, the recognition of the "Knave" and his being knighted, are also treated in Heinrich Heine's ballad "Knave of Bergen" (1846)—although Zuckmayer does not mention Heine among his sources.[3] Both Heine and Zuckmayer, incidentally, use the term *Schelm* ("knave") in its older meaning of executioner. Yet in both the ballad and in the drama there are traces of the modern *Schelm* or rogue. Heine's ballad relegates the events depicted to history, and in its concluding line states that the knave of Bergen and his offspring now rest in coffins made of stone. Similarly, Zuckmayer's drama does not seem to have any relevance to contemporary affairs. One critic, for example, attributed the play's lack of popularity to the playwright's inability to provide an answer to the pressing social needs in the aftermath of the economic crisis during the late twenties and early thirties.[4] Another critic saw in the play an expression of the "creative crisis" that resulted from the author's exile.[5]

True, the Berlin stages with their wealth of talented directors, actors—many of whom were exiled themselves—and appreciative audiences were no longer at Zuckmayer's disposal. The Nazis' takeover also meant that neither the ironic voice of Alfred Kerr, which had accompanied Zuckmayer with both censure and encouragement from *Crossroads* to *The Captain of Köpenick*, nor that of Kerr's authoritative antipode, Herbert Ihering, were available to provide critical comment and discern future trends of the theater. The evidence suggests that the reviews of the Vienna premiere of *The Knave of Bergen* were laudatory rather than penetrating; precisely the lyrical and picturesque qualities of the play made it noncontroversial in a political sense—even in Berlin.[6]

The lack of contemporary significance supposedly lent the drama universal validity and enabled the playwright to represent a higher reality.[7] Still, *The Knave of Bergen* cannot be entirely divorced from the time of its origin. Despite the almost miraculous social rise of the executioner's son, Zuckmayer places great emphasis on social order and class *(Stand)*. Unlike Voigt in *The Captain of Köpenick*, who pleads eloquently for the rights of the individual that are threatened by the enormous military-bureaucratic establishment, the courtier Lemosier in *The Knave of Bergen* underscores the importance of rigid social classes to which the individual has to subject himself. In his admonition to the empress, whom he wishes to remind of her duties, Lemosier offers a "metaphysical" explanation of the social hierarchy that he declares to be immutable and governed by eternal laws: "Just as the constellations in the sky are immutable, never coming into contact and yet supporting each other—so every human being belongs to his class. And whoever abandons his class will fall into a bottomless void" (*WA*, 8:63).

When compared to the gentle political satire to be found in *The Captain of Köpenick*, not political abstinence but rather a conservative tendency is to be encountered in *The Knave of Bergen*. Zuckmayer's elevation of the emperor to an idealistic representative of everything that is noble in the German character [8] as well as his portrayal of the people in the execution scene as both bloodthirsty and naively superstitious (*WA*, 8:75–80) tend to reinforce this conservative tendency. At any rate, one cannot entirely disregard the similarities between Zuckmayer's concept of a society structured into rather rigid classes—even if this concept is presented in medieval guise—and that of the Austrian Chancellor Dollfuss. Dollfuss, who was murdered in July 1934, promoted an Austrian brand of Fascism that many exiled writers considered to be a far lesser evil than that represented by Hitler. Although one should be careful not to overestimate the political message of *The Knave of Bergen*, the playwright's implicit political stance in a seemingly nonpolitical play, in which the private love affair between the empress and the knave is given more prominence than the emperor's actions to preserve the unity of the empire, merely demonstrates that the exile imposed upon the writer affected his creativity far more seriously than is ordinarily assumed.

## II   Bellman

In contrast to the usual practice of Zuckmayer criticism, the drama *Bellman* will be discussed in the context of the playwright's exile plays. Although the second version, *Ulla Winblad, or Music and Life of Carl Michael Bellman*, which premiered in 1953 and was published in the same year, is better known than the first version, there are rather compelling reasons to deviate from standard practice. Since the basic concept of the play remained largely intact in the second version, the drama qualifies as an exile drama rather than a post–World War II play.[9]

As the titles of the two versions indicate, *Bellman* revolves around the historical figure of Carl Michael Bellman (1740–1795), "the Anacreon of the Scandinavian rococo, poet, composer, instrumentalist" (*PoM*, 202), who is to this day beloved in his native Sweden, and his muse Ulla Winblad, whose role in Bellman's life is only sketchily documented.[10] In choosing Bellman as the main character of his play, Zuckmayer continued to seize upon materials that, at first glance, were far removed from contemporary events. To be sure, as in *The Knave of Bergen* private love affairs and politics tend to mingle, particularly through the introduction of King Gustav III of Sweden who ascended the throne in 1772. His reforms, which limited the power of the aristocracy, and his murder by a rebellious member of that aristocracy in 1792 are part of the plot and provide what Zuckmayer later came to regret as encumbering the character of Bellman with weighty affairs of state.[11] But the playwright warns that "action and characters are only loosely related to history" (*WA*, 9:143) and that the play is "not at all to be understood as a representation of historical events" (*WA*, 9:245).

Actually, Zuckmayer's acquaintance with and performance of Bellman's songs go back to his student days in Heidelberg in 1919.[12] It is clear, then, that the playwright's choice of a presumably noncontroversial subject matter cannot be exclusively attributed to his exile situation and his wish not to become embroiled in politics. But despite his taking refuge in the realm of love, music, and poetry that pervades *Bellman*, politics drastically asserted itself. It is bitterly ironic that while Zuckmayer was inside a Viennese theater participating in the rehearsals for *Bellman* and succumbing to the "irresistible magic exercised by the theater" (*WA*, 1:69), outside in the streets of Vienna another drama unfolded—the collapse of independent Austria that resulted in the *Anschluss* of 13 March 1938.

After an adventurous flight from German-occupied Austria—a flight that Zuckmayer explicitly compared to the escapades of his captain of Köpenick (*PoM*, 54–71)—the playwright found temporary refuge in Switzerland. On 17 November 1938 *Bellman* premiered in the Zurich Schauspielhaus, the foremost stage among the only remaining free German-language theaters, that is, those of Switzerland. In reference to the political aspects of his play Zuckmayer remarked that "poets and musicians are not dramatic agents and their activities exhaust themselves in simply existing but not being actively engaged in anything extrinsic to them."[13] But the "realm of imagination and love" proved an insufficient haven in the face of the deteriorating political situation after the Munich Agreement of 1938 and the Western European powers' attempt to appease Hitler. The playwright was given to uncharacteristic bouts of pessimism; *Bellman*, he assumed, would be the last of his plays to be performed in a German-speaking country. Fortunately, Zuckmayer erred; on 14 December 1946 *The Devil's General*, a play written in Vermont during the last years of World War II, was performed in the Zurich Schauspielhaus and began its conquest of the stages in that part of Germany that was occupied by the Western allies.

After the abortive play *Somewhere in France*, to be discussed below,[14] Zuckmayer did portray a man of action in General Harras, the devil's general, who atones for his support of Hitler's military machine by submitting to divine judgment and, in effect, committing suicide.[15] Zuckmayer strongly identified with Harras, the man of action; even more strongly he identified with Bellman who, unlike Harras, is a poet, singer, and musician, but who, like Harras, is also "a drinker and great lover."[16] While Bellman's carefree life, which exhausts itself in just being rather than acting, may appear as an ideal existence, it is evident that it does not provide protection against the intrusions of politics.

In the very first scene of *Bellman* there are references to the contemporary situation in Germany, specifically to the position of the artist in a totalitarian state. In this scene Ulla Winblad breaks with Bellman, motivated by both jealousy and, to a lesser extent,

by her desire to find economic security as the wife of Baron Lindkrona. In explaining Bellman's inability to repay his debts, Ulla
remarks: "You know, it is these times. It's politics. Now they have
founded an office for cultural affairs. For the poets that's no laughing
matter" (WA, 9:156). In contrast to the totalitarian state's efforts to
have cultural and intellectual endeavors politicized and closely su-
pervised by bureaucrats, Bellman proclaims: "No politics. . . .
Only the kings in fairy tales protected their singers and understood
the signs of their poets. Perhaps we shall meet them on a different
star. Here it may suffice . . . to sing, to love, to dream" (WA,
9:173).

Despite the clearly apolitical nature of Bellman's program, in the
third scene the encounter between the king and politician Gustav
III and the poet and singer Bellman takes place. Although the historical Bellman enjoyed the protection of Gustav III, it is justified
to see in this meeting of an aesthetically inclined and liberal king
with a poet who is oblivious of social rank an expression of Zuckmayer's longing for a free and unrestrictive relationship between
the spheres of politics and art.[17] Ultimately, however, politics and
reason on the one hand and love and poetry on the other are antithetical entities. They can only be reconciled temporarily through
the existence of such a "fable king" (cf. WA, 9:144) as Gustav III.
A king for whom politics is of interest only "as far as it concerns
man and serves life" (WA, 9:200) is a rarity, indeed. It requires a
high-minded statesman to pattern the state after a work of art that
is characterized by both "extreme liberty and extreme discipline"
(WA, 9:200).

Zuckmayer's hopes, then, seemed to rest on the enlightened individual rather than the masses. Although the king institutes a number of democratic reforms, the concept of democracy does not appear
in a positive light, as is evidenced, for example, in the "Drum March
of the Little Man" (WA, 9:203–204). Again, the politicization of the
masses in the Third Reich, albeit in a strictly controlled fashion,
may have influenced Zuckmayer's views.[18]

In scenes 4 and 5, which take place in the park of a royal castle
and a primitive tavern respectively, the different and contrasting
social milieus of the play are juxtaposed. In these two pivotal scenes,
both of which are named after Bellman's songs, the further course
of action, which will directly affect Bellman's fate, is decided. Lindkrona, who so far had resisted the entreaties by rebellious members
of the aristocracy to join their ranks, decides to become one of the

conspirators. Jealousy rather than considerations about the welfare of the state—as perceived by the aristocracy—motivate Lindkrona. He realizes that a strong bond still exists between Ulla Winblad and Bellman and that without the protection of Gustav III Bellman would be a far less formidable threat to his marriage. In scene 5 the final confrontation between Lindkrona and Bellman takes place. Lindkrona's musically and poetically inspired youngest son by a previous marriage has joined Bellman and his motley troupe and refuses to return to his father. Bellman's slightly elegiac "Soliloquium" at the conclusion of scene 5 is in stark contrast to the Dionysiac "Great Drinking Minuet" at the end of scene 4; it foreshadows the subsequent course of events.[19]

Bellman's belief in the power of love—"nothing lasts in the world, nothing is real except love" (*WA*, 9:227), he declares—is ultimately proved true as far as Ulla Winblad is concerned. The new government, which has assumed power after the murder of the king in scene 6, acts on the basis of different premises, however. The nonpolitical Bellman is arrested on the grounds of "machinations detrimental to the state" (*WA*, 9:234), and the arrest itself in its combination of stealth and brutality is strongly reminiscent of the methods employed by Hitler's secret police, the Gestapo.

Although Bellman's escape is accomplished by bribing the prison guards, his planned flight abroad has to be abandoned. In his "protective custody" (*WA*, 9:244)—a euphemism used in Nazi Germany for imprisonment in concentration camps—the poet has become physically weakened to such an extent that he dies in the arms of Ulla Winblad. Ulla left Lindkrona once she learned that he was responsible for murdering the king and incarcerating Bellman.

It is fairly obvious that Bellman's programmatic exclamation "no politics" is rather ineffectual in a world in which the life of each individual is affected by political events. To be sure, Bellman does not go down in ignominious defeat but, like all of Zuckmayer's heroes, accepts death as an inseparable part of life itself.[20] The "hidden topicality"[21] of the play, as expressed in the allusions to the contemporary situation in Germany, clearly reflects the experiences and preoccupations of an exiled writer. But Zuckmayer was not concerned with the analysis of social and political conditions in general and an exploration of the poet's role in society in particular; rather, the figure of Bellman may be seen as an embodiment of the playwright's wishful thinking. For example, Bellman's lack of a passport or an identification card (cf. *WA*, 9:211) suggests Zuckmayer's longing for a life unhampered by bureaucratic restrictions. One need only recall the role identification papers played in *The Captain of Köpenick* to realize the enormous significance proper documents could assume in the life of an individual. In fact, the homeless cobbler Wilhelm Voigt anticipates in many respects the experiences of exiled writers. In his *Conversations of Refugees* Bertolt Brecht has one of his characters remark with wistful irony: "The passport is the noblest part of a human being. It isn't produced in such a simple fashion as a human being. . . . Therefore, it is recognized if it is valid *(gut)*, whereas a human being can be as good as possible and still not be recognized."[22]

Similarly, Bellman's toast in the last scene reflects the sentiments of a writer who has been expelled from his homeland: "How often have I longed to travel and to see the world. Now, when I am forced to, I would much rather stay. . . . To every, every home in the world" *(WA*, 9:242–43). We may assume that Zuckmayer, like Bellman, would have preferred to remain in Europe; yet circumstances beyond his control compelled him to seek refuge in the United States, the country that eventually was to become his new home. Only in the United States did Zuckmayer abandon his political abstinence and return to topical plays somewhat in the fashion of *The Captain of Köpenick*—first in the abortive *Somewhere in France* and then in the successful but problematic *The Devil's General*.

## III   *Prose Fiction, Filmscripts*, Pro Domo

The publication history of the novel *Salwàre* is indicative of the tightening of the grip the Nazis began to hold on cultural life. The prologue appeared as late as November 1935 in the prestigious periodical *Die Neue Rundschau*;[23] however, in the same year the entire first edition of the book was seized in the bindery and destroyed.[24] In 1936 the novel was brought out by Bermann Fischer, who through a special arrangement with the authorities had been able to move from Berlin to Vienna and, like his author Zuckmayer, had become an exile.[25] Zuckmayer now was an "undesirable author" and his books were no longer distributed in the Third Reich as, somewhat ironically, Zuckmayer's own publishing company informed a customer from Germany.[26] Zuckmayer explored publication possibilities abroad. In the case of *Salwàre* his efforts were successful and the novel appeared in English translation in both London and New York.[27]

Curiously, Alfred Kazin, in his review of the American translation, divided contemporary novelists writing in German into émigrés and mystics and assigned Zuckmayer to the latter group.[28] Other American critics simply considered Zuckmayer an Austrian writer. To be sure, such a view was not entirely unjustified because Zuckmayer had established his residence in Henndorf near Salzburg long before his involuntary exile from Berlin. Moreover, according to the note in a 1968 edition, the novel originated in Henndorf in 1934 and 1935 and takes place in the Southern Tyrol near Bozen or Bolzano in Italian, the German-speaking region that Austria had to cede to Italy after World War I.

The novel is the first-person narrative of the amateur painter and explorer Thomas Stolperer who feels compelled to tell his unidentified friend about the strange events that occurred during his extended visit to the castle Salwàre in the Tyrolese mountains. The castle is inhabited by the overrefined descendants of an aristocratic family of ancient lineage. Notably Count Stries, a writer, and his sister Magdalena, upon whom the full moon exercises a mysterious influence that changes her from a slightly eccentric creature to an almost demonic one, epitomize the spirit of fatalism that may be discerned in the novel. The narrator Thomas, who is of a more robust constitution, seeks refuge from his attraction to the delicate Countess Magdalena in the arms of her flesh-and-blood namesake, the waitress of an inn near the castle. The novel ends on a tragic note after the waitress has left the inn and both the count and his sister fall to their deaths when mountain climbing.

True, in contrast to Thomas Mann's *The Magic Mountain*, to which *Salwàre* bears a superficial resemblance because of its setting, a "philosophy of genteel fatalism" and an air of "perplexity and evasion"[29] are discernible in Zuckmayer's novel. Without doubt, the writer's belief in the influence of cosmic forces on human fate contributed to that atmosphere.[30] There are also subtle indications, however, that the contemporary political situation helped determine the somber mood of the novel. Although the Italian officer Mario does not win any converts to Fascism—as a pathetic suitor of Countess Magdalena he appears in a somewhat comical light—the count's aristocratic aloofness is anachronistic in the face of the collectivist movement of Fascism that threatens to extinguish individuality. In fact, in one of many poignant discussions about subjects covering a broad spectrum of intellectual and artistic endeavor that form an essential ingredient of the novel, America is mentioned as the last refuge for creative people because there is increasingly less room for them in Europe.[31] The allusion to an America that is no longer populated by the Indians and pioneers of *Pankraz Awakens* or *Sitting Bull* but, instead, is associated with Broadway and Hollywood clearly indicates Zuckmayer's awareness of his precarious status as a writer in exile—even if, at the time of composing the novel, Austria might have appeared to be a comparatively safe haven. At any rate, the American publication of the novel prior to Zuckmayer's arrival did not significantly enhance his stature in the United States. At best, although one critic granted that it was "really beautifully written,"[32] *Salwàre* may have enjoyed the "quiet vogue" predicted by another American critic.[33]

Just as Berlin had provided the setting for Zuckmayer's prose works in the years preceding his expulsion from Germany, Austria began now to play a larger role. Apart from the novel *Salwàre*, there are the short story *A Walk in Spring* (1935), the largely autobiographical *Henndorf Pastorale*, and a harmless trifle, the novel-length narrative *A Summer in Austria* (1937).[34] Both *A Walk in Spring* and *Henndorf Pastorale* were only published after World War II;[35] especially the latter work in its evocative mood recalls the chapter devoted to Austria in Zuckmayer's autobiographies and the narrative *The Soul Brew*.[36] *A Summer in Austria* betrays its origins as a film-script; it exhibits elements of both the provincial and folkloristic *Heimatfilm* and the travelogue in its depiction of a group of slightly eccentric English tourists who have rented a castle in the vicinity of Salzburg and seek to emulate the natives in their costume, if not in their manners. Perhaps the unmitigated hilarity by which *A Summer in Austria* is inspired is merely an escape mechanism, an attempt to counteract the anxiety caused by threatening political developments. This is evident from Zuckmayer's retrospective observation that, for example, the poem "Cosmic Interference," written in 1937 and included in *Henndorf Pastorale* (WA, 4:79), should not merely be interpreted as a nature poem but as an indication of apprehension and, at the same time, life-affirming courage in the face of imminent threats. Actually, Zuckmayer's poems from this period are essentially nature poems or, rather, poems concerned with the relationship of man to nature, the elements, and the Creator.[37] If contrasted, for example, with Brecht's well-known poem "To Those Born Later" from the same period, in which the poet declared it to be "almost a crime" to speak about trees in "dark times,"[38] Zuckmayer's essentially nonpolitical stance becomes quite evident.

Perhaps it was appropriate that *A Summer in Austria*, with its unclouded gaiety, represented Zuckmayer's unwitting farewell to Austria; it was the last of his works to be published in that country before the *Anschluss* of March 1938.

In the six years from 1925 to 1931 six Zuckmayer plays (from *Pankraz Awakens* to *The Captain of Köpenick*), two adaptations, and a play for children had premiered in Berlin. However, from 1933 to 1938 only two new plays and one adaptation were performed. This "free adaptation" of the old Indian play *Vasantasena* was staged in London in 1934.[39] The production impressed one critic through "the splendour of its pageantry and the shimmering richness of its décor" rather than through its dramatic substance.[40] Zuckmayer himself attributed so little significance to his adaptation that he failed to mention it explicitly in his autobiography. Without doubt the adaptation, possibly inspired by Lion Feuchtwanger's previous German version of *Vasantasena*, was one of those jobs merely undertaken for securing a livelihood. The emphasis, however, on visual effects, relates the production of *The Golden Toy* to Zuckmayer's activities for another medium, the film. Writing for the European film industry became an increasingly important aspect in the exiled writer's efforts to compensate for the loss of the German theater—discernible in the comparative paucity of dramatic productions from 1933 to 1938—and book market. Although he speaks disparagingly of "earning my bread doing movie work" (*PoM*, 38), under the best of circumstances such "movie work" could yield artistically satisfactory results. Such is the case with *Master of Life and Death* (1938), originally intended as a film story.

In its setting—Paris and London but also rural Northern France—this prose narrative exhibits the cosmopolitan character desirable for a film appealing to an international audience. But it is rather far removed from previous settings used by Zuckmayer. The "master of life and death," the famous heart surgeon Sir Norbert Stanhope, marries Lucile, a French girl from an impoverished aristocratic family. A deep gulf opens between husband and wife when Sir Norbert is on the point of killing their newly born infant who has suffered severe brain damage. His self-assurance and rational approach to life make the physician a proponent of euthanasia; only when faced with the possibility that his wife might commit suicide is he able to release his rigidly controlled emotions and forgive her deception and infidelity. Lucile had fallen deeply in love with the young French doctor Raymond, whose practice of medicine was infused with that spirit of compassion that Sir Norbert's clinical approach lacked.

The action of the prose narrative is fast-paced and the prose tends toward being taut; however, such coincidences as Sir Norbert's meeting with Raymond on a train and Raymond's subsequent death in a train wreck on the eve of his elopement with Lucile may destroy the reader's suspense of disbelief.

Zuckmayer was, of course, no stranger to the film industry, as his collaboration on *The Blue Angel* has shown.[41] In addition, as Zuckmayer became better known, films were made of his own works— beginning in 1927 with *Schinderhannes*.[42] But the "struggle for existence" (*PoM*, 76), which became particularly acute after Zuckmayer's flight from Austria to Switzerland in 1938, resulted in greatly increased productivity. Zuckmayer mentions that he turned out "six movie scenarios" (*PoM*, 77) in one year. Apart from *A Summer in Austria* and *Master of Life and Death*, works that could only be distributed to a German-speaking public outside the Third Reich, such foreign-language films as *Escape Me Never* (1935), based on the dramatization of Margaret Kennedy's bestseller novel *The Constant Nymph* (1924) and starring Elisabeth Bergner; *Rembrandt* (1936), directed by the British "*grand seigneur* among movieland's adventurers" (*PoM*, 76), Alexander Korda, with Charles Laughton in the title role; and *Mayerling to Sarajevo* (1940), a romantic love story directed by Max Ophüls, attracted international attention.[43] Needless to say, Zuckmayer's share in these films tended to be overshadowed by the achievements of stars and directors.[44] That, ultimately, Zuckmayer did not consider himself a screenwriter is demonstrated by the fact that he left Hollywood with its promise of a secure livelihood, when he was thwarted in his attempts to complete his screen adaptation of Arnold Zweig's novel *The Case of Sergeant Grischa*.[45] Nevertheless, Zuckmayer's work for the film industry cannot be ignored altogether, particularly since film stories such as *A Summer in Austria* and *Master of Life and Death* were conceived in epic rather than dramatic, dialogue-oriented terms and hence tended to reinforce the "epic" tendencies in Zuckmayer's drama.[46]

Of greater consequence than Zuckmayer's film stories is his autobiographical essay *Pro Domo*, an attempt to define his position after the flight from Austria. *Pro Domo* was the last of Zuckmayer's works to be published in Europe before his emigration to the United States;[47] we may then consider this intellectual and spiritual stock-taking as the sum of an important phase in Zuckmayer's life almost exactly at its midpoint.[48] At the same time, however, Zuckmayer looks to the future in the antifatalistic, life-embracing fashion of Nietzsche's *amor fati*. In five sections he sketches his intellectual development from boyhood and youth, the impact of World War I, the revolutionary postwar era with its flourishing of the arts, to the present. Although *Pro Domo* is not autobiographical in a strict sense, the various phases of Zuckmayer's life, as they are also to be found in *Second Wind*, emerge quite clearly. Although the Nazis are never mentioned by name, it is obvious that Zuckmayer opposed their ideology—notably in his disquisition on anti-Semitism. Zuckmayer's Jewish heritage was of no consequence to him—his mother's father had been a converted and thoroughly assimilated Jew—and he professed himself to be a German who viewed Zionism with caution. As a German, however, he was aware of the flaws in the German character. Those flaws he had portrayed, for example, in such a figure as Knuzius in *The Merry Vineyard;* but he had opposed to him the representative of the "true" German, Gunderloch.[49] In endowing his dramas with "metaphysical" qualities, Zuckmayer opted for a theater that was the opposite of tendentious, didactic, ideological drama and instead founded on "beauty, truth, humanity."[50] These ideals could not be accommodated within the confines of narrow nationalism; hence for Zuckmayer being both German and a citizen of the world were not incompatible. *Pro Domo* ends with a profession of *Weltbürgertum*. That concept of *Weltbürgertum* was, however, inspired by elevated sentiments rather than founded in the political realities of the day. Thus the satirist Alfred Polgar, a fellow exile, admired Zuckmayer's vision but also noted cautiously that survival in exile was not merely a matter of will and high-principled intentions but quite often a matter of chance.[51]

## IV  Second Wind, Somewhere in France, *Prose Writings*

Despite the optimistic predictions of a Theatre Guild director that Broadway would not only be able to absorb the sudden influx of talented playwrights, actors, stage designers, and directors but also ultimately benefit from it,[52] the fact is that the vast majority of exiles from Hitler's Germany and Austria did not make much of an impact on the theatrical scene. Franz Werfel's play *Jacobowsky and the*

*Colonel* which, in S. N. Behrman's adaptation, premiered in New York on 14 March 1944 and ran for over a year, is most decidedly an exception. In contrast to the theater, the film industry seemed to offer better opportunities for writers, especially since a large German colony had become established in Hollywood. Zuckmayer, now deprived of his German citizenship, arrived in New York in June 1939 with his family on visitor's visas but had to immigrate officially via Cuba later during the same year. Despite the material security of a seven-year contract as a motion picture scriptwriter, he found the artificial life-style of that "anteroom to hell called Hollywood" (*PoM*, 346) abhorrent and the restrictions placed on his artistic freedom of expression too confining. He returned to New York and obtained a job as lecturer in Erwin Piscator's Dramatic Workshop, a branch of the New School for Social Research.

His negative experience in Hollywood notwithstanding, it seemed that Zuckmayer was getting a good start, in contrast to many less fortunate exiles. As early as July 1940, excerpts from *Second Wind* were published.[53] The autobiography itself, with an introduction by the eminent journalist, Dorothy Thompson, appeared in December 1940.[54] Unlike *Pro Domo, Second Wind* concentrates on occurrences and people rather than presenting an essayistic philosophy of life. It is remarkable that in many respects *Second Wind* anticipates *A Part of Myself*; the seven chapters correspond closely to the main sections in Zuckmayer's later autobiography and clearly demonstrate that, by this time, certain phases in the writer's life, such as World War I, the postwar era, life during the Weimar Republic in Berlin and during exile in Austria, had assumed their unalterable significance as distinct building blocks for a future autobiography that would also take into account the years in the United States. To be sure, in *A Part of Myself* the chapters appear greatly expanded so that the subtitle of the English translation, *Portrait of an Epoch*, is justified. But the principle of beginning the autobiography with an incisive period and only then proceeding in chronological fashion is already in evidence in *Second Wind*.

Although the autobiography was well received by the critics— "a book outstanding in emigrant literature," wrote one reviewer [55]— *Second Wind* remained the only American publication of a book during Zuckmayer's stay in this country. It took thirty years before another book of his, *A Part of Myself* (1970), attracted considerable attention. We are hence faced with the curious fact that not the dramatist Zuckmayer but Zuckmayer, the writer of memoirs, achieved a very limited success in this country.

But in 1940, after the abortive Hollywood venture, Zuckmayer was eager to try his hand at a play that would enable him to gain access to Broadway. For Zuckmayer, who in *Pro Domo* had spoken up for the values he believed in and who in *Second Wind* had expressed his readiness to come to terms with the strange New World he now inhabited, a different orientation seemed to be called for. Politics had asserted themselves as a decisive factor in Zuckmayer's life; hence it is safe to assume that the political events of 1940, especially the defeat of France at the hands of Hitler's armies and the subsequent armistice of 22 June 1940, provided the impetus for the collaborative effort with the actor Fritz Kortner. Zuckmayer had known Kortner from his Berlin years during the twenties; they now wrote a play first entitled *The Last Round* and later *Somewhere in France*. The exiled artist Kortner felt it to be his duty to wage the fight against Hitler from the stage, and it was he who supplied the basic idea of the play.[56] *Somewhere in France* constituted Kortner's second venture as a playwright in America after his and Dorothy Thompson's *Another Sun*, a drama about refugees in New York, had failed after only eleven performances.

In their attempt to elucidate the defeat of France as a warning against the aggression of Nazism by dramatic means, Zuckmayer and Kortner availed themselves of the popular-didactic play, *The Fourth Commandment*, by the nineteenth-century Austrian playwright Ludwig Anzengruber. In order to exemplify his thesis that parents are only deserving of the respect and obedience of their children if they have their offspring's interest at heart, Anzengruber introduces three families. But Zuckmayer and Kortner transplant only the most degenerate family from late nineteenth-century Vienna to a small French town. The children of the Viennese Schalanters do not fare well at all. Goaded on by her frivolous, pleasure-seeking mother, the daughter turns into a prostitute; the son follows in the footsteps of his father, who much prefers carousing to a day's work. He ends as a convicted murderer. Although the French Marignacs are financially better off than their Viennese models—father Marignac is the proprietor of an inn whereas Schalanter is a craftsman who has fallen on hard times—they share in the moral bankruptcy of their literary precursors. Hence we may infer that Zuckmayer and Kortner intended to draw attention to the corruption of segments of the French populace as it manifests itself in the

Marignacs. Through their political blindness, egocentricity, and, ultimately, collaboration with the Germans they contribute to the collapse of France. For example, despite warnings about imminent war in the politically volatile situation of May 1939, we see father Marignac full of hopes for expanding his business at the beginning of act 1. Although his son André enlists in the French army, he does so less out of patriotic fervor than for the enhancement of his masculinity. His violent temper, a character trait adopted from his Viennese model, finally causes him to kill a superior officer. To be sure, Marignac's daughter Odette does not engage in actual prostitution like Josepha Schalanter; however, she commits an act of political prostitution by supporting her lover, the industrialist Laboureur. Laboureur sabotages defense installations and actively collaborates with the Germans because he believes that the strongman Hitler will establish a new order in Europe, an order in which all social forces inimical to the vested interests of the ruling classes will be suppressed. There are further indications in the play that the Nazi ideology has found sympathizers among members of the French establishment since the local prefect also supports Laboureur. In the face of such formidable obstacles, the true patriot Mercier, who in act 2 is in charge of the defense measures against the advancing German armies, does not have much of a chance.

The play opened in Washington, D.C., on 28 April 1941 and ran for a week. In addition, there were several benefit performances in New York; but the planned Broadway production by the Theatre Guild was first postponed and then withdrawn.[57] The theater critics acknowledged the "timeliness and significance"[58] of the play that depicted the "spiritual sterility of France, the confusion, venality and treason that preceded the débâcle;"[59] however, they also noted a "tremendous diffusion of interest"[60] that rendered it ultimately impossible to decide whether the play was a love story about the romantic entanglement of André and the kitchen maid Marie or a political drama. What was missing, one critic claimed, was the "driving, hard-hitting impact upon American consciousness"[61] that transmitted an unambiguous message to the audience—a message, incidentally, that is clearly discernible in Anzengruber's play.

To be sure, Zuckmayer and Kortner did not confine themselves to the depiction of France before and during the collapse. Rather, they took issue with Nazism in the character of Buerzenich, a traveling champagne salesman from Cologne in act 1 and an officer of the German occupation army in act 3, scene 2. Buerzenich is characterized by Mercier as a representative of Germany's ancient and obsessive desire for world domination—a desire that is in stark contrast to the spirit of the other Germany as embodied by Goethe, Heine, and Stresemann. When compared with such an exile play as Bertolt Brecht and Lion Feuchtwanger's *The Visions of Simone Machard*, a play that likewise deals with the fall of France, it is obvious that Zuckmayer and Kortner's attempt to come to grips with the phenomenon of Nazism remains very much in the realm of the metaphysical and abstract and thus foreshadows Zuckmayer's later play *The Song of the Fiery Furnace*. Hence the play's political message appears blunted and André's final act of resistance not very convincing.

In retrospect, Zuckmayer blamed the failure of *Somewhere in France* on his inability to conform to the norms of Broadway.[62] There is, without doubt, some truth in such an explanation. More importantly, with *Somewhere in France* Zuckmayer had returned to the political and topical play in the manner of *The Captain of Köpenick*. At the same time, Zuckmayer resorted to the milieu of his adaptation of Anderson and Stallings's *What Price Glory*—an adaptation that Herbert Ihering had then found lacking in an unambiguous antiwar statement.[63] In a sense, in 1941 the American critics merely reiterated and paraphrased the objections Ihering had voiced some twelve years before. In the final analysis, then, it was not Zuckmayer's nonconformist stance vis-à-vis Broadway that led to the failure of *Somewhere in France* but rather the play's insufficiently clear message.

For all practical purposes, the failure of *Somewhere in France* meant that Zuckmayer had not succeeded in becoming established on the American literary scene. In 1941 Zuckmayer had rented a farm near Barnard, Vermont, and his existence as a farmer precluded further sustained literary efforts.[64] Actually, there is a noticeable dearth of publications between 1942 and 1945—a dearth to which, without doubt, the difficulty of being required to write in English greatly contributed. In his "Verses Written in Linguistic Exile," dedicated to Thomas Mann on occasion of his seventieth birthday on 6 June 1945 (*WA*, 3:113–14), Zuckmayer whimsically reflected on the problems created by the endeavor to express oneself in a different linguistic medium. Matters were not necessarily facilitated by the employment of translators. For example, in the case of *Second Wind* Zuckmayer had offended the feminine sensibilities of his translator Elizabeth Reynolds Hapgood with his explicit depiction of gruesome war experiences.[65] A problem of a different kind was posed by the quality of the translations. When the fellow exile Hermann Kesten asked Zuckmayer for a contribution to a planned anthology of modern European literature, the playwright wished to have a scene from the English version of *The Captain of Köpenick* included—despite his serious reservations about the inadequate rendering.[66] Ultimately, not the scene in question (act 2, scene 14) but the poem "My Death" in the translation of E. B. Ashton was printed in the anthology.[67] That the publication of a single poem—moreover, a poem that first appeared in print in 1937[68]—is noteworthy at all, is indicative of both the exiled writer's diminished production and his severely limited publishing opportunities. A few times Zuckmayer succeeded in placing short stories in magazines with a national distribution; none of these prose narratives, however, can be counted among the writer's stronger artistic achievements. Thus "The Swiss Pension" (1942),[69] a story based on childhood memories; "Don't Give Your Animals a Name" (1945),[70] humorous episodes of farm life in Vermont; and "A Tiger's Heart" (1947),[71] a circus story, are not to be found in either the *Gesammelte Werke* or the *Werkausgabe*—an indication that Zuckmayer himself did not think too highly of these literary efforts whose sole purpose presumably was to earn some money.

With the exception of "Don't Give Your Animals a Name," these stories do not reflect the writer's experiences in the United States. At the same time, nostalgia for a lost world is not very much in evidence either. In fact, there is one facet of Zuckmayer's literary activity that attests to his awareness of, and concern for, the plight of the exile. When on 23 February 1942 the internationally renowned and materially successful Austrian-born émigré writer Stefan Zweig and his second wife committed suicide in Petropolis, Brazil, their deaths were interpreted by many exiles as a defeat of one of the chief representatives of humanitarian pre-Hitler Europe in the face of naked aggression. For at the beginning of 1942 Hitler and his allies controlled practically all of continental Europe and considerable parts of North Africa; even the Atlantic Ocean did no longer seem to offer an insurmountable barrier to them. In order to combat the hopelessness and despair among the refugees that were either caused or intensified by Zweig's suicide, Zuckmayer, who himself was deeply affected by his friend's death, penned his "Appeal to the Living."[72] Without mentioning Zweig by name, he exhorted his fellow exiles in rhetorically skillful fashion but with great emotional intensity not to surrender to despair but to fight for the freedom of the spirit. Not a program for any specific action, the "Appeal" nevertheless cannot have failed to instill confidence in those tempted "to cast off this weary burden of life."[73] The "Appeal" is, without doubt, a moving and important document from the period of exile; Zuckmayer himself attributed so much significance to it that, much later, he used it as the title for his first collection of essays.[74]

Although Zuckmayer claims that "Appeal to the Living" was the only pamphlet *(Flugblatt)* he published during World War II,[75] once more he felt compelled to address himself to an issue that was of concern to most exiles. In 1944, Germany's defeat at the hands of the allies seemed to have become inevitable. At that time the discussions about Germany's postwar future intensified. The "Council for a Democratic Germany," one of the organizations of exiles, sought, supported by American sponsors such as John Dewey, the publisher B. W. Huebsch, and Dorothy Thompson, to influence the future course of events by advocating a "just peace." However, there was no unanimity as to which political goals, if any, the exiles should pursue on the eve of the allied invasion of France. Thomas Mann's daughter Erika, for example, sharply disagreed with the thesis of the Council that a distinction should be made between the Nazis and other Germans.[76] In his open letter to Erika Mann, Zuckmayer emphasized that he had deliberately refrained from joining any committees of German or Austrian emigrants but stressed that, for reasons of fairness, he could not support a wholesale condemnation of the entire German people. In addition, he argued, such condemnation would be detrimental to an eventual normalization of international relations in the postwar period.[77] The brief controversy between Zuckmayer and Erika Mann, incidentally, recalls the much better known one in which Brecht and Thomas Mann debated exiles' politics, the postwar future of Germany, and related issues.[78]

To be sure, Zuckmayer's attitude was dictated less by political considerations than by his desire to be "just" toward the German people, even "in their darkest hour."[79] The desire to be just ultimately also inspired *The Devil's General* and led to charges of ambiguity and a conciliatory attitude toward Nazism.[80] The play originated in Vermont but was not performed and published until after World War II. Although Zuckmayer repeatedly stressed his inability to concentrate on writing because farm chores required his undivided attention, he managed to contribute smaller pieces both to *Aufbau*—strictly speaking, a periodical of Jewish immigrants rather than exiles[81]—and other publications founded by refugees.[82] Apart from those lesser literary efforts he succeeded in completing, but not publishing in this country, both the prose narrative *The Soul Brew* and the play *The Devil's General*—works that in their decidedly Austrian and German orientation show no trace of their place of origin but demonstrate Zuckmayer's intense concern with German affairs.

## CHAPTER 4

# Post–World War II Works

## I The Devil's General

ZUCKMAYER reports in his autobiography how in December 1941 he read a brief notice in American newspapers about the death of Ernst Udet, World War I flying ace and, at the time of his death, chief of the Air Force Supply Service of the German army.[1] Almost a year later, the word "state funeral" that had appeared in the news item (*PoM*, 382) set in motion the playwright's creative energies. According to his account, the sudden inspiration resulted in a complete plan for the drama: "The whole story was there in my mind—without a gap" (*PoM*, 382). However, the play was not completed until more than two years later owing to Zuckmayer's demanding chores as a farmer in Vermont. Unlike *Somewhere in France*, *The Devil's General* was a play intended for a German audience—although the playwright could not, at the play's inception, hope for a performance in Germany. Even when, after the decisive battle of Stalingrad (November 1942–February 1943) the tide began to turn and eventually the defeat of the Hitler regime became inevitable, the prospects for seeing the play on a German stage seemed remote. There was, after all, no possibility of assessing the chances of a drama that addressed itself to Germany's immediate past. In Udet, opponent and yet collaborator, Zuckmayer had found a model that could offer an explanation as to why many Germans, although they were not Nazis themselves, ultimately supported Hitler. Zuckmayer recalled that Udet had offered his considerable talents to the new masters for no other reason than his belief that only in Germany would he be able to indulge his passionate love of flying.

It is understandable that the allied occupation forces did not look favorably upon a play that seemed to offer too sympathetic a portrayal of a Nazi general. Hence the drama premiered in Switzerland, in the Zurich Schauspielhaus on 14 December 1946.[2] Curiously, just as the performance of *Bellman* on the same stage in 1938 had signaled Zuckmayer's imminent departure from Europe, the premiere of *The Devil's General* augured the exile's triumphant return to Europe in general and to Germany in particular. Such return was the exception rather than the rule, but Zuckmayer was able to be present at the Zurich premiere—as a civilian employee of the United States government he had been sent to Germany in the fall of 1946 to study the state of cultural affairs in the war-ravaged country.

Even before the play reached German theaters—strictly speaking, those of the American, British, and French occupation zones; it was not performed in the Soviet occupation zone—*The Devil's General* had attracted such a degree of advance publicity that the German premieres in Hamburg and Frankfurt (November 1947) were eagerly awaited. When the play was finally staged in Germany, it had a profound impact and stimulated intense debates wherever it was performed.[3] A glance at the text may help explain why it was so widely debated.

The first act, by far the longest, takes place in the private dining room of an elegant Berlin restaurant. It is entitled "The Time Bomb" (911)[4]—a reference to a newly installed device through which the secret police, the Gestapo, hope to record General Harras's remarks about the Führer and the Nazi regime. Harras, a member of the air force, is known to be an opponent of Hitler; at the same time, he has no qualms about enjoying the privileges, including the delicacies from the occupied countries with which the table is laden, which accrue to his high military rank. His entrance in "full dress uniform" (912) and the festive atmosphere that develops with the arrival of other guests belie the fact that the year is 1941 and America is on the point of entering the war.

Harras's invited and uninvited guests belong to those circles who hold positions of influence in the Third Reich. There is, for example, the industrialist von Mohrungen. He is an honorable man according to Harras; nevertheless, he helped finance Hitler during the Weimar Republic in the hopes of using him against Communism. The diplomat, Baron Pflungk, however, secretly despises the "plebeian" Nazis yet serves them willingly in order to advance his career. Conversely, the narrow-minded and doctrinaire Dr. Schmidt-Lausitz is an ardent supporter of National Socialism. In fact, apart from functioning as an agent of the Gestapo, he is officially charged with disseminating its ideology.[5] Colonel Eilers, leader of a fighter squadron, shows yet a different attitude; he represents those younger, idealistic officers who serve Hitler out of conviction and patriotism and not for material gains or personal advantages.

There are other characters on stage whose attitudes toward Nazism are developed in numerous discussions but who do not significantly contribute to advancing the action.[6] Only the confrontation between Harras and Schmidt-Lausitz results in a dramatic conflict that requires an eventual resolution. The Nazi Schmidt-Lausitz and the anti-Nazi Harras have become irreconcilable opponents and it is clear that the former will do everything in his power to destroy the latter. But Schmidt-Lausitz is only the external agent of Harras's eventual perdition that is preceded by the inner drama of a process of recognition; through his heated exchange with Harras about the exiled writer Erich Maria Remarque he forces Harras to take stock of the situation and to become aware of his morally ambivalent position as both an opponent of Hitler and his servant.

The second act, entitled "Stay of Execution or The Hand" (932), takes place approximately two weeks later. Harras returns to his flat from the prison of the Gestapo where he had been incarcerated. Again Schmidt-Lausitz and Harras engage in a confrontation that brings out their profound personal and ideological differences. Harras is granted ten days during which he is to find the causes for the defects in new airplanes that cause them to crash. The externally imposed "stay of execution" forces Harras to act if he wishes to survive. But as the further events reveal, the general is less interested in solving the mystery of the sabotaged airplanes than in coming to terms with his awakening conscience. His second encounter with the young actress Diddo Geiss evokes the fleeting vision of flight and happiness with Diddo outside Germany. This encounter is followed by the "turning point" of the inner action of the play.[7] The singer Olivia Geiss hands Harras a letter from a Jewish surgeon, inmate of a concentration camp, whom Harras had planned to help escape. The surgeon, however, committed suicide, partly because of his desire not to cause Harras even greater difficulties. The surgeon's death moves Harras deeply. For the first time, he formulates an admission of guilt: "Everybody has his conscience-Jew or several of them so he can sleep nights. But you can't buy yourself free with that. That's self-deception. We're guilty for what's happening to thousands of people we don't know and can never help. Guilty and damned for all eternity. Permitting viciousness is worse than doing it" (940).

Despite the almost naturalist milieu depiction of the first act, Zuckmayer employs symbolic elements fairly consistently. Thus Harras's feeling of guilt manifests itself in his seeing the gigantic five fingers of God's hand (mentioned in the title of the second act) when the searchlights of a flak station light the dark sky. Harras's allusion to the biblical writing on the wall (Dan. 5:25–27) is a further indication that Zuckmayer conceived of Harras's inner struggle in moral terms. Although *The Devil's General* is not a "religious" play by any means, one encounters religious allusions fairly frequently. The regime of the "devil" Hitler uses "hellish" devices (the German term for the aforementioned recording machine in the first act is *Höllenmaschine*) and holds great promise and rewards for those willing to serve it. Toward the end of the second act the dedicated National Socialist Pootsie von Mohrungen, who in every respect presents a complete contrast to Diddo Geiss, tempts Harras with the offer of great power if he would only abandon "that old drivel about freedom, humanity" (948) and join the ranks of the new masters. In analogy to the biblical temptation of Christ through the devil (Matt. 4:8–12; Luke 4:5–8) Harras resists and again sees the threatening hand of God in the sky. His final vision of a better future, exclusively devoted to love, is ultimately relegated to the realm of wishful thinking.

The third act, "Damnation," takes place on the last day of the period of grace granted Harras. Apart from the fact that his life is at stake, Harras has now an additional motivation for finding those responsible for the defective airplanes: his friend Colonel Eilers crashed in one of those ill-fated machines and was killed. But Harras's efforts to find the culprits have been in vain. Ironically, for a long time he believed that the Gestapo and SS had instigated the sabotage to undermine his authority and to gain control of the air force. The results of a series of discussions propel Harras further along on his way toward "damnation." In his talk with Lieutenant Hartmann, whose belief in the ideals of sacrifice and purity, propagated by Nazi ideologists, has been shattered by his witnessing the killing of Jews, Harras formulates his conviction that divine justice will prevail in the end. That this divine justice will also be meted out to himself and that he cannot escape his damnation for the guilt he incurred by supporting an evil government is forcefully brought home to Harras by Colonel Eilers's widow, who accuses him of lacking the courage of his true conviction. In his discourse with Oderbruch, an engineer in the air administration, Harras finally is enlightened about the cause of the crashes. Oderbruch confesses to have sabotaged the planes in order to hasten the demise of the Nazis' shameful and evil rule. Although Harras has the option of either being completely rehabilitated by denouncing Oderbruch or—as Oderbruch suggests—of attempting to flee abroad and to work for the resistance movement, he rejects both possibilities. With his often-quoted words, "Whoever has been the devil's general on earth and paved the way for him with bombs, he also has to prepare lodgings for him in hell" (*WA*, 8:230),[8] Harras submits to "divine judgment" by flying a defective airplane in which he promptly crashes and is killed. Schmidt-Lausitz has the last word in the play when, after reporting the accident by phone, he reiterates the instructions he receives: "State funeral, with full military honors" (958). Those words, it will be recalled, initially triggered Zuckmayer's creative response and eventually led to the completion of *The Devil's General*.

Zuckmayer's play elicited divergent critical reactions. From the very beginning, political aspects predominated in the discussion. Whereas conservative and liberal critics tended to praise the lack of tendentiousness, reviewers with leftist leanings faulted the drama for precisely the same reason, that is, the absence of any discernible ideology on the part of the author.[9] For example, one critic lauded Zuckmayer's portrayal of the demonic powers of evil—a portrayal that transcended mere milieu realism[10]—yet another literary scholar charged the playwright with misrepresenting such socioeconomic facts as the collaboration between German industrialists and Nazis and thereby shrouding historical reality with a veil of mysticism.[11]

But it was Harras, the central character, who was most widely debated. Although Zuckmayer presented him as an individualized character, his actions assume general significance in that they provide at least a partial answer to the question why so many Germans in influential positions became willing tools of the Nazis even if they despised them.[12] As several critics noted, however, the vitality, charm, loyalty toward friends, and appeal to women that Harras exudes particularly during the lengthy and festive first act make it somewhat difficult to accept his ultimate atonement for his cooperation with the powers of evil. Paradoxically, with Harras's growing awareness of his moral failure in the course of the play he loses in dramatic substance and theatrical appeal. Luise Rinser argues convincingly that the portrayal of Harras in the second and third acts was influenced by Zuckmayer's serious doubts about his original concept of Harras, that is, a man of action who shuns contemplation in favor of attacking the tasks at hand with vigor and self-assurance.[13] While using Udet as his model, Zuckmayer projected his own wishful thinking into the character of Harras, who appears to have several traits in common with the playwright himself.[14] Yet there is no total identification with Harras on Zuckmayer's part; Harras's increasing moral stature and ultimate atonement reveal the playwright's dissociation from his youthful dreams about an active life unencumbered by introspection and awareness of moral categories.

For critics of leftist persuasion such psychologizing explication would not do. In a fierce diatribe Paul Rilla castigated Harras as an unprincipled, characterless scoundrel who, unlike Schmidt-Lausitz and his ilk, disguised his bestiality with aesthetic sentiments.[15] Although many critics expressed reservations about Zuckmayer's sympathetically drawn Nazi general, Rilla went furthest in his condemnation of Harras, whose moral purification he almost entirely ignores.

Next to Harras it was Oderbruch who was most widely discussed. As the representative of active resistance against Nazism his actions are in sharp contrast to those of Harras. Yet, curiously, he does not emerge as an opponent of Harras but rather as his friend. Moreover, Oderbruch's character is not nearly as fully developed as that of Harras and his presence on stage is rather limited. Thus his first appearance does not occur until the end of the second act. Oderbruch's moral rigorism—he places the dictates of his conscience higher than loyalty toward his country—brings into sharp focus the problems related to engaging in acts of resistance against a totalitarian state. For Oderbruch's sabotage results in the loss of the lives of those who, like Colonel Eilers, may be accused of misguided idealism but cannot be counted among the criminal perpetrators of injustice. Oderbruch, one critic pointed out, acts as a Machiavellian for whom the end justifies the means, rather than as the true Christian as whom Zuckmayer portrays him. For he does not avail himself of the only permissible recourse, that is, the murder of the chief source of evil—Hitler himself.[16]

Zuckmayer himself wavered in his assessment of Oderbruch. At first, he declared him to be an "ideal figure"[17] for future generations, but not much later he modified his view by stating that he could not endorse Oderbruch's actions even if they were inevitable.[18] In an attempt to remove all misunderstandings, Zuckmayer in 1963 no longer permitted the performance of his play and slightly revised it in 1966.[19] The rewritten passages of the discussion between Oder-bruch and Harras in the third act do not remove all ambiguities, however. Those ambiguities can, ultimately, be traced to the con-ception of Oderbruch in 1942 when Zuckmayer had called for an uncompromising fight against National Socialism in his "Appeal to the Living."[20] On the one hand, Oderbruch's stance corresponds to Zuckmayer's uncompromising attitude in 1942; on the other, the playwright's realization "of having to wish for the defeat of my own nation" so that Hitler might be "overthrown and his reign of terror ended" (*PoM*, 368) resulted in an irreconcilable conflict that pre-vented Zuckmayer from wholeheartedly endorsing Oderbruch. In fact, in his *Memento*, dedicated to those officers and politicians who made an attempt on Hitler's life on 20 July 1944,[21] Zuckmayer casts the resistance fighters in the same role as Oderbruch. They were motivated by their conscience to disregard their oath of loyalty to the Führer; the guilt they incurred they atoned for through their deaths; they were not privileged to help build a new and better world.

In contrast to both Harras and Oderbruch, young Lieutenant Hartmann, who becomes disillusioned with National Socialism and turns toward the resistance movement at the end of the play, is an essentially positive figure in that he seems to point the way toward a better future. In his exhausting discussions with Germany's youth, which lasted from late 1947 for more than a year until he collapsed from a heart attack, the playwright noted that many young men tended to identify with Hartmann—a further indication of how ac-curately he had depicted the situation within Nazi Germany from abroad.

The play had its greatest impact in the late forties and early fifties. Although the stormy debates of the immediate postwar years have subsided, the play remains, quite justifiably, not only the best-known dramatic treatment of the Nazi period but has played a vital role in Germany's coming to terms with its past, a process called *Vergangenheitsbewältigung*.[22] True, the drama is decidedly prob-lematic in its sympathetic portrayal of the fellow traveler Harras. One does well to remember, however, that "it required a higher degree of justice to plan such a drama on a farm in Vermont during the cold winter of 1942–1943 than to interpret it as an apology of Nazism in a warm editorial office during the sixties."[23] This statement is, without doubt, also applicable to the seventies.[24]

## II   Barbara Blomberg

Despite the enormous success Zuckmayer had achieved with *The Devil's General*, a drama that anticipated in several respects another controversial play about the Third Reich, Rolf Hochhuth's *The Deputy*,[25] and was praised as recently as 1978 as a mine of information about such issues as the persecution of the Jews, concentration camps, Gestapo tactics, and propaganda methods,[26] the playwright focused his attention on a historical subject matter in his next play. To be sure, in the early thirties Zuckmayer had likewise turned from the exceedingly topical *The Captain of Köpenick* to the pseudo-historical *The Knave of Bergen*—although in that case the playwright's political abstinence may have been attributable to conditions imposed upon him by his beginning exile.[27]

Curiously, the first plans for *Barbara Blomberg* date back to Vermont;[28] again we are faced with the phenomenon that Zuckmayer is not yet exploring authentic American themes and topics but that he is oriented toward Europe in general and Germany in particular. *Barbara Blomberg* takes place in the Spanish-occupied Netherlands and in Spain toward the end of the sixteenth century. In choosing a historical background that involves the political and religious clashes between the Spain of Philip II and the Netherlands, between Catholics and Protestants, Zuckmayer invited comparison with German classical drama, notably with Schiller's *Don Carlos* (1787) and Goethe's *Egmont* (1788). Unlike Schiller and Goethe's heroes, however, Zuckmayer's heroine does not appear as an advocate of freedom against an oppressive, absolutist regime. Surely, the fact that the playwright chose a comparatively minor historical figure contributed to the different emphasis in his play. More importantly, Barbara Blomberg's inner development from fatalistic indifference through her struggle for power and final acceptance of her fate, that is, her voluntary quasi-exile in Spain, resembles that of General Harras and thus demonstrates that, despite the play's historical guise, it does not represent a complete break with the playwright's concerns and preoccupations as evidenced by *The Devil's General*.[29] Further, the problem of the individual's relationship to power, the fact that one central character dominates the scene, and the implicit demand that actions in the political realm should be ultimately governed by one's conscience relate *Barbara Blomberg* to *The Devil's General*.

The heroine's claim to historical fame is that, as a young girl, she briefly became the mistress of the aging Emperor Charles V during his stay at the diet of Regensburg in Southern Germany and gave birth to a son whom the emperor acknowledged as his own and upon whom he conferred the title of Don Juan d'Austria. The mother was married off to an officer in the Spanish army after the child had been taken away from her to be educated in Spain. The play begins with the somber prologue in which officials question the dying former companion of Don Juan d'Austria about the identity of the mother of the emperor's illegitimate son so that this potentially damaging information may possibly be used against the popular Don Juan, victor in the naval battle against the Turks near Lepanto in 1572, by his half-brother, King Philip II. But the inquisitors obtain only insufficient evidence; Don Quixada merely reveals that Don Juan's mother was a beautiful commoner.

At the beginning of the play proper Barbara Blomberg is introduced. She is now Mrs. Pyramis-Kegel, married to an officer in the Spanish service, mother of two children fathered by Kegel, and living in a dilapidated apartment in Brussels. She has kept her oath not to betray the fact that she gave birth to the emperor's son. But now she is suddenly confronted with the past when the depraved musician Massi, who is familiar with the entire affair, appears and proposes to blackmail the Spanish authorities. In the ensuing quarrel between Massi and the drunkard Kegel the latter is accidentally killed and Barbara Blomberg turns Massi over to the police. Massi betrays Barbara's secret when he is tortured by the Spanish. Barbara, who has been hitherto living in very reduced circumstances, cleverly exploits her newly acquired prominence by demanding and receiving the means for living in accordance with her social station.

The second act takes place in a small castle near Brussels where Barbara now resides. She soon becomes engulfed in both personal and international intrigues. She falls in love with the English adventurer Ratcliff but is asked by the all-powerful Spanish regent in the Netherlands, the duke of Alba, to spy on her lover and report on his political activities. Her daughter Caroline is in love with the Flemish aristocrat van Hoghstraate and, for personal and moral reasons, sides with the cause of the Netherlands. She accuses her mother of benefitting from the system of injustice and oppression the Spaniards have imposed upon the land.

A turn for the better seems imminent when the duke of Alba, a ruthless law-and-order man, is relieved as regent and Don Juan d'Austria is appointed to the position. But in her discussion with her son Barbara realizes that her claims to a happy life with Ratcliff—who is actually an agent of Queen Elizabeth of England, foe of the Spanish Empire—and loyalty to her son are irreconcilable. For Don Juan pursues the ultimately futile plan to liberate Mary, Queen of Scots, from Queen Elizabeth's prison, marry her, and combine the Scottish-English crowns with that of Spain. Although Barbara dissuades Don Juan from his adventure, she also renounces Ratcliff and agrees to go into voluntary exile in Spain—something that she had refused to do before. The epilogue in rhymed verse is spoken by Miguel de Cervantes, participant in the battle of Lepanto. He relates Don Juan's death—presumably, Don Juan was poisoned on orders of Philip II. At the same time, the epilogue contains what almost amounts to a "literary program."[30] This program, to be sure, gains in significance by being spoken by the author of the immortal *Don Quichotte* who proclaims that depicting man's image is the poet's worthy object.

Neither history nor politics are, then, of primary importance in the play. In his stage directions Zuckmayer stated that the historical background had been freely treated and that historical accuracy in scene design and costumes could be dispensed with. Conversely, he claimed that *Barbara Blomberg* was not intended as an allegory that depicted a modern dictatorship in terms of a historical one, that is, that of Philip II.[31] Nevertheless, particularly the tactics and views of the duke of Alba and Albornoz, chief of the secret police in Spanish-occupied Brussels, evoke those of similarly ruthless oppressors from Germany's Nazi past. Ultimately, however, the problem of man's relationship to power, as especially exemplified in the main character's grasp of power and its renunciation, is seen by Zuckmayer as transcending specific historical situations.

The lack of overt historical and political significance induced one Marxist critic to fault Zuckmayer with both evading contemporary problems and misrepresenting historical reality by neglecting to concentrate on the socially relevant aspects inherent in the topic.[32] Instead of depicting the fight of the Netherlands against Spanish suppression or a woman's desire to achieve justice for wrongs suffered at the hands of the ruling classes, the same critic argues, Zuckmayer maintains an impartial stance by having Barbara enjoy, albeit briefly, her parasitic existence. Further, he counterbalances the methods of suppression used by the Spaniards with atrocities committed by the populace of the occupied countries against Catholic priests.[33] But then Zuckmayer had anticipated such criticism when, in 1949, he explicitly stated that his drama was not intended as an "ideological thesis, as a dogma."[34] Curiously, in a 1976 revival of the seldom performed play the director saw it as his main task to represent Barbara as a woman struggling with emancipation and overcoming traditional forms of dependence.[35] Such interpretation is not entirely farfetched, yet the comparison with Brecht's heroine Mother Courage, whose fate demonstrates that poor people must be opportunists in order to survive,[36] is a clear indication that there are decided limits to an "ideological" interpretation.

*Barbara Blomberg* is, after all, a play of great theatricality and desirable roles for actors; it is not, however, a play from which emerges a clear message or a drama that can be said to have broad social implications.

## III  The Song of the Fiery Furnace

In his next play Zuckmayer returned to the immediate past, to the time in which *The Devil's General* takes place. He conceived of the idea to *The Song of the Fiery Furnace* when, in October 1948, he read two unrelated news items in the *Basler National-Zeitung*. The first report stated that French authorities had sentenced to death a Frenchman who had betrayed a group of resistance fighters to the German occupation troops. This betrayal resulted in a singularly gruesome act: in 1943 the German military police had set fire to the castle in which the resistance fighters were celebrating Christmas and those attending the celebration either perished in the flames or by the bullets of the military police. Whereas this factual occurrence would seem to point in the direction of a documentary drama about the French resistance movement in World War II, the second report was of a totally different nature. It stated that forty-four whales swam ashore at a beach in Florida; those that could not be dragged back into deep water by fishermen died shortly thereafter.

The connection between these two apparently unrelated events is established by one of the characters in the play, the pious German soldier Martin, who explains to his comades that every thousand years the fish leave the water to die and that then "is the time when Lucifer comes to earth and nobody knows what is good and what is evil" (WA, 9:80). Hence it is evident that Zuckmayer was not primarily interested in exploring the political aspects of the resis-

tance movement but rather in probing metaphysical problems—
problems that transcend the specific historical situation in the Savoy
mountains of Southeastern France in 1943 and 1944. Such metaphysical tendencies are already evident in *The Devil's General;* but
in *The Song of the Fiery Furnace* Zuckmayer intensifies his metaphysical probing by having the action take place on both a realistic
and allegorical-symbolical plane.[37] In fact, the director of the
Göttingen premiere on 3 November 1950, Zuckmayer's long-time
friend and associate Heinz Hilpert, divided the stage into an upper
and a lower level and thereby provided a visual demonstration of
the division into a natural and a supernatural realm almost in the
fashion of the medieval mystery plays.[38] However, as the introduction on the stage of the allegorical, elemental forces of wind, frost,
and fog presented some difficulties, Zuckmayer, in cooperation with
the director Heinrich Koch, presented a somewhat different version
of *The Song of the Fiery Furnace.*[39] This version was performed in
Hamburg only ten days after the Göttingen premiere, and Zuckmayer expressed his hope that the revised play would continue to
convey its message of *überpolitische Menschlichkeit* ("humanity beyond politics").[40]

The very beginning of the play establishes its metaphysical context
and, at the same time, anticipates its ending by confronting a Judas
figure, the traitor Louis Creveaux, with his victims who have come
to accuse him and bear witness against him. In the "heavenly"
courtroom the two angels do not pronounce judgment but acknowl-
edge the earth, the "impersonal unifying force of good and evil" as
the "final arbiter."[41] They then ask the actors, especially those who
will be the dead victims at the end of the play, to go and "dream"
their lives (*WA,* 9:15), that is, act out their predestined roles in the
play. The second part of act 1, scene 1, concludes with the angels
enjoining the spectators to bind that which has become disjointed,
to overcome that which separates men from each other by their
common humanity.[42]

The play proper begins with the arrival of both Sylvaine Caston-
nier, the daughter of the local innkeeper, who returns from a forced
labor camp in Germany, and Sylvester Imwald, the replacement for
the radio operator who has been killed by the resistance movement,
in the village of Haut-Chamond in December 1943. The similarity
in the names of these two characters provides a hint of their affinity
and eventual love for each other that will ultimately enable them
to bridge the gulf separating the French and the Germans. The

driving force behind the German efforts to quell French resistance is warrant officer Sprenger of the military police, "the terror of Oslo and scourge of Tripolis" (*WA*, 9:18), whose very name betrays his destructive and evil nature (*sprengen*, "to explode"). The German soldiers under his command hail from a variety of backgrounds; their counterparts in the French Garde Mobile, the police force of the Vichy government, are played by the same actors. In this fashion Zuckmayer deemphasizes national characteristics and draws attention to the problem of good and evil that transcends national boundaries. Thus the French soldier Pierre, who hails from Paris, has his counterpart in the German soldier Peter from Berlin; the French soldier Martin from Brittany corresponds to the German soldier Martin from Masuria. While Pierre/Peter and Martin/Martin are, owing to their essential humanity, sympathetically drawn, Albert/Albert and Georges/Georg have abdicated all individual responsibility and tend to carry out orders unquestioningly and unhesitatingly.

The desire to distribute good and evil equally among the French and the Germans is also evident in the almost symmetrical configuration of the remaining characters. Thus Sprenger has his evil counterpart in the traitor Creveaux, son of a German prisoner of war during World War I and a farm maid, whose name (*crever*, "to burst," "to crack") suggests his affinity with Sprenger. But Sprenger's antagonist is Marcel Neyroud, head of the local resistance group. Major Mühlstein, the local commandant, has, despite his humanitarian instincts and anti-Nazi convictions, resigned himself to following orders while still endeavoring to maintain good relations with the French. Similarly, the French policeman Neyroud, Marcel's father, upholds the existing order by halfheartedly cooperating with the German occupation troops.

Sylvaine and Sylvester's arrival, mentioned above, sets in motion the chain of events that culminates in the "fiery furnace" alluded to in the title of the play. The gradually increasing attraction between the two young people fuels Creveaux's hatred and desire for revenge. Although he managed to join the resistance movement, he has worked as Sprenger's agent and betrays to him a Jewish family, including a wanted fugitive, whom he had promised to conduct to safety in Switzerland for a hefty sum. Creveaux's destructive and, in the final analysis, deadly actions are contrasted to the tender love scene between Sylvester and Sylvaine that, significantly, takes place in a barn where they help a cow give birth to a calf, that is, in the creation of new life.

Marcel, the resistance fighter, had found refuge and a hiding place in the church of the Catholic priest Francis when he was on the point of being arrested. He and thirty-five other female and male members and sympathizers of the resistance movement have gathered in the vaults of an old castle near the village to celebrate Christmas. Unbeknown to them, Creveaux has betrayed their meeting place to Sprenger who, in the absence of the local commandant, is preparing the operation "fiery furnace" against the group in the castle. In the philosophical discussion between Marcel and Francis that precedes the operation, however, nature and function of the resistance are defined. Whereas the atheistic and materialistic Marcel sees the issue at stake in nationalistic terms as one of freedom versus slavery and advocates force as the only means to achieve his goal, Francis's perspective is entirely different. He poses the question of individual responsibility in the face of force that produces counterforce, terror that produces counterterror, and attracts all those "who murder for murder's sake" (WA, 9:100). According to Francis, each human being is faced with the question whether to denigrate life, that is, giving in to blind and bestial instincts, or to love it as "God's gift, in all of his creatures, even in the enemy, in death and destruction" (WA, 9:102). Although no resolution of the ideological differences and antithetical world views of Marcel and Francis is given, it is not difficult to see that Francis acts as Zuckmayer's spokesman. In fact, when the castle is burned down by Sprenger and his troops and those assembled in the castle are faced with the choice of either perishing in the flames or by the bullets of the Germans surrounding the castle, Marcel, perhaps somewhat unconvincingly,[43] comes close to accepting Francis's creed by making peace with his former enemy Sylvester.

Sylvester had come to warn Marcel and his group as soon as he had learned of Sprenger's impending action. Although his warning comes too late, Sylvester's union with Sylvaine is a demonstration of that love that overcomes hatred and transcends earthly concerns. Thus death does not hold any threat for them, comforted by the thought of the Nietzschean "eternal return"[44] they succumb with dignity. The last sound to be heard from the castle is Francis's voice singing the Ambrosian "Te Deum Laudamus"—the apocryphal "Song of the Fiery Furnace."[45] In having all members of the resistance movement perish in the fire, Zuckmayer metes out a fate to them that prevents them from incurring guilt for the deaths of innocents—precisely the destiny that Oderbruch in *The Devil's General* could not escape.[46]

The final scene begins with the allegorical figures of wind, frost, and fog proclaiming the revenge of the dead and the revulsion of the debauched earth. The tide of war has turned, and Sprenger and two of his men are fleeing. They are joined by Creveaux, visibly disfigured by a wound that resembles the mark of Cain, but they reject him and leave him to his doom. The mother herself, into whom the elemental Mother Frost has been transformed, delivers her wayward son into the hands of the French authorities.

*The Song of the Fiery Furnace* elicited a mixed response. While its theatrical success was largely confined to the 1950–1951 season, the reactions of the critics were, inevitably, influenced by their ideological persuasions. On the one hand, the play was, on the basis of its "new realization of *Humanität*" proclaimed to be "quintessential Zuckmayer";[47] on the other, the drama was declared to support the politics of the cold war by endeavoring to eliminate national differences and "supporting the expansive cosmopolitanism of the USA."[48] Needless to say, there is an inherent element of unfairness in the attempt to cast Zuckmayer in a political mold. After all, the playwright was quite explicit in emphasizing that his concerns were not primarily political; hence they should not be confused with those of either his contemporary Brecht or postwar playwrights like Rolf Hochhuth and Peter Weiss who launched the documentary drama in the early 1960s.[49] The following discussion of Zuckmayer's play *Cold Light* will tend to emphasize the differences between Zuckmayer and those playwrights who hewed to the presentation of documented historical facts on stage.

## IV  Cold Light

*Cold Light*, a drama that premiered in Hamburg on 3 September 1955 and subsequently appeared on the program of more than thirty theaters in the Federal Republic during the winter season 1955–1956, follows *The Devil's General* and *The Song of the Fiery Furnace* in that it attempts to come to grips with political and topical issues resulting from World War II and its aftermath.

On the surface, the play seems to recreate the story of the German émigré scientist and naturalized British citizen Klaus Fuchs, whose betrayal of atomic secrets to the Soviet Union was discovered in

1951 and whose subsequent trial attracted much publicity. It seems, indeed, that Kristof Wolters, the main character of *Cold Light*, has been patterned after Fuchs, for both the historical figure and the fictitious character have a number of traits in common. For example, both are the offspring of Protestant ministers, both were engaged in leftist politics as students, both were forced to emigrate when Hitler came to power, both were deported as enemy aliens from Britain to Canada after the outbreak of World War II, both returned to England and collaborated in the theoretical development of the atom bomb, and, above all, both betrayed atomic secrets to the Soviet Union. However, in his afterword to the play Zuckmayer shifts the focus of the drama from a purely political, topical level to the individual and spiritual plane. He states that "the theme of the play is not the splitting of the atom but rather the crisis of trust. In a larger sense: the crisis of thinking and faith in the present" (*WA*, 9:391). Consequently, the drama is essentially concerned with Wolters's struggle for finding a clear orientation in a confused and divided world, his incurring guilt by betrayal, his suffering pangs of conscience because of the betrayal, and, finally, his confession and atonement for his betrayal.[50] To be sure, this "inner" action occurs within a framework of realistic, and even humorous scenes that provide the theatergoer with the tangible theatrical fare he has come to expect from a playwright like Zuckmayer.

The play begins in London's Green Park in September 1939, shortly after the outbreak of World War II. The "professional revolutionary [and] party soldier" (*WA*, 9:259) Buschmann attempts unsuccessfully to recruit Wolters for the goals of the Communist party. For Wolters has become thoroughly disillusioned; after rejecting conventional, orthodox religion he is not about to become a follower of a substitute religion—Communism. Instead he has opted for a rational, mathematical, and scientific approach to life that will enable him to have access to the true power governing modern man's destiny. In somewhat heavy-handed symbolism Zuckmayer has Wolters play with a child's ball while he proclaims: "Power on earth—that is concentrated in a few formulae. And he who knows them could hold the globe in his hand like this, weigh it, and throw it away, if he doesn't like it any longer" (*WA*, 9:263). Wolters's reliance on abstract science demonstrates that there is "an emotional vacuum" in him, that his emotional life has remained "underdeveloped."[51] How easily Wolters's self-proclaimed security can be shaken becomes evident in the following scene that takes place in the austere hold of a British transport vessel in May 1940 after the invasion of France by German troops. Wolters, who had applied for British citizenship, is deported to Canada—curiously, in the company of Nazis. He now has become receptive to Buschmann's ideas—Buschmann is likewise a deportee. Despite his reservations about the "lacking elegance" (WA, 9:269) of Buschmann's economic solution to the problem of human freedom, Wolters opts for it and professes not to see any difference between Nazi Germany and the Western democracies. He is deeply hurt by his treatment that resembles that of a common criminal and, as a consequence, he will serve Buschmann's cause voluntarily. Wolters can even retain the illusion of independence; he will not be required blindly to toe the party line but will be able to decide of his own free will "which part of the world shall possess the armaments of the future" (WA, 9:281). Strictly speaking, Wolters's impending decision to serve the cause of Communism cannot be classified as an "ideologically" or even "idealistically" motivated betrayal of which Zuckmayer speaks in his afterword (WA, 9:391) because Wolters's rekindled sympathies for Communism can be largely explained in terms of the treatment he received at the hands of the British. Thus, what Wolters conceives to be a rational decision is colored by personal motives. Nevertheless, Zuckmayer added to the scene on the transport vessel the figure of the worldly-wise yet pious Jew Friedländer who, in contrast to Wolters, realizes full well that life cannot be mastered exclusively in terms of rational calculation. This point is underscored in the chess match between Friedländer and Wolters in which the former, clearly the underdog, checkmates the latter by means of a bold move that defies cold logic.

Fifteen months later Wolters is back in London because he is needed by Sir Elwin Ketterick, a physicist engaged in atomic research. Sir Elwin is the ruthless British imperialist par excellence; despite his openly stated goal of working toward the annihilation not only of Nazism but of all of Germany, he does not hesitate to accept Wolters, both a German—though an exiled one—and a leftist, as a member of his team. The common bond that unites Sir Elwin and Wolters is their belief in science as God. A gentlemanly handshake suffices for the British physicist to establish a relationship with Wolters that is based on trust—precisely the quality Wolters cannot afford, as Buschmann will inform him in the following scene. When he meets Sir Elwin's wife, Hjördis, a former fellow student with whom Wolters is secretly in love, he realizes that he will incur guilt in accepting the position. But Hjördis's words persuade him not to forfeit such a singular research opportunity.

Almost two years later, in May 1943, Wolters and Buschmann meet again in London's Green Park. In this fourth and final scene of the first act Wolters has become what he refused to be at the beginning of the play: a spy who betrays atomic secrets to the Soviet Union. Yet he has doubts about his activities and endeavors to justify his betrayal of classified information by partially contradictory reasons. On the one hand, he explains to Buschmann that he had turned over only information he considered his own intellectual property; on the other, he deeply resents Ketterick and "the world, the class, the kind of people he represents" (WA, 9:300). Finally, Wolters professes to believe that the results of research should be made available to all mankind and should not be shrouded in secrecy. Although Buschmann considers himself an agent of an irrevocable historical process, "fuel" for "the motor of an irresistible development" (WA, 9:305), he is not without redeeming humane qualities. Yet he points out that Wolters has embarked upon a course that cannot be reversed. Hence Wolters must ultimately suffer the consequences of his actions.

In the Hamburg premiere the director Gustav Gründgens omitted the first scene of the second act for a very valid reason: the scene does not advance the action of the play in any significant way. Rather, it introduces a down-and-out character, a bum in New York City's Central Park West in the summer of 1943. Hence the scene is somewhat reminiscent of the broadly and humorously developed milieu of the flophouse in *The Captain of Köpenick* (act 1, scene 6). Interestingly, Zuckmayer composed the bum scene originally in English—though hardly in idiomatically accurate speech—presumably in the hope of having the entire play translated and seeing it performed in the United States.[52] At any rate, Wolters's encounter with the bum that results in his failure to establish contact with a Soviet agent provides a contrast between the individual freedom the bum enjoys—to be sure, a freedom devoid of social responsibility—and the collectivist mentality of the Soviet agent Jurew.

The following scenes (act 2, scenes 6–8) take place in Las Mesas, the thinly disguised atomic research center Los Alamos, in 1945. Ketterick and his collaborators Wolters and the naive supporter of the Soviet Union, Fillebrown, have joined the cultured and humanitarian director of the research center, Nicolas Löwenschild, and his team. In these scenes the theme of betrayal *(Verrat)* and trust *(Vertrauen)* is repeatedly alluded to, particularly in the discussion about Judas in the eighth scene. Löwenschild's slim hopes for a peaceful application of atomic power after the war rest on the assumption that nonproliferation will preclude the possibility of an arms race—hence it would be treasonous to share atomic secrets with the Soviet Union. Without doubt, the assumptions of the fictional character Löwenschild are based on Zuckmayer's conviction that the Western democracies ultimately serve mankind far better than totalitarian states. It is interesting to note in this context the ideas and attitudes of both the naturalized and native-born Americans among the group of international scientists who have assembled at Las Mesas in strictly enforced isolation.

The Americans, it seems, adhere to values that tend to exclude the flagrant misuse of atomic power. Löwenschild, a naturalized American of both German and Russian descent, expresses fears about the consequences of the use of the atomic bomb—although he and his team were instrumental in developing it. Similarly, the American test pilot Roy opposes Ketterick's imperialist views, reminiscent of the Nietzschean "Beyond Good and Evil," by emphasizing the ultimate authority of a duly elected legislative over all warlike actions and thus contrasts the functioning of a democratic society to that of one ruled by a dictator. Finally, Frederick Schiller Lee, an American of Negro descent, is supposed to symbolize in his existence the contradictions of America itself. His very names are said to have been derived from both the herald of freedom, Friedrich von Schiller, and the well-known general of the anti-abolitionist Confederacy, Robert E. Lee. Despite the many disappointments he experienced as a Negro, Frederick Schiller Lee professes his belief in the redeeming and regenerative virtues of his country: "For we believe in the paradox that is America, we love it, and we are confident that from the free interplay of opposites something beautiful and fertile will be born into this world" (WA, 9:342).

In contrast to Wolters, Frederick Schiller Lee's severe personal disappointments have not induced him to become a traitor. As is made abundantly clear, especially in scenes seven and eight—they may be considered the turning point of the play[53]—Wolters has violated the trust and confidence of those with whom he works. He has, indeed, become a Judas figure. The parallel between Wolters and Judas is made more explicit by the fact that Wolters eventually is forced by the Soviet agent to accept money for his treason. Wolters's acceptance of money is equivalent to the sealing of the pact of treachery, as Löwenschild had stated earlier (*WA*, 9:341).

Although Löwenschild and those associated with him do not suspect Wolters of any wrongdoing, his personal relations are seriously affected by his actions. Hjördis, who is planning to leave Ketterick, accidentally discovers a note stating the date, time, and location of one of Wolters's regular meetings with the Soviet agent. Since Wolters cannot reveal to her whom he is meeting, Hjördis, probably suspecting another woman, feels deceived and betrayed. The scene in question (act 2, scene 8) ends with Wolters's realization that he does not deserve Hjördis's trust.

Appropriately, the "American" scenes of the play end with the news about the bombing of Hiroshima in August 1945. Zuckmayer withholds all comment by having the momentous news announced as a radio broadcast at a moment when all the characters have temporarily left the stage. As throughout the play, it is evident from the last scene of the second act—which again takes place in London's Green Park—that Zuckmayer's concern is not world politics in the era of the atom bomb but Wolters's individual conscience. The traitor must now accept the monetary wages of sin from the Soviet agent Jurew. How ruthless the representatives of the cause he is serving really are is brought home to Wolters by the news that Buschmann has been liquidated and that his name is no longer officially mentioned.

The third act—it takes place four years after the end of World War II—introduces a new and important character, the British secret agent Northon. Northon devotes his time and energy to the task of eliciting a confession of guilt from Wolters not by cloak and dagger tactics but rather by acting as a mixture between confessor and psychoanalyst. Northon's task is complicated by the fact that the only piece of evidence—the note Hjördis had discovered accidentally—is destroyed. Ketterick, who had stumbled upon the note, is bent on revenge and intends to deliver it to Northon. But in his agitated state he has a car accident. Somewhat melodramatically both Ketterick and the piece of evidence perish in the flames of the wrecked car—albeit offstage. In the end, Wolters's conscience prevails and he confesses his guilt after a final discussion with Northon in which the latter suggests that the proper course for a true believer would have been to emigrate to the Soviet Union rather than to engage in acts of treason.

Northon's use of religious terminology—he speaks, for example, of the "martyrdom" (WA, 9:377) that Wolters will have to endure as a consequence of his actions—suggests that, in the final analysis, metaphysics rather than politics are at issue. To establish the proper framework for his drama Zuckmayer explained Wolters's guilt in terms of Greek tragedy. In the author's view, Wolters's attempt to influence the fate of the world (*Weltschicksal;* WA, 9:391) constitutes a moral transgression that can only be atoned for by Wolters's acknowledging his guilt, the first step on the road to a possible redemption. But it requires precisely such an "intact" character as Northon to bring about Wolters's acknowledgment and confession that, in turn, pave the way for a nontragic ending of the play. It is true, "Wolters never does come to experience deeply the international consequences of his betrayal";[54] hence his transgression consists more of a failing of personal loyalty than an act of treason. Thus the play ends on a conciliatory note with the suggestion that Hjördis will be waiting for Wolters once he is released from prison.

Zuckmayer's reduction of the play to an essentially personal conflict induced an influential Viennese critic to label it a failure.[55] It should be remembered, however, that in 1955 Zuckmayer was the only living German playwright comparable in stature to Bertolt Brecht. The fact that Brecht, after his return to Europe from the United States in 1947, eventually settled in East Berlin, where he and his wife, the actress Helene Weigel, established the famed Berliner Ensemble, invited without doubt implicit or explicit comparisons between Zuckmayer and Brecht and contributed to an interpretation of the play along ideological lines. It was, after all, Brecht who in his *Life of Galileo* had posed the question of the scientist's responsibility in the face of his obligations toward society or, in a more encompassing sense, mankind. Under the influence of contemporary events such as Niels Bohr's splitting of the uranium atom and the dropping of the first atom bomb on Hiroshima on 6 August 1945, Brecht arrived at an increasingly austere view of the scientist's functions and obligations in his most heavily reworked play—a play that is extant in three versions and occupied him from 1938 until his death in 1956. In the third and final version, first performed on 16 April 1955 in Cologne, that is, before the premiere of *Cold Light,* Galileo accuses himself of cowardice at a historically pregnant juncture when his defiance of the church as the representative of authority might have induced other scientists to develop a kind of Hippocratic oath, "the vow to use their knowledge only for the good of mankind."[56]

In Zuckmayer's play the scientist's responsibility for the welfare of "mankind"—in the context of Brecht's play to be conceived of as the poor and oppressed—is only peripherally referred to. Zuckmayer's focus on the individual's decision produced widely divergent assessments of the play that did not, by any means, receive exclusively good marks from critics in the West. On the one hand, one reviewer praised Zuckmayer's noble stance and considered *Cold Light* an "effective weapon against Communist barbarism."[57] On the other hand, critics in the German Democratic Republic sharply rejected the play. Curiously, they did so for precisely the same reason, that is, because the play was assumed to constitute "an ideological weapon in the Cold War."[58] The Marxist critic Adling even went so far as to term *Cold Light* the nadir of Zuckmayer's development as a dramatist.[59]

Among the several dramas on physicists[60] those by Heinar Kipphardt and Friedrich Dürrenmatt should be singled out. Kipphardt, in his *In the Matter of J. Robert Oppenheimer*, intended, by strictly adhering to the facts, to present a shortened version of the proceedings against the well-known physicist and former director of the Atomic Weapons Laboratories that were conducted by a Personnel Security Board of the Atomic Energy Commission in 1954. Kipphardt deviated from the documentary character of his play by putting concluding words into the mouth of his character Oppenheimer—words the real Oppenheimer objected to as a distortion of the historical truth.[61] When Oppenheimer ponders the question whether he and his fellow scientists had not perhaps become "traitors to the spirit of science when we handed over the results of our research to the military, without considering the consequences,"[62] Kipphardt's drama is most reminiscent of Brecht's *Life of Galileo*, particularly Galileo's self-condemnation. At the same time, the concept of "ideological treason" that is used by the chief counsel for the Atomic Energy Commission to establish the physicist's disloyalty to the government because of his loyalty to his Communist friends recalls Kristof Wolters's predicament. Ultimately, however, most critics tended to give preference to Kipphardt's higher degree of authenticity and considered the documentary drama a more adequate vehicle for conveying the transpersonal conflict between science and politics than Zuckmayer's largely fictional treatment.[63] That under present-day conditions this conflict may defy a rational resolution is indicated by Dürrenmatt's *The Physicists*, a comedy that relies heavily on the absurd and grotesque but also on elements of the detective story. The physicist Möbius considers an insane asylum the last refuge that will enable him to keep his scientific discoveries to himself and prevent them from falling into the wrong hands. In the asylum he is joined by two secret agents, likewise physicists and likewise pretending to be insane. They have been charged by their respective governments to obtain Möbius's secret formula. But Möbius convinces them that inevitable, large-scale destruction would result from the application of his discovery—regardless of whether it would be acquired by the West or by the East. When the three physicists decide to spend the rest of their lives in the insane asylum, Dürrenmatt seems to suggest a solution, if a whimsical one, to the dilemma of the scientist in the modern world. But in a paradoxical turn of events the director of the asylum, a hunchbacked spinster, who is the descendant of a family of dubious mental stability, announces that she has managed to avail herself of Möbius's discovery that will now serve as the basis for her striving for the domination of the world.

Dürrenmatt thus shares neither Brecht's optimistic belief in a purposeful historical process that can be decisively influenced by human action nor Zuckmayer's trust in the individual's potential to distinguish good from evil and to decide autonomously on the right course of action.

## V  *Adaptations*

Although Zuckmayer's major creative efforts during the war years had been directed toward themes and topics primarily of interest to (future) German audiences, there are indications that the playwright began to draw on his experiences in the United States and started incorporating them in his work. Thus the American journalist Buddy Lawrence, who appears in the second act of *The Devil's General*, is the first genuine contemporary American to appear in Zuckmayer's *oeuvre*. True, his main dramatic function is to provide a wholesome contrast to the perverted mentality of segments of German society that Nazism exploited. Yet we may conceive of Buddy Lawrence as a forerunner of those characters who make their appearance in Zuckmayer's "full-fledged" American plays of the sixties, that is, *Dance of the Herons* and *The Life of Horace A. W. Tabor*.[64]

America had, of course, occupied a prominent place in Zuckmayer's creative imagination long before the dramatist had set foot
on American soil. Apart from the early play *Pankraz Awakens*,[65] his
two dramatic adaptations from the late twenties and early thirties
testify to Zuckmayer's interest in the United States and its literature.
However, both Anderson and Stallings's *What Price Glory* and
Hemingway's *A Farewell to Arms*[66] presumably appealed to Zuckmayer because they dealt with soldiers at war. World War I, it will
be recalled, had profoundly affected Zuckmayer and had found its
reflection in his own works.[67]

The third work hailing from the United States that Zuckmayer
chose to adapt bears hardly any thematic resemblance to the two
previous adaptations. Conversely, it may be said to be more genuinely American in that it does not deal with Americans in a European theater of war but rather in a more genuinely American
milieu. John van Druten's Broadway success of the forties *I Remember Mama*—revived as a musical in 1979—is based on Kathryn
Forbes' [Kathryn McLean's] novel *Mama's Bank Account* (1943). It
depicts the trials and happy moments of a Norwegian immigrant
family in San Francisco around 1910. As the title indicates, it is the
mother who successfully manages to protect her family from all
adversity. In 1947 Zuckmayer's adaptation was performed in Zurich
under the title *Die Unvergessliche* [The Unforgettable One] and in
1948 in Berlin under the title *So war Mama* [That Was Mama].[68]
In his program notes to the Zurich production Zuckmayer stated
that he was motivated to translate van Druten's play precisely because it portrayed life in the United States in a fashion that differed
considerably from European notions but was "at the same time,
more characteristic and significant than one might surmise."[69]

Without doubt, the adaptation must be seen in the light of Zuckmayer's efforts to explain the phenomenon of America to his European audience. Zuckmayer had undertaken a similar task in his
public lecture "America is Different" (1948) that was also repeatedly
published thereafter.[70] In his essay Zuckmayer provides a sympathetic but not, by any means, uncritical account of his years in the
United States—at this time still his official residence. While the
essay is not entirely free of idealizing tendencies in, for example,
its implicit assumption that hard work will eventually receive its
just rewards or in its extolling of the participatory democracy in
small New England towns, it is, perhaps, an overstatement to claim
that Zuckmayer had created an American myth.[71] At any rate, both

the fact that Zuckmayer had found not only a refuge but a new home in America and that this country had been instrumental in defeating Hitler Germany contributed to Zuckmayer's positive view. Such a view was not necessarily shared by Zuckmayer's younger colleagues—nor, for that matter, his contemporary Brecht—like Hans Magnus Enzensberger and Reinhard Lettau who, under the impact of the Vietnam War, no longer conceived of the United States as the guardian of freedom and democracy but considered it a ruthlessly aggressive and oppressive superpower.[72]

That Zuckmayer did not entirely escape the danger of idealizing is evident from his professed predilection for van Druten's play, a drama that depicts the virtues of an idyllic family life but is almost totally devoid of serious conflict and indications that the domestic sphere is not self-sufficient but subject to socioeconomic forces. In comparison to the profoundly moving *The Devil's General* that had premiered in Zurich approximately nine months before *The Unforgettable One*, Zuckmayer's adaptation attracted little notice and scant praise. After all, one critic observed, the adaptation consisted merely of "harmless trifles."[73]

Although not a notable stage success, Zuckmayer's next adaptation elicited far more critical comment. The dramatist's affinity to Gerhart Hauptmann, whose literary production spanned the period from the late eighties of the previous century to almost the middle of ours, had been noted by critics at the beginning of Zuckmayer's dramatic career in the early twenties.[74] Zuckmayer himself explicitly acknowledged Hauptmann as one of his literary ancestors in the case of his first play *Crossroads* (*PoM*, 220) and paid repeated tribute to him.[75] Zuckmayer's esteem continued unabated; even the fact that Hauptmann chose to remain in Nazi Germany whereas Zuckmayer was forced into exile, did not appreciably alter the latter's attitude toward the former. On the occasion of the centennial of Hauptmann's birthday on 15 November 1962, Zuckmayer read a eulogy in Cologne, Vienna, and Zurich in which he professed his belief that Hauptmann was the last *Dichterfürst* ("princely poet"), towering like a tree or mountain in the literary landscape.[76]

In view of both Zuckmayer's repeatedly expressed admiration for Hauptmann and the often noted affinity between the two writers, it was, perhaps, entirely appropriate that Zuckmayer was entrusted by Hauptmann's widow with the reworking of a drama that Hauptmann had essentially completed in the early twenties. Hauptmann had briefly returned to it in 1941 but, presumably because of the impossibility of having a drama with pacifist sentiments published or performed during World War II, had left it in its not quite finished form.[77]

*Herbert Engelmann*, the drama in question, was published in both Hauptmann's original and Zuckmayer's adaptation in 1952;[78] the Zuckmayer version premiered in the Vienna Burgtheater in March 1952. In structure and plot Zuckmayer essentially adheres to Hauptmann; however, he did change the dialogue and Hauptmann's concept of the main character. *Herbert Engelmann* is an "analytical" drama, that is, the decisive event, Herbert Engelmann's murder of a mailman entrusted with delivering cash to postal customers, has taken place before the action of the play begins in Berlin around 1923, at the height of inflation. Only the consequences of the murder constitute the action. The occurrence of a murder suggests that the play has elements of the detective story.[79] One strand of the action is, indeed, concerned with the efforts of two undercover policemen to bring Engelmann to trial. More importantly, however, the drama may also be considered a *Heimkehrerstück*, a play that pits the returned soldier against postwar society somewhat in the fashion of Brecht's World War I soldier Andreas Kragler in *Drums in the Night* or Wolfgang Borchert's World War II noncommissioned officer Beckmann in *The Man Outside*. Engelmann's murder of the mailman can be linked directly to his World War I experiences that result in his becoming a member of the "lost generation." He volunteered for the German Army in 1914, served with distinction, and received the Iron Cross for his bravery. After returning to Germany from a Siberian prisoner of war camp he has difficulties adjusting to civilian life and resents the apparent lack of gratitude for his sacrifices at the front. In a state of depression he robs and, accidentally, kills the mailman.

The action proper begins in Frau Kurnick's boardinghouse, the scene of the first and second acts, where Herbert now lives in the midst of a group of heterogenous characters whose diverse and, in some cases, highly suspect backgrounds indicate the social, economic, and cultural uprooting of society that has taken place as a result of the war. But whereas most of the other characters endeavor to make the best of life, if an unstable one, Engelmann has been permanently scarred—both physically (he has uncontrollable fits of shaking) and emotionally. A turn for the better seems imminent when he marries Christa, his landlady's daughter, and the couple moves to a Berlin suburb, the scene of the third and fourth acts.

But Engelmann's newly found tranquillity is shattered when he is arrested by the two policemen who had formerly been Frau Kurnick's boarders. At his trial—it takes place between the third and fourth acts—Engelmann defends himself successfully and is acquitted, albeit "for lack of evidence." Although his defense lawyer, a former friend of the family, offers him the possibility of resuming his university studies, which were interrupted by the war, and beginning afresh, Engelmann can no longer endure life and commits suicide.

Although both versions of the play adhere to the same plot and end with Engelmann's suicide, the context in which the suicide is presented provides a final indication that Zuckmayer did not adopt Hauptmann's concept of Engelmann's character upon which much of the drama's meaning depends. True, in both versions Christa "absolves" Engelmann before his death on the basis of his suffering before and after the murder. But Zuckmayer adds a passage in which he has Engelmann proclaim the sanctity of each individual life and declare any offender against it sentenced or condemned (*gerichtet;* 271). Hence it appears that Zuckmayer's Engelmann carries out a self-imposed sentence and commits suicide as a final act of atonement, almost in the fashion of General Harras in *The Devil's General*. Hauptmann's Engelmann, however, in accordance with several of Hauptmann's male characters,[80] simply seeks release from the burden of a life that has, despite his acquittal, become unbearable. Further, Frau Kurnick, who had only very reluctantly accepted the marriage of her daughter to Engelmann, explicitly states at the end of Hauptmann's version that God will forgive her son-in-law's suicide. Zuckmayer's Frau Kurnick avoids any specific reference to God's forgiveness and merely states that Engelmann has achieved peace: "Er ist im Frieden" (273).

In brief, Zuckmayer imposes a pattern on the play that consists of the hero's incurring guilt by a moral transgression, his becoming fully aware of his guilt and acknowledging it, and, ultimately, atoning for his transgression. Such a pattern is familiar from both *The Devil's General* and the drama *Cold Light* that, however, was written after *Herbert Engelmann*.[81]

The transgression of Zuckmayer's Engelmann is evident from the fact that he committed the murder in a frame of mind akin to the Nietzschean contempt of the common herd and disregard of the lives of "inferior" individuals.[82] Engelmann's attitude, incidentally, also resembles that of Dostoevski's Raskolnikov in *Crime and Punishment*, who likewise eventually acknowledges his guilt.[83]

The question of guilt is debated in both versions. Zuckmayer has Christa conclude that, strictly speaking, the crime cannot be called murder because the mailman had been tied to a chair and accidentally strangled himself when his plight was not immediately discovered. But Herbert retorts that regardless of the accident a murder had been committed. By invoking in a paraphrase the stern Mosaic law of an eye for an eye he demands punishment: "A life for a life" (238). Characteristically, this passage is missing in Hauptmann's version; here, in fact, it is Herbert who virtually proclaims himself to be innocent by insisting that there had been no murder.[84]

Without going into further detail, it seems clear that Zuckmayer changed the thrust of Hauptmann's play by presenting Engelmann as an autonomous individual who is fully responsible for his deed. Precisely the opposite is true of the main character in the original version. Here Engelmann appears as a victim of circumstances, as an individual who cannot escape the baleful influences of both heredity and environment.[85] As a youth Engelmann had been afflicted with a form of epilepsy. Although there seems to have been no recurrence of these seizures, the savagery of war proved a devastating experience for the extremely gifted but high-strung young man. Even Christa's love ultimately fails to save him from his fate. Moreover, Hauptmann's Engelmann cannot even be held legally responsible for the murder—so that, in the final analysis, war and the society that caused it emerge as the real culprits in Hauptmann's play. By focusing attention on the murder itself rather than presenting it as an extension of the wholesale slaughter of war preceding it Zuckmayer weakens the antiwar message of the play and removes it from the realm of the contemporary, topical drama (*Zeitstück*).[86]

In Zuckmayer's view—stated in the afterword to *Herbert Engelmann*—the drama is a "human tragedy" that takes place " 'between the times' " (274) rather than in a specific period. Conversely, Zuckmayer rooted the play more firmly in the twenties by providing explicit references to concrete historical events and persons, albeit from a post–World War II vantage point. Thus the Treaty of Locarno (October 1925), generally considered an important step in securing peace in Europe because of the rapprochement between Germany and France, and such contemporary statesmen and politicians as the French foreign minister Aristide Briand, the German foreign minister Gustav Stresemann, and Hitler, who had been imprisoned after his abortive Munich attempt to seize power in November 1923, are mentioned.[87] In addition, Zuckmayer vividly evokes the intellectual-cultural climate of the times by developing, on the basis of Hauptmann's stage directions, a dinner conversation for Frau Kurnick's boarders in which he gives full rein to his penchant for the comical.[88]

The critics' opinions concerning the success of Zuckmayer's adaptation have not been entirely unanimous. On the one hand, Zuckmayer has been praised for having created a "succinct and intricately drawn psychological study."[89] On the other, one critic went so far as to question the necessity for Zuckmayer's adaptation.[90]

Whether one gives preference to Hauptmann's original or to Zuckmayer's version, the preceding discussion has demonstrated that Zuckmayer, despite his often expressed admiration for Hauptmann, is no mere imitator but a playwright in his own right. Zuckmayer's vitalistically oriented response to the problems posed in the play is indicative of his belonging to a generation following in the wake of expressionism for whom the representative poet of "Naturalism and social compassion"—epithets generally applied to Hauptmann[91]—could provide inspiration but not a model to be slavishly followed.

An altogether different adaptation is Zuckmayer's revision of his own play *Bellman*. The new version premiered in 1953 in Göttingen under the title *Ulla Winblad, or Music and Life of Carl Michael Bellman* and was published in the same year. Since, as far as could be ascertained, the changes in the new version are not significant enough to change the substance or thrust of the play, the drama has been discussed in its proper chronological context.[92] In a manner of speaking, the Göttingen premiere and the performances in its wake constitute a revival of a play that, because of the volatile political situation in 1938 and the exigencies of Zuckmayer's exile, had attracted only scant notice and had fallen into virtual oblivion.

## VI Prose Fiction

At first glance, it would appear that Zuckmayer's prose fiction of the forties and fifties is only tenuously related to such plays as *The Devil's General*, *The Song of the Fiery Furnace*, and *Cold Light*— all of which explore topical issues. Yet, apart from the humorous *The Soul Brew*, in which Zuckmayer avoids deeper probing, the remaining two prose narratives deal, despite their noncontemporary settings, with such problems as guilt and innocence—problems that are familiar from the post–World War II plays.

The tale *The Soul Brew* is a nostalgic evocation of the "lost paradise" Henndorf near Salzburg.[93] Zuckmayer wrote it to conquer his homesickness and fear for the lives of his parents, who had remained in Germany, during the last months of World War II. The significance that Henndorf had assumed in Zuckmayer's life is evident from the fact that both in *Second Wind* and *A Part of Myself* individual chapters are devoted to Henndorf and that, late in life, Zuckmayer once more, in *Henndorf Pastorale* (1972), reminisced about a place where he once had experienced unadulterated happiness.

Not surprisingly, then, Henndorf provides much of the general atmosphere, local color in dialect and customs, and even some characters for the fictitious events in *The Soul Brew*. But the story takes place at an "indefinite time" and it seems as if time had been suspended and caught in a trap like a "careless mouse" (*WA*, 6:95). Two characters dominate the tale, the rich brewer Matthias Hochleithner, a massive man with an unbridled zest for life reminiscent of Gunderloch in *The Merry Vineyard*, and the unsophisticated village priest, whose girth is hardly less impressive than that of the brewer. Both men preside over their respective realms, the worldly and the spiritual, with absolute authority. The priest, alas, has developed a strong passion for music whose strength is in inverse relation to his musical talents. It is this musical passion that provides both the title of the story and the source of conflict. In the work of a second-rate composer the church choir performs on festive occasions, there is a part for bass and soprano sung by the priest himself and one of the female pillars of his choir. In this part the words "Du Seelenbräutigam" occur; while *Seelenbräutigam* ("bridegroom of the soul") carries with it the proper spiritual connotations, the pause after the first three syllables of the word results in *Seelenbräu* ("soul brew")—a term that elicits decidedly more worldly associations and automatically leads to suppressed merriment in the pews.

Conflict becomes inevitable when a young teacher arrives in the village of Alt-Köstendorf. Like the priest, he is a devotee of music and openly criticizes the priest's antiquated musical taste and methods of instructing his choir. Moreover, he offends the brewer, in contradistinction to the priest named "body brew," by falling in love with the brewer's niece Clementin and dedicating one of his compositions to her. For Clementin is the connecting link between the two dominant figures in the story who otherwise encounter each other with "the mutual respect of enemy powers who know that they possess equal strength" (*WA*, 6:108). The unmarried brewer dearly loves his niece, who has been living in his house since the death of her parents; the priest is likewise very fond of her because Clementin has become one of the chief supports of his choir and has tactfully refrained from challenging him in musical matters.

However, the peace of the village idyll is not permanently threatened. The brewer consents to Clementin's marrying the teacher; the priest is won over by a Bach cantata performed in his honor by the children of the church choir under the direction of Clementin and the young teacher. Thus in *The Soul Brew* Zuckmayer's optimism and his belief in the basic harmony between man and nature, between man and his fellow man asserts itself. The good-natured and down-to-earth humor, the colorful and vigorous language, the deft characterizations of the main figures, and the realistic depiction of events are, surely, qualities that recommend the tale. However, it is well to remember that this idyllic, harmonious world belonged essentially to the past—to the time before the "European catastrophe" as one critic, a fellow exile, put it.[94] The paradise Zuckmayer evoked had been permanently lost and could not be regained. Thus the story could afford his German readers of 1945, when the story was first published,[95] escape from the cataclysm of World War II. Unlike *The Devil's General*, however, *The Soul Brew* was hardly designed to confront its readers with their immediate past and its consequences.

Shortly before leaving Europe, in July 1938, Zuckmayer and his wife had visited the village of Saas-Fee in the Swiss canton of Valais. Rendered speechless by the breathtaking beauty of the alpine village, the Zuckmayers returned again and again until in 1957 they were able to purchase a house and permanently settle in Saas-Fee the following year. Although Zuckmayer claims in his autobiography that it would require a second Jeremias Gotthelf, the nineteenth-century Swiss writer renowned for his realistic depictions of the farmers' lives, to do justice to the landscape and the people of the upper Valais,[96] the prose narrative "The Walking Huts"[97] takes place in the region where Zuckmayer spent the last two decades of his life. Zuckmayer takes one of the striking features of the Valais villages as the starting point for his tale—the *Mazots* or storage huts built on short, plump "legs" or stilts to prevent both rodents and flood waters from destroying the accumulated goods. Yet the peculiar looking huts harken back to an earlier time, and to Zuckmayer, who had published his essay *The Brothers Grimm* in the same year as "The Walking Huts,"[98] they conveyed "another, secret, lost sense, . . . a mythical, cultlike, and slightly uncanny meaning" (*WA*, 6:174).

Thus the prose narrative proper begins like a fairy tale "a long time ago" (*WA*, 6:175) and makes ample use of the supernatural. Two families inhabit the valley of the little river Vispach that empties into the Rhône. Whereas the Balfrins (the name is derived from a mountain near Saas-Fee) are efficient farmers and expend their energies primarily on the acquisition of material wealth—as manifested in the growing number of their well-filled *Mazots*—the Holdermattens (the name ending -*matten* is also indigenous to Saas-Fee)[99] are artistically gifted but incline toward raptures of enthusiasm. In contrast to the ungainly *Mazots* of the Balfrins, they construct tastefully designed houses and chapels.

The latent, but mostly friendly rivalry between the two families escalates into open conflict when a Holdermatten, Peter Marie, asks for the hand of the beautiful Isola Balfrin. During the wedding feast Isola's excessively proud brother Lucas insults Peter Marie and demands quick payment for the debt the latter has incurred while gambling with Lucas as if obsessed. Peter Marie, who possesses a mysterious affinity with nature, promises to pay his debt with precious stones he will gather in the mountains. He is on the point of handing over an extraordinarily beautiful stone to Lucas at the local inn, but the stone has slipped from his pocket to the floor and the ill-disposed Lucas covers it with his foot. Peter Marie, unable to pay his debt, vows to return to the mountains and find even more precious stones. But when Peter Marie swears by the eyesight of his first-born child, the glass face of the clock in the inn shatters. It is not struck by a stone, as the innkeeper assumes, but destroyed by supernatural powers whose warning Peter Marie can no longer heed for he is irresistibly drawn back to the mountains where he disappears.

His wife Isola gives birth to a daughter named Petra who, alas, is blind. Thus Peter Marie's oath has come true. After Isola's death within a short time after giving birth, Petra is adopted by Peter Marie's grandfather. As the years pass, the Holdermattens become completely impoverished and fall as serfs to Lucas, now the head of the Balfrins. Lucas feels irresistibly drawn to Petra who, however, shrinks from him in revulsion. When he beseeches and then commands her to become a member of his household, she flees from him. Miraculously, the mountain stream in which she had been bathing forms a barrier between her and the pursuing Lucas and the wind carries her cries for help to her grandfather and an orphaned Italian boy named Salvatino also living in her grandfather's household. Lucas, frustrated and furious, dismisses the Holdermattens from his employment and has their house destroyed so that they are forced to spend the winter in a hut in the high Alps where they are threatened by death from starvation and freezing. The earnest requests by respected members of the community to reconsider his action spurn Lucas on to ever greater recklessness; he swears that his own *Mazots* will sooner march up the mountain than he will rescue the Holdermattens.

At the same time, Petra implores nature to come to the aid of her family. Lo and behold, Lucas's *Mazots* start on their slow but irresistible march up the mountain and simply squash Lucas, who tries to stop them. Just as Lucas is blinded by the stump of one of his own *Mazots* before an avalanche carries his mangled body away— similarly to Peter Marie Lucas had sworn by his own eyesight not to help the Holdermattens—so Petra's eyesight is restored after Lucas's death. After Lucas, the incarnation of evil,[100] has disappeared from the scene, there are no further obstacles to a fairy-talelike happy ending. Salvatino marries Petra and when Peter Marie's body is discovered—it has been perfectly preserved by the ice—it turns out that a vein of silver is nearby whose exploitation restores the Holdermatten's wealth. They, however, use it wisely by not only building houses and chapels "in praise of eternal beauty" (*WA*, 6:193) but also helping their fellowmen.

"The Walking Huts" is then not a realistic tale in the manner of Jeremias Gotthelf but rather an evocation of legend and myth in the form of the fairy tale as it was conceived by the brothers Grimm: "Like Wilhelm Grimm, Zuckmayer sees the *Märchen* as a symbolic revelation of fundamental human values. Hence the constant juxtaposition . . . of innocence and guilt, altruism and materialism, beauty and ugliness."[101] Ultimately, the struggle waged is that between good and evil, and the evil spirits who possessed, though to varying degrees, Lucas as well as Peter Marie and his wife Isola are vanquished by the "strength of a mild and pious soul" (*WA*, 6:175).[102]

Perhaps it is only appropriate that the writer, in his last work of prose fiction, should return to his origins, that is, select as the setting of *Carnival Confession* the ancient city of Mainz where he had spent his youth. The prose narrative was published more than ten years after "The Walking Huts"[103]—an indication that, with the availability of stages for producing his plays after World War II, the drama assumed renewed significance for Zuckmayer. The short story "Angela of Leuven," first published in German in 1952, cannot really be considered a post–World War II work because it originated much earlier.[104]

Although *Carnival Confession* achieved some kind of international success by being translated into more than ten foreign languages,[105] its appeal to the German reading public was overshadowed by that of Zuckmayer's autobiography, *Als wär's ein Stück von mir* (1966), that clearly ranks as the major prose work and is considered a classic among autobiographies. Although not a work of prose fiction, the autobiography exhibits "the range of a great novel"[106] and provides, indeed, the *Portrait of an Epoch*, as the subtitle of the English translation states. The autobiography was preceded by the essay *Long Walks* (1952),[107] a statement of personal views in the manner of *Pro Domo*,[108] and followed by two minor prose pieces of an essentially autobiographical nature, *Henndorf Pastorale* and *A Walk in Spring*, both of which have been briefly discussed before.[109] The predominance of the autobiographical element in the sixties and early seventies confers upon *Carnival Confession* the distinction of being the last work in a small, but by no means insignificant prose *oeuvre* that spans, as far as the time of origin is concerned, the time from the early twenties to the end of the fifties.[110]

*Carnival Confessions* begins like a detective story when, during one of the last days of the famed Mainz carnival season in February 1913, a man clad in the uniform of the Mainz dragoons enters the cathedral to confess. But before he can utter more than the beginning of the formula used in confessions, he collapses and it is discovered that he has been stabbed between the shoulder blades with a stiletto of Italian origin. Although the police search for the murderer, it is not primarily through their efforts that he is eventually found. In fact, Zuckmayer's emphasis is on the confrontation of the various characters with the guilt they have incurred rather than on the resolution of the crime by a sleuth. The technique used recalls that of the nineteenth-century dramatist Heinrich von Kleist who, in some of his novellas, for example, *The Marquise of O.*, only gradually unravels the meaning of, and reasons for, the bizarre event with which the story began.

In the course of the story it develops that the murdered man is both victim and culprit—a culprit who is prevented from confessing his sins and achieving absolution. The dead man is identified as Ferdinand Bäumler who had fled the country after embezzling money, had joined the French Foreign Legion, and was believed to have been killed in action in Africa. As a result of the interrogation of Clemens Bäumler, Ferdinand's steadfast and honest brother, it is established that Ferdinand had suddenly and surprisingly surfaced in Mainz and had endeavored to persuade him to flee with him to America to begin a new and better life. Before the planned departure, however, Ferdinand wanted to return to his native village near Mainz to see his mother and, above all, to settle scores with an unnamed party. In order not to be recognized he put on Clemens's uniform.

The unknown person with whom Ferdinand hoped to meet before he was murdered turns out to be the wealthy vineyard owner Panezza. He has been elected carnival prince and, together with his princess, must preside over the gay and often raucous festivities. After having been asked by the police to identify the corpse, Panezza feels compelled to unburden himself to the same priest, a canon, to whom Ferdinand had intended to confess. He reveals that Ferdinand was his illegitimate son. Although he had provided educational opportunities for him, Panezza had refused to bail him out when the discovery of Ferdinand's embezzlement was imminent. In the priest's opinion, Panezza cannot be held legally responsible for Ferdinand's murder. But because he had wished Ferdinand dead and had not helped him in time of need, the priest admonishes him to relinquish all thoughts of ever being united with the carnival princess, a young girl, with whom he has fallen deeply in love.

The discovery of yet another corpse, the victim of a street brawl, leads to the resolution of the murder case. Viola Moralta, a distant relative from Sicily, had unexpectedly appeared at the Panezzas' home in a state of great agitation. She now identifies the dead creature—with animallike features—as her half-brother Lolfo and unravels the mystery. Lolfo, who adored Viola because of the kindness she had shown him, had distrusted and hated Ferdinand when he appeared at the Moralto's estate under the name of Viola's cousin Jeanmarie de Panezza. As a relative, Ferdinand was welcomed with open arms, and eventually he became secretly engaged to Viola. Viola even entrusted the family jewels to him to help Ferdinand out of a momentary financial embarrassment. But he disappeared and Viola had no other choice but to follow him with faithful Lolfo to retrieve the jewels and to induce him to marry her so that her child would not be born out of wedlock.

Like Panezza, Viola is not guilty in a legal sense. However, she also had wished Ferdinand—whom she mistook for her cousin—dead if she could not possess him alive. Thus she also feels compelled to confess in the last of the series of confessions revolving around the problem of human guilt. Actually, it is Viola's confession—again, to the same priest—that lends the prose narrative its title. For Viola bares her soul on Ash Wednesday at the so-called carnival confession that was intended to provide instant purification for those who had excessively indulged in the exuberant festivities of the preceding days. But the priest absolves her and thus emerges as the human representative of divine mercy and forgiveness.

The suspenseful story unfolds against the background of the Mainz carnival. The carnival provides not only local color but also emphasizes the contrast between appearance and reality, between the masks that the characters wear in a both literal and figurative sense until they are stripped away to reveal their true selves. The exuberant carnival atmosphere further tends to underscore the proximity of life and death, as there is always the danger that the unbridled gaiety of the masses may assume a Dionysian and even demonic and destructive quality.[111] Despite its serious theme of "contrasting the weakness and fallibility of man with the infinite wisdom and mercy of God,"[112] Zuckmayer alleviates the somber mood by humorous and ribald touches. For example, at the beginning of the story the priest is shown in a somewhat ironical light; there appears a loquacious madame of a whorehouse who insists on the French pronunciation of her name; a detective bursts out in genuine Mainz dialect at the inquest; and there is a bicycle club with an obscene name whose members impatiently wait their turn in the madame's establishment. All these characters and incidents provide comic relief.

Zuckmayer's mastery is also evident in such telling episodes as the brief exchange between the Prussian prosecutor and a court-appointed Jewish defense attorney; in a brief vignette both the latent and the official anti-Semitism are exposed. In the case of the lawyer (*Assessor*), who aspires to marry the carnival princess, Zuckmayer gives in to his satirical penchant by presenting a caricature remotely akin to Knuzius in *The Merry Vineyard*. But for Zuckmayer unbridled, unreflected zest for life was no longer a viable goal; this is evident, for example, in Panezza, a potential Gunderloch. In contrast to Gunderloch, Panezza is not permitted to live life to the fullest but must renounce his love because of his previous moral transgressions. Even his son Jeanmarie, a fairly guileless character, experiences the transitory nature of happiness and love when he realizes that his passion can be easily transferred from Viola to his family's servant girl whom, in her mask, he had mistaken for Viola. The transitoriness of life in the midst of the carefree and self-indulgent carnival atmosphere is underscored when Jeanmarie has a fleeting vision of his death—a foreshadowing of the outbreak of World War I. Nature itself occasionally assumes an oppressively intense quality that is reminiscent of Büchner's novella *Lenz*. But the somber mood of guilt and remorse is not all-pervasive. In contrast to Panezza, who must seek fulfillment in altruistic rather than carnal love, and Viola, who will give birth to a fatherless child, the truly good and innocent Clemens Bäumler will find happiness. It is both an indication of Zuckmayer's faith in the capacity of man to do good and of his unorthodox, unconventional views that Clemens's future wife is an ex-prostitute whom he accepts without question or reproach—thus practicing truly unselfish love.

CHAPTER 5

# The Last Plays

## I  The Clock Strikes One

After the production of *Cold Light* in 1955 there was an uncharacteristic lapse of six years before another Zuckmayer premiere—still an event that demanded the critics' attention—took place. The drama *The Clock Strikes One* is, in many respects, a continuation of themes and problems dramatized in the preceding plays. In Zuckmayer's own view the play deals with that "tragic guilt that all men incur more or less 'innocently' in times of dishonor—unless they are martyrs or saints."[1] Unlike *The Devil's General, The Song of the Fiery Furnace,* and *Cold Light, The Clock Strikes One* was not based on an actual occurrence, or so the playwright claimed.[2] Further, whereas the former plays tended toward fairly lengthy discussions at the cost of dramatic action, the present drama almost achieved the opposite effect by presenting too much action in a comparatively brief drama.[3]

The drama that premiered on 14 October 1961 at the Vienna Burgtheater has the slightly paradoxical subtitle *A Historical Drama of the Present.* The striking of the clock referred to in the title denotes that it is past midnight and a new day is beginning; at the same time, the subtitle suggests that the problems of the past continue to haunt the present—a present, however, that by the time of the play's writing had become almost historical.[4]

The play is, then, an attempt to come to terms with Germany's Nazi past, a contribution to the so-called *Vergangenheitsbewältigung*—although in a distinctly Zuckmayerian mode. The action takes place in 1953 and 1954, that is, during a period when Germany's economic recovery often referred to as economic miracle *(Wirtschaftswunder)* set in. The material prosperity of Jörg Holtermann, a successful industrialist, belies the shadows of the past that beset his family. It is ultimately the aura of guilt intuitively sensed by Gerhard, the

120

youngest of the Holtermanns' two children, that impels him to reject his parents' life style and strike out on his own. Curiously, however, he joins a gang of criminals whose leader, Turo von Heydenkamp, he adopts as a model. Gerhard's mother Gudula, next to him the main character in the play and the one perhaps most likely to arouse the spectators' sympathy and pity, has never been able to overcome her past and continues incessantly to probe her guilt. Gerhard's going astray exacerbates her problem; whereas her daughter from a previous marriage serves as a constant reminder of her culpability, Gerhard held the promise for a brighter future—a promise that now will not be fulfilled. As she confesses to Turo, whom she had asked to release his hold on her son, she was previously married to a successful Jewish musician who, when the Nazis came to power, was beaten and tortured so severely that he asked his wife to end his suffering by giving him poison—a request to which she acceded. In order to save herself and her daughter she had to swear that her daughter was the offspring of an adulterous union with her present husband, Holtermann, who, in 1933, had come to her aid. Turo, chief of a gang of men who have become criminals as a consequence of their having been uprooted and emotionally scarred by their experiences in World War II, has a past that even surpasses Gudula's in its gruesome and not entirely unsensational aspects.

As a young child Turo witnessed how his father, a Latvian estate owner, was carried off and his mother raped and then killed by a mob. Later in life Turo joined the German army and became officer of a unit at the Russian front in World War II. In memory of his mother, a beautiful Tartar princess, he called his outfit "The Golden Horde"—the same name he has given his gang—and waged his private war against the Soviet Union not for ideological reasons but to punish the presumable murderers of his parents.

Unlike Gudula, Turo has accepted his guilt by adopting a nihilistic and stoic stance—he reads Seneca. He does not provide any particular justification for his recent activities except the need to go underground after the war in order to escape punishment. Curiously, the previous victims do not seem to be better off than their oppressors; one of the members of Turo's gang is a fatalistic Jew who survived the concentration camps but is shot by police during an unsuccessful hijacking attempt.

The third character whose guilt is most obvious but who, as a man completely without conscience, almost totally ignores it, is Dr. Flühvogel, a university lecturer and Gerhard's tutor. There is bitter

irony in the fact that Flühvogel asks for the hand in marriage of
Gudula's daughter—who could have been one of his potential victims. For Flühvogel is a former concentration camp doctor who had
been charged with selecting those who in the Nazis' view were
"superfluous eaters." Gudula, who has gone insane after learning
that Turo and Gerhard have left the country as a result of the abortive
hijacking at which a policeman was killed, instinctively recoils from
Flühvogel. The enormity of his crimes becomes apparent in Gudula's use of Christ's words to the devil, "Get thee hence" (WA, 10:65).
But there is no accounting for Flühvogel's further fate, no attempt
at poetic justice, and no effort to elucidate the function of ex-Nazis
in post–World War II German society.

With the eighth scene the place of action shifts to Hanoi, then
in French Indochina, where Turo and Gerhard, soldiers in the
French Foreign Legion, spend their off-duty hours in an establishment of doubtful reputation. Zuckmayer, intimately familiar with
a soldierly milieu, provides some colorful touches for this scene.
But his tendency to rely on exaggerated effects and stereotyped
characters is also in evidence here. Just as Flühvogel corresponds
perhaps too closely to the cliché of the brutal, inhuman doctor of
a concentration camp, so the girl, with whom Gerhard flees, turns
out to be a Communist agent. Gerhard, however, does not become
a deserter because of qualms about his role in the Indochina War
but as a consequence of his having killed his corporal out of jealousy.

The last scene takes place in the hospital of a French garrison.
Gerhard has been caught but, in view of a rare tropical disease he
has contracted, been given a brief reprieve before being shot as a
deserter. His father comes to see him; his last act of mercy is to
empty the hypodermic needle that was intended to make Gerhard
fit for the execution. In the end, in a departure from realism, the
attending nurse assumes the features of Gerhard's dead mother—
she had been killed in a car accident after Gerhard's flight—and,
reconciled with his fate, Gerhard dies.

In the dialogue of the final scene questions such as the responsibility of the individual for his actions, human guilt, and God's
mercy are voiced once more. But one wonders whether Gerhard's
recognition that he failed his mission in life is convincingly presented; unlike the tale *Carnival Confession*, in which the carnival
atmosphere provides a perfect foil for the exploration of the main
characters' guilt, the thrilling events in *The Clock Strikes One* tend
to obscure the inner action, that is, Gerhard's spiritual purification.

One wonders further whether a drama that is ostensibly concerned with coming to terms with the political past should entirely dispense with the ideological dimension. True, "Zuckmayer places all his hope and faith for the future in the individual, because . . . the individual alone is capable of insight, spiritual growth, and the conscious shaping of his life."[5] Yet even a rudimentary degree of political awareness on the part of the main characters might have added to their depth.

Some reviewers of the Viennese premiere guardedly applauded the drama or rather the performance—and especially that of Paula Wessely in the role of the mother[6]—although they did not fail to point out that the play relied on thrilling effects. Other critics were less charitable. The weekly news magazine *Der Spiegel*, renowned for its caustic style, seized upon the opportunity for a pun provided by Zuckmayer's title. Instead of *Die Uhr schlägt eins*, *Der Spiegel* headlined its review "Schlägt dreizehn" (*es schlägt dreizehn*, / "that's the limit") and termed the action of the play "monstrous."[7]

For good reasons, the drama is rarely performed and seldom mentioned in the secondary literature.

II   Dance of the Herons *and* The Life of Horace A. W. Tabor

Although published in 1961,[8] the drama *Dance of the Herons* was not performed until 1967 when the Zurich Schauspielhaus honored the playwright, a Swiss resident for more than a decade, on the occasion of his seventieth birthday. The gap between the publication of the play and its premiere—unprecedented in Zuckmayer's career—can be explained by the fact that *Dance of the Herons* is a one-act play requiring only approximately thirty minutes for its performance. Hence a suitable opportunity had to present itself before the play could be staged.

Curiously, whereas Zuckmayer professes to have conceived the idea for *The Clock Strikes One* in the American jungle,[9] his first drama that has an entirely realistic American setting seems to have originated after the playwright's permanent return to Europe. Like *The Clock Strikes One*, the play takes place in the present; however, in *Dance of the Herons* Zuckmayer confines himself to the domestic sphere and develops the dramatic conflicts from there instead of attempting to deal with a host of problems within the confines of a play. By limiting himself to the domestic sphere and a correspondingly small number of characters, Zuckmayer achieved a degree of density, economy, and concentration that induced many critics to compare *Dance of the Herons* to the last act of a tragedy in which pent-up emotions explode in a sudden outburst of violence.[10]

The play takes place in the living room of an old farm house in New England during the morning hours of a spring day. The preservation of the classical unities of time and place in combination with the limited number of characters—five, in all—sustains the forceful unified action. Loren King, manager of the Atwoods' farm, sees his dream of again acquiring a farm owned and operated by his own family shattered when his son Dave marries a model who poses for underwear ads and whom he therefore considers to be disreputable. The conflict between father and son results from an irreconcilable difference in outlook; whereas the father plans and builds for the future, the son belongs to a generation that is content to live day by day and enjoy instant gratification.

The day of reckoning has also come for Rhoda, an extraordinarily strong-willed woman, and her husband Jolly Atwood, the owners of the farm. When Jolly, a weakling and alcohol-addicted playboy, returns from a hunt, he imitates the mating dance of the male heron. Rhoda, transformed into the hunter, shoots her husband whom she both despises and pities. She rejects the suggestion by Loren, presumably her lover, to declare the shooting an accident and accepts full responsibility for the murder. In a final evocation of Greek tragedy, the stage direction at the end of the play states that she looks upon the corpse with the glance of both "priestess and victim" (*WA*, 10:104).

Although Zuckmayer could hardly have written the play without having spent a number of years as a farmer in Vermont, its merits do not primarily derive from its "Americanness." To be sure, the playwright provides local color by, for example, liberally sprinkling his text with slightly Germanized Americanisms such as "Front-Porch, Locust-Pond, Deerland-Country, Greyhound, Lumberjack." Ultimately, however, the tragic resolution of the conflict tends to transcend the geographical and chronological limitations of the setting. Conversely, it was precisely Zuckmayer's realism that induced one critic to observe Zuckmayer had demonstrated that naturalist theater continued to be a legitimate theatrical mode of expression in the sixties.[11]

*Dance of the Herons* had signaled Zuckmayer's adopting a somewhat different direction in his choice of topics to be dramatized. In his second-to-last drama, *The Life of Horace A. W. Tabor*—written after *Dance of the Herons* but first performed on 18 November 1964, approximately three years before the one-act play—Zuckmayer again drew on his experiences as an American resident and seized upon a genuinely and uniquely American subject: an authentic hero's rise from rags to riches and, in a significant deviation from the pattern of the success story, his sudden downfall. It is hardly surprising that, in 1939, the story of the erstwhile "silver king" Tabor and his wife Baby Doe was recommended to the newly arrived immigrant as a project with the potential of a surefire Broadway success.[12] Only a few years before Zuckmayer had set foot on American soil, in 1936, newspapers had reported Baby Doe's demise; she had been found frozen to death in her dilapidated shack in Leadville, Colorado. Until the very last she believed—contrary to the opinion of the experts—that the silver mine "The Matchless" she had inherited from Tabor would yield new treasures.

But at that time the dramatist lacked sufficient familiarity with his host country to tackle indigenous material that Douglas Moore, composer of the opera *The Ballad of Baby Doe* (1956), considered a "great American story."[13] In addition, Zuckmayer was too preoccupied with the fate of Europe in general and Germany in particular—as both the unsuccessful *Somewhere in France*[14] and the hugely successful *The Devil's General*[15] demonstrate to varying degrees. As a consequence, we are faced with the somewhat paradoxical fact that, despite its authentic American subject, the play was not written during Zuckmayer's stay in the United States but rather after the playwright's return to Europe. It was also in Europe, at the Zurich Schauspielhaus, that the play premiered some twenty-five years after Zuckmayer had first heard of Tabor and Baby Doe.[16] Needless to say, the expectations of the German-speaking public differed considerably from those of American theatergoers; they may well have influenced Zuckmayer's dramatic concept.

Despite Zuckmayer's insistence that he had not intended any evocation of the Wild West, it is fair to say that he did not entirely escape the danger of making concessions to popular European preconceptions about the United States. Many critics, at any rate, made explicit references to the Wild West in the headlines of their reviews.[17] A closer look at the text reveals, however, that *The Life of Horace A. W. Tabor* is not, by any means, simply an improved version of the early drama *Pankraz Awakens*.[18] On the contrary, although the first act begins in the run-down golddigger town of Leadville in 1879, the playwright endeavors to de-emphasize the adventuresome and exotic elements by referring to phenomena of the modern industrial world such as environmental pollution and social problems. Only as part of the exposition, presented by means of reports, dialogue, and as a play within a play, does the colorful past of the pioneer and the fight against the Indians play a role. Other conflicts, that is, primarily those between workers and their employers, dominate the present.

Tabor himself—he and his wife Augusta run a post office and general store in Leadville—has renounced the false romanticism of golddigging and succumbed to a pessimistic attitude that is quite uncharacteristic of an inhabitant of the New World. But by a stroke of luck he is able to acquire cheaply two thirds of a silver vein from two German immigrants that proves to be almost inexhaustible. Only two years later—the second act takes place in 1881—Tabor, now a wealthy man, fully subscribes to the idea of progress that for him is almost synonymous with prosperity and profit. Hence he considers a strike by his workers a criminal act; if necessary, he is prepared to use his private army in order to preserve law and order.

The third act takes place one year later and shows Tabor at the height of his power; his economic rise from rags to riches is reflected in his newly gained political prominence. He has been elected governor of Colorado; somewhat later he will become senator. In addition, Tabor's fabulous wealth has excited the people's imagination; his extraordinary good fortune provides the stuff for popular lore and legends. When Tabor first sets eyes on Baby Doe, she appropriately sings the song of silver king Tabor. The song emphasizes Tabor's foremost characteristic—his luck. According to the playwright, Tabor lived in the "time of great improvisations . . . in the world of unheard-of strokes of luck and enormous losses" (WA, 10:107). As the subtitle of the play, *A Drama from the Days of the Last Kings*, suggests, Zuckmayer conceived of Tabor's wealth as being of magical origin.

Tabor's ostentatious display of wealth and his illicit relationship with Baby Doe have alienated him from his wife Augusta who, motivated by social compassion, tends to the needs of the exploited miners. Although she grants him a divorce so that he is free to marry Baby Doe, it is precisely at the moment when his fortune seems to have reached a new peak, at the lavish and spectacular wedding feast, that his empire begins to crumble as a consequence of unfavorable developments in the stock market. In only a little more than three years—the wedding scene in act 4, scene 3 takes place in

Washington in 1883, the following first scene of act 5 in Denver, Christmas 1886—Tabor has lost his entire fortune and is reduced to poverty again. Miraculously, however, Augusta returns to Tabor, and Baby Doe remains faithful to him. In the last scene of the play Tabor dies a poor but happy man in a play that in almost Brechtian "epic" fashion spans twenty years of his life[19]—from 1879 to 1899— yet essentially concentrates on the seven years—from 1879 to 1886—of Tabor's rise and fall.

In the view of a number of critics Zuckmayer's play lacked relevance in the middle sixties, at a time when the documentary drama had begun to assert itself. Both Zuckmayer's choice of subject matter—usually decried as a Western or golddigger story—and the artistic means chosen to present this subject—essentially realism— these critics argued, lacked modern appeal and were an insufficient attempt at historical analysis. In fact, one critic went so far as to charge that Zuckmayer had dramatized material that was also used by Hollywood for "the creation of the American myth."[20] To be sure, Zuckmayer delights in the creation of a milieu that is populated by colorful characters whose very names hint at the unusual. Thus we encounter John Savage, a former medicine man of the Cheyenne Indians, Buckskin Joe, an old golddigger, "Chicken-Bill" Lovell, a prospector, and Harvey "Vulture" Doe, the former husband of Baby Doe. Particularly the last named appears as the prototypal Chicago gangster when, during his brief presence on stage, he successfully blackmails Tabor. At the same time, however, in accordance with his avowed intention of minimizing the ingredients to be found in Westerns, Zuckmayer stressed the "documentary" character of his drama by appending a list of works he consulted (*WA*, 10:261–62)— a procedure far more familiar from, for example, Rolf Hochhuth's documentary drama *The Deputy* (1963) than from Zuckmayer.

At any rate, in the final analysis it was not the playwright's aim to explore the social dimensions of an important phase of American history; rather, Zuckmayer was fascinated by the figure of Tabor whose rapid rise and fall—despite its peculiarly American traits— seems to transcend the specific time and place of the action. That Tabor's fate is not primarily determined by socioeconomic factors and that he refuses to be cast in a mold is evident, for example, from the apt characterization of one of his fellow bonanza millionaires who calls him a "mystic, . . . not an entrepreneur, . . . not a modern man" (*WA*, 10:235). On the one hand, Tabor is not a true capitalist in the fashion of Pierpont Mauler in Brecht's *Saint Joan of the Stockyards;* on the other, as an avowed individualist he neither fully grasps nor sympathizes with the ideas of social reform that are advocated in the play by the character Stratton. Stratton, incidentally a historical figure, is presented by Zuckmayer as a Marxist millionaire—the seeming contradiction notwithstanding.

Tabor's existence is, in the last analysis, little affected by the laws of economics. The repeated references to his fortune, the subtitle, and initial stage directions of the play suggest—quite apart from Zuckmayer's additional comments—that the atmosphere of the fairy tale, in which riches and power are bestowed upon the pure in heart, pervades the drama. There is, indeed, a popular play *(Volksstück)* by the nineteenth-century Viennese playwright Ferdinand Raimund, entitled *The Farmer as Millionaire*, that bears a remarkable structural-thematic resemblance to Zuckmayer's drama. Raimund presents, although within the confines of the *Romantic, Original, Magic Fairy Tale* (thus his subtitle), the rise and fall of a humble man, his temporary delusion, and ultimate happiness that is preceded by the recognition of the errors of his ways. Zuckmayer's drama lacks Raimund's didactic application; however, like Raimund Zuckmayer is primarily interested in the "purely human" devoid of its social and political implications.[21] *Der Spiegel*, hardly noted for subtle understatement, was quick to seize upon the fairy-tale aspects of Zuckmayer's drama and recommended it to the children's hour of the German broadcasting companies.[22] Other critics expressed more balanced but not entirely positive views. The astute Friedrich Luft, for example, asseverated in his review that one could no longer write naively realistic plays as if Brecht, Beckett, or Ionesco had never existed.

The objections raised against Zuckmayer's play concerning the choice of subject matter, the lack of social relevance, the realistic means of presentation, and the creation of a fairy-tale atmosphere have their common denominator in the implicit or explicit assumption that Zuckmayer is no longer "modern" by virtue of the fact that he adhered to both his dramatic creed and his essential means of expression. Lack of modernity, in turn, almost automatically denotes a dramatist of less consequence, many critics seem to infer. Yet such views have not remained unchallenged. One perceptive reviewer observed correctly that critics form only part of the theatrical establishment.[23] Some directors, many actors—for whom Zuckmayer wrote highly rewarding roles—and large segments of the theater-going public constitute Zuckmayer's following. To be sure, these followers tend to be less vociferous and articulate than the critics. Nevertheless, their loyalty to Zuckmayer provides an indication that the playwright continued to be a viable force in the theater—even if, as in the case of *The Life of Horace A. W. Tabor*, he shunned the message play and made an only partially successful transition from the exoticism, inspired by Karl May, of *Pankraz Awakens* to a play in which the social dimensions, represented by the ideas of Karl Marx as interpreted by Stratton, come clearer into focus.

## III   The Pied Piper

Literary history in general and theater history in particular do not abound with writers and dramatists who achieved a ripe old age of undiminished creativity. Goethe, George Bernard Shaw, and Gerhart Hauptmann come readily to mind as examples of productive longevity. If we leave the complex question of artistic stature aside, Zuckmayer can easily be added to this list of creative grand old men of letters. What to many might have appeared to be the sum of his life and literary output, the autobiography *A Part of Myself* (1966), should prove not to be Zuckmayer's last work. A few weeks after the playwright had celebrated his seventy-eighth birthday, his last drama, *The Pied Piper*, premiered at the Zurich Schauspielhaus on 22 February 1975. The Swiss theater thereby continued a tradition of first performances of Zuckmayer's plays that reached as far back as the premiere of *Bellman* in 1938 and included such notable events as the first performance of *The Devil's General* in 1946 as well as the premieres of the third-to-last and second-to-last dramas *Dance of the Herons* and *The Life of Horace A. W. Tabor*, respectively.

Curiously, *The Pied Piper* appears to be less a work inspired, in the Goethean sense, by the wisdom, maturity, and contemplative attitude of old age than a play that exhibits youthful impetuosity and partisan overtones. Zuckmayer achieved this effect by reinterpreting the ancient legend of the Pied Piper of Hamelin, a subject to which a prominent citizen of Hamelin had drawn his attention approximately ten years before the play was actually completed. In fact, my English rendering of Zuckmayer's original title *Der Rattenfänger*[24] as *The Pied Piper* has been prompted by Robert Browning's beloved "Child's Story" in verse, entitled *The Pied Piper of Hamelin* (1842), rather than by the attempt to provide a literal translation.[25] Precisely the fact that there is only one document relating the event of 26 June 1284, an inscription on the so-called Pied Piper's house in

Hamelin, which briefly reports the abduction of one hundred thirty children, enabled Zuckmayer to give his own interpretation of the legend. Apart from Browning's humorous verse narrative with its gentle moral, there are other literary reworkings. Suffice it to mention Goethe's playful "Rattenfängerlied" [Song of the Pied Piper, 1804] and Achim von Arnim and Clemens Brentano's inclusion of the orally extant "The Pied Piper of Hamelin" in the first part of their famed collection of folk songs, *The Boy's Magic Horn* (1806). The freedom from the restraints of historical accuracy induced the nineteenth-century novelist Wilhelm Raabe to offer his own version of the events in his prose narrative *The Children of Hamelin* (1863). Raabe dispensed with a vital ingredient of the legend, the invasion of Hamelin by the rats, altogether. Instead of having the Pied Piper rid the city of the rats and then, when he is refused his promised reward, disappear with the children in a small mountain near the city, he has the socially rejected Pied Piper lead the city's male youths into an ambush where they are slain by their enemies.

We may infer from Zuckmayer's afterword to his dramatization that he studied the historical literature on the subject rather than the literary interpretations of the legend. The dramatist retained all important elements of the legend such as the rat plague, the city's deliverance from the rats by the Pied Piper, the withholding of his just reward, and his disappearance with the city's children. However, from the very beginning it is clear that Zuckmayer's reinterpretation differs from those of his predecessors by virtue of the fact that the social tensions existing in medieval Hamelin assume utmost importance. Actually, the *dramatis personae* are grouped according to their social status, and the inhabitants are rigidly divided into the patricians of the city proper and those lesser citizens who live outside the city walls. Before the play begins, a narrator draws the spectators' attention to the rigidly enforced class distinction that separates the city.

The rat plague that besets Hamelin turns out to be a monstrous scheme on the part of the ruling class in general and of the city's regent in particular. The rats are allowed to multiply—in the quarter of the poor outside the city walls it is even prohibited to kill them—because they devour everything and thus keep the price of flour at an artificially high level. The city regent's greed and desire to reap windfall profits, however, threaten to destroy the entire city, owing to the fact that the rats can no longer be contained outside the city walls. Social unrest among the poorer populace is rampant; in addition, the children of the well-to-do have turned away from their morally corrupt parents and established an anachronistic hippie counterculture replete with drug or rather herb sniffing.

Bunting, so called on account of his colorful dress (*bunt*, "colorful"), arrives at Hamelin during this politically volatile situation. He has fled the Eastern territories where he had been educated by the Teutonic Knights but where, as a Slav, he was destined to spend his life in servitude. Bunting finds employment as the assistant to the executioner with jurisdiction over the poor. His curious power over rats by means of playing his pipe—construed by the superstitious to be magic but explained by Bunting to be a natural phenomenon—does not remain unnoticed for long. An agreement is reached between Gruelhot, the city regent, and Bunting. Rather than money Bunting demands a parcel of land and all rights of a free citizen if he should succeed in leading the rats out of the city to the Weser river where they will drown. Despite Bunting's success in ridding the city of the rats, he is denied his recompense. Instead, the authorities make a counterproposal to the effect that Bunting will be handsomely rewarded if he leads the undesirable poorer citizens into virtual slavery by inducing them to become colonists in the Eastern territories. Bunting refuses to have any part in such a devilish scheme and demands both political rights and economic fair play for the poor citizens. But the planned uprising of the underprivileged is prevented by the arrival of the duke of Brunswick's soldiers. They, unlike their predecessors in previous Zuckmayer plays, have no redeeming qualities whatsoever and are depicted with severity. Thus Rikke, the executioner's daughter with whom Bunting is in love, commits suicide in a particularly grisly fashion to avoid being ravished by the soldiers. Meanwhile Bunting, who had escaped the authorities, is recaptured again and sentenced to death for inciting a riot. At the last moment, Gruelhot is presented with an ultimatum. His two children are being held hostage by the other children of the city and will die unless Bunting is released unharmed. The voluntary departure of the children with Bunting in search of a better and freer land concludes the play proper.

In a sense, *The Pied Piper* represents the sum of Zuckmayer's dramatic efforts, owing to the fact that he displays a considerable range of techniques and devices.[26] It sports, for example, a narrator who, however, is less evident in the text than he was at the Zurich premiere.[27] Further, songs interrupt the action, and vivid scenes taking place among the people interchange with highly stylized

scenes in the milieu of the upper classes. The entire play is structured loosely into twenty-one scenes, of which eighteen were performed in Zurich, in two "sequences," and thus exhibits an "epic"
tendency slightly reminiscent of Brecht's theater.

In fact, it is not entirely unjustified to see Brecht's influence at
work.[28] Apart from the aforementioned narrator and the songs (such
as Zuckmayer had used before, however), the rigid division of the
characters into rulers and ruled, into exploiters and exploited, and
the absence of a middle class corresponds somewhat to the Brechtian
scheme of things in which the tendency toward social polarization
is quite pronounced. Further, the use of the profit motif, that is,
that the rats are being permitted to eat wheat in order to keep prices
high, results in a scathing indictment of an unjust social order that
rivals Brecht's condemnation of a society split into antagonistic
classes.

At the same time, these points of comparison should not obscure
the fact that the play is essentially Zuckmayerian in spirit. For
example, it does not end with a clearly stated moral or with an
appeal to the spectators to change that which is rotten in Hamelin
and, by inference, elsewhere; rather, the promised land to which
Bunting leads the children appears dimly on the horizon. It is a
hope-inspiring vision, not necessarily a concrete goal that can be
achieved by means of concerted action. In contrast to such plays as
*Cold Light* and *The Clock Strikes One*, however, Zuckmayer places
his hope and trust not solely on the individual but on an entire
generation of disenchanted children and youths who, to be sure, are
dependent on Bunting's leadership.

The process of regeneration is aided by the fact that poetic justice
prevails in the case of the chief perpetrator of evil, Gruelhot, and
his informer, a baker of consecrated wafers. Gruelhot commits suicide by hanging himself after his wife's death and his children's
turning against him; the baker, ironically, meets his end when he
is on the point of claiming his reward for the betrayal of Bunting.
But Zuckmayer only condemns the worst offenders. The old and
humble Bishop Ludger, who significantly speaks the last words of
the play, will, together with a crippled youth left behind in the
exodus, endeavor to heal the wounds in the bereft and leaderless
city. Ludger thus clearly emerges as the moral victor over his opponent, the proud and power-wielding prior.

Zuckmayer's concept of Bunting, the central figure of the drama,
does not correspond to the character of the medieval legend. To be

sure, like the traditional Pied Piper Bunting has power over animals and men; however, he uses his power not to entice but to advance progressive social ideas. Yet even Bunting succumbs briefly to the lust for power, although in the end he assumes the role of the children's leader to the promised land.

Whereas Zuckmayer retains the medieval setting and alludes both to such ingredients of the legend as the disappearance of the children in the Koppen, a modest hill near Hamelin, and their resurfacing in Transylvania, there are aspects of the play that clearly relate it to the present. Thus Bunting appears as a man of reason in a world of medieval superstition. This superstition is manipulated by Gruel-hot to a certain extent when he proposes to charge Bunting with the use of black magic. Gruelhot, at any rate, occasionally uses the modern bureaucrat's phraseology and avails himself of the services of an informer to assess the mood of the populace. The entire power structure functions in modern fashion; it is replete with such types as the executioner who willingly carries out orders without ever asking for their justification until he realizes that he contributed to upholding social injustice. Further, there are allusions to racial per-secution; Bunting himself suffered at the hands of the Teutonic Knights precisely because he was a member of an "inferior" race. The baker of consecrated wafers incites a riot against the Jews of the city—an event indicative both of medieval pogroms and modern-day oppression of racial minorities. Finally, there are the youths of the city who, in rejecting the world of their parents, have adopted the life-style of the Hippies.

Several critics, although they were not necessarily persuaded by the virtues of the play, noted that *The Pied Piper* represented a convincing demonstration of Zuckmayer's essential humanity, such as he had retained throughout his life. In the final analysis, one critic remarked, it was beside the point to charge Zuckmayer with the failure of providing new directions either in the theater, in the underlying philosophy of his plays or their social implications.[29] In fact, Bunting's "Psalm of the Murdered Souls" (*WA*, 10:360–61) uses the motifs of drowning and decay that are familiar from the brief cooperation in the twenties between the pre-Marxist Brecht and Zuckmayer.[30] But whereas there is no room for God in Brecht's universe, in Zuckmayer's play God is not totally absent even in the face of intense suffering. Thus Bunting asks after the death of his beloved Rikke: "Is there Someone who permits all this to happen and is yet merciful?" (*WA*, 10:360). Exactly the problem of human suffering had been declared the "bedrock of atheism" by one of the characters in *Danton's Death* by Georg Büchner,[31] that eminent precursor of the moderns, approximately one hundred sixty years before. As is evident from the conclusion of his play, Zuckmayer viewed man's existential situation less bleakly than either Büchner or Brecht. Such guarded optimism may, perhaps, be unjustified; still, one cannot but respect the tenacity with which Zuckmayer continued to present his vision of man.

CHAPTER 6

# Conclusion

UNTIL his death in 1977 Carl Zuckmayer was a curious phenomenon in the realm of postwar German letters. On the one hand, the premieres of each of his plays attracted considerable attention and numerous stages usually acquired the rights to produce them. Moreover, with the exception of the German Democratic Republic, Zuckmayer's plays were performed in all the German-speaking countries—in Austria, the Federal Republic, and Switzerland; official honors were bestowed upon the playwright by the three European countries in which he had established roots: in Germany, the country of his birth, where he resided until the Nazis seized power, in Austria from 1926 until the *Anschluss* of 1938, and, after his permanent return from the United States in 1958, in Switzerland.[1] Further, at least some of Zuckmayer's plays continue to be repertory mainstays of many theaters; his readers are served by S. Fischer, Zuckmayer's publisher since the thirties, which keeps most of his works in print. Some of them, for instance *The Captain of Köpenick*, have become perennial best-sellers in inexpensive paperback editions. Television and radio broadcasts also have contributed to popularize Zuckmayer's works. Hence it is fair to conclude that the author continues to attract a wide following among both readers and theatergoers.

On the other hand, there has been growing, sometimes vociferous disenchantment among critics who consider Zuckmayer's dramas outmoded on two counts. First, these critics argue, the dramatic techniques employed, that is, an essentially "epic" structure without the Brechtian ideological foundation, tend to present plot for plot's sake rather than adhere to a specific purpose; second, Zuckmayer's underlying individualistic and humanitarian world view that endows man with the moral responsibility for his acts and places him in an ultimately meaningful, God-controlled universe, is, in the opinion of many critics too inadequate to render the complexities of the modern world on the stage.

The controversy that ensued upon the city of Düsseldorf's decision in 1972 to award Zuckmayer the newly created Heine Prize may serve to bring into focus the objections raised against the writer. Zuckmayer was awarded the prize on occasion of the one hundred seventy-fifth anniversary of Heine's birth on 13 December 1972 despite a statement the playwright had made earlier to the effect that, although he admired Heine's brilliance and poetic prowess, he did not feel any affinity with him.[2] When Zuckmayer accepted the prize *in absentia* because of an illness and hence could not give his planned formal address in which he redefined his view of Heine,[3] objections were raised in the press on the grounds that Zuckmayer had little in common with one of the most contradictory but, at the same time, clearly liberal and progressive figures of German literary history.[4] In the essay, an implicit reply to his critics, Zuckmayer points out that a common bond existed between Heine and himself—the incisive experience of exile that tended to transcend their differences. The fact that Zuckmayer emphasized Heine's turning to religion when he was confined to his bed during the last years of his life merely illustrates that the many facets of Heine's work and personality admit of different interpretations. Yet the objections raised were not entirely unjustified owing to the fact that Zuckmayer can hardly be compared to Heine, the writer of commitment who, with caustic wit and devastating irony furthered the cause of liberalism but, at the same time, possessed an exceedingly vulnerable ego.

Nevertheless, Zuckmayer had accomplished the remarkable feat of launching what amounted to a second career after the demise of the Nazi regime and his return from exile. He achieved this not by remaining aloof from contemporary issues but by dramatizing them in a fashion that corresponded to his nonideological artistic creed and by employing the artistic means at his disposal. Generally speaking, Zuckmayer had proved himself to be a contemporary fully attuned to the problems of his times. In his best plays, *The Merry Vineyard*, *The Captain of Köpenick*, and *The Devil's General*, he transcended mere topicality and succeeded in presenting in masterly realistic fashion dramatic portraits of decisive moments in twentieth-century German history. Precisely the fact that Zuckmayer refrained from adopting the message play or using the stage as a pulpit assured the general acclaim his best plays, and foremost among them his masterpiece, *The Captain of Köpenick*, received. It is well to recall that literary merit and popular appeal do not necessarily coincide; in the case of Zuckmayer's three plays this not entirely common phenomenon did, indeed, occur.

There is no denying that after *The Devil's General* Zuckmayer's fortune began to decline and criticism of his plays grew more vociferous. It has been argued that once Zuckmayer abandoned the encompassing realism of his earlier plays and concentrated instead on mere topicality, the substance of his plays grew weaker while his persistently proclaimed moral convictions began to ring hollow.[5] Still, Zuckmayer can boast of a not entirely unenviable record: at least three plays out of the fifteen included in the 1976 ten-volume edition of his works have been acknowledged as either masterpieces or plays of superior merit. It is also well to bear in mind that Zuckmayer was not, by any means, passé after the singular success of *The Devil's General* had begun to wane in the early fifties. Until Brecht's death in 1956 he was often cited as the only playwright living in the West comparable in stature to his erstwhile friend and fellow returnee from exile.

The publication of *A Part of Myself* in 1966 confirmed Zuckmayer's position as the "grand old man of German letters."[6] No matter that, as a dramatist, he had begun losing ground to such acclaimed newcomers on the drama scene as the Swiss Friedrich Dürrenmatt and Max Frisch in the fifties; the representatives of the documentary drama Rolf Hochhuth, Heinar Kipphardt, and Peter Weiss in the sixties; and Thomas Bernhard, Peter Handke, and Franz Xaver Kroetz in the seventies. Zuckmayer's autobiography is, whatever yardstick one may apply, not only a moving but also a superbly written document that evokes the political, social, and cultural climate of the first half of our century.

In a manner of speaking, *A Part of Myself* is a thoroughly "German" book—if for no other reason than that it deals with the fate of a German author who witnessed important phases of German history. In her introduction to *Second Wind* (1940), the forerunner of *A Part of Myself*, Dorothy Thompson called Zuckmayer a "German and a patriot" and wrote that he was, in both appearance and outlook, "German blood and soil."[7] Although Zuckmayer became an American citizen and, after his return to Europe, settled in Switzerland rather than Germany, he never succumbed to a wholesale condemnation of the German people. He clearly distinguished between Nazis and non-Nazis and retained a nonvindictive attitude during and after his years in exile. Moreover, Zuckmayer's three most important dramas have been termed a "German Trilogy"[8]— precisely because they penetratingly and, in a theatrical way, convincingly mirror three decisive epochs of Germany's twentieth-century history: Empire (*The Captain of Köpenick*), Weimar Republic (*The Merry Vineyard*), and Third Reich (*The Devil's General*).

The question arises, then, as to whether or not Zuckmayer's "Germanness" proved to be an obstacle for the reception of his works in other countries. Without doubt, his intense preoccupation with German problems—as evidenced by *The Devil's General*— and his inability to adjust to both the linguistic and cultural climate of his host country significantly reduced his chances of becoming established as a man of letters in general and a dramatist in particular during his residence in the United States. Not surprisingly, these efforts resulted in almost total failure. In fact, the exigencies of exile were a formidable hurdle that was overcome by only a very few writers from the German-speaking countries, notably Lion Feuchtwanger, Thomas Mann, and Franz Werfel. The example of Bertolt Brecht, whose works began to be widely received in America only after his return to Europe, demonstrates that an author's physical presence is not a prerequisite for the acceptance of his works in that country. In Zuckmayer's case, however, no such boom in the reception of his works ensued after he had left the United States, although they did not remain completely unnoticed.

It remains to chart briefly the impact of Zuckmayer's works, that is, those that became available in English translations for the American book market or the theater, in order to be able to assess the degree of recognition he achieved in at least one country beyond the German-speaking lands. The international recognition, as expressed in such quantitative criteria as the number of works translated, seems to be an indispensable prerequisite for any author laying claim to belonging to that elusive category of world literature. Curiously, a brief survey reveals that the small number of translations are decidedly weighted in favor of Zuckmayer, the prose writer and not, as one might have expected, Zuckmayer, the dramatist. It is a further irony of the reception process that the first work to be published in 1928 was the short story "Bal" about which Zuckmayer later expressed ambivalent feelings.[9] It was not until approximately ten years later that the second translation, the novel *The Moons Ride Over* (1937), became available.[10] There was a noticeable increase in the number of translations after Zuckmayer's arrival in the United States; however, apart from the first version of his autobiography *Second Wind* (1940),[11] few of these pieces, some of which have been discussed in a different context,[12] were particularly noteworthy. Only thirty years later another major work was published: the fairly extensively reviewed and generally acclaimed but abridged English version of *A Part of Myself* (1970).

Whereas there are three independently published prose works in English translation—one novel and two autobiographies—Zuckmayer fared worse in the realm of the drama. The Berlin correspondent of the influential *New York Times* reported in fairly detailed fashion about the premieres of Zuckmayer's plays during the last years of the Weimar Republic.[13] The same newspaper also acknowledged Zuckmayer's contribution to the film as both playwright and scriptwriter.[14] However, the planned New York production of *The Captain of Köpenick* did not materialize despite the fact that an English translation that was apparently not distributed on the American market was available as early as 1932.[15] In the United States a translation of the play did not appear until 1972[16]— after a second British adaptation had been published and the play had had a very successful run at the National Theatre (London).[17] The American translation of *The Captain of Köpenick* had been preceded by that of *The Devil's General* in 1962;[18] like the former play the latter was performed in London but not in New York.[19] Apart from the short-lived *Somewhere in France*,[20] there were, in all likelihood, no performances of Zuckmayer's plays by American professional companies before 1959.[21] Only recently there has been some minor theatrical activity with regard to Zuckmayer's plays.[22] The result of this brief survey is not, by any means, awe-inspiring. In the almost fifty years from 1928 to 1972, there were published in the United States one early prose narrative (in an anthology), one novel, two autobiographies, a handful of mostly minor short stories and essays—among the essays, "Appeal to the Living" deserves special mention[23]—and two plays.

The survey tends to corroborate the statement made by one literary historian in 1959 that Zuckmayer, together with Heinrich Mann, Ernst Jünger, and Gottfried Benn, is "underrepresented" in this country.[24] But the application of the quantitative yardstick does not reveal the entire story. Perhaps it is the kind of works that have been translated rather than their number that has led to Zuckmayer's underrepresentation. Surely, one can hardly quarrel with the translation of *A Part of Myself;* at the same time, it seems desirable to have his plays performed more often so that Zuckmayer, the dramatist, emerges more clearly in the public's consciousness.

That it is all too easy to do a writer an injustice by succumbing to hackneyed clichés is apparent from the following. In 1932 an essay appeared on "The Young Writers of Germany." The caption of Zuckmayer's picture in this essay reads: "Carl Zuckmayer. Born 1896. A playwright. He adapted 'What Price Glory' for the German stage, and wrote the scenario of 'The Blue Angel', for Marlene Dietrich and Emil Jannings."[25] Approximately fifteen years later, in 1947, *Life* magazine published an essay by Zuckmayer and included a small photo with the following caption: "Author Zuckmayer is best known to Americans for his script for *The Blue Angel*, the movie which introduced Marlene Dietrich to the United States."[26] Finally, in 1977 the *New York Times* referred prominently—in both subtitle and subheading—to Zuckmayer's script for *The Blue Angel*.[27]

That Zuckmayer should be remembered for his contribution to a film that indubitably achieved both world-wide success and critical acclaim is highly ironic in view of the fact that the merits of his contribution have been seriously questioned by the film's director.[28] It is only small solace that a considerable part of the Zuckmayer research has been carried out by literary historians and critics residing in the United States.[29] Scholarly publications ordinarily do not reach the general reader and hence are usually not instrumental in establishing an author's reputation by increasing the circulation of his works—although, in a modest way, academic publications may pave the way for an author's wider acceptance.[30] Academic and scholarly criticism may, however, set intrinsic standards by which an author can be judged. Judged by those standards, Zuckmayer falls ultimately short of the genuine accomplishments in the realm of world literature by the likes of Rilke, Kafka, Thomas Mann, and Brecht. At the same time, on the basis of those same criteria Zuckmayer deserves a wider recognition in this country than he has been accorded so far.

# Notes and References

## Chapter One

1. Carl Zuckmayer," The Devil's General," trans. Ingrid G. and William F. Gilbert, in *Masters of Modern Drama*, ed. H. M. Block and R. G. Shedd (New York, 1962), p. 930.

2. Cf. Luise Rinser, "Porträtskizze," in *Fülle der Zeit. Carl Zuckmayer und sein Werk* (Frankfurt, 1956), pp. 13–30, and Henry Glade, "Carl Zuckmayer's *The Devil's General* as Autobiography," *Modern Drama* 9 (1966–1967): 54–61.

3. Carl Zuckmayer, "1896–1914: A Look at the Rhine," in *A Part of Myself. Portrait of an Epoch*, trans. Richard and Clara Winston (New York, 1970), pp. 97–134.

4. Carl Zuckmayer, *Pro Domo* (Stockholm, 1938), p. 92.

5. Carl Zuckmayer, "The Captain of Köpenick," trans. Carl Richard Mueller, in *German Drama between the Wars*, ed. George E. Wellwarth (New York, 1974), p. 191.

6. Carl Zuckmayer, *Werkausgabe in zehn Bänden 1920–1975* (Frankfurt, 1976), 7:307. Subsequently referred to as *WA*.

7. Zuckmayer's autobiography (*PoM*) begins, in defiance of chronological order, with the chapter "1926–1934: A Moment [lived] in Paradise." The chapter heading is a quotation from Schiller's drama *Don Carlos*.

8. Zuckmayer, *Pro Domo*, p. 92.

9. Carl Zuckmayer, *Die Brüder Grimm: Ein Beitrag zur deutschen Humanität* (Frankfurt: Suhrkamp, 1948), p. 24; reprinted in Carl Zuckmayer, *Aufruf zum Leben: Porträts und Zeugnisse aus bewegten Zeiten* (Frankfurt, 1976), p. 264.

10. In his autobiography Zuckmayer specifically mentions and partly quotes the doggerel about a Dog Barber (*PoM*, 109), "Pessimistic Tales" (*PoM*, 126), and "poems in the manner of Heine" (*WA*, 1:168; not included in *PoM*).

11. According to a note on the typescript of "Auch bei uns wird es Frühling. Brief aus der Westfront" (10 April 1915), Zuckmayer's letter was published by the *Frankfurter Zeitung*. However, the letter is not listed in Arnold John Jacobius, *Carl Zuckmayer. Eine Bibliographie 1917–1971* (Frankfurt, 1971).

12. Carl Zuckmayer, "Zwei Gedichte. I. Wir treiben durch die Nebel einander zu. II. Auf beiden Ufern ist die Not geringer," *Die Aktion* 8, nos. 9–10 (9 March 1918): 121; reprinted in Carl Zuckmayer, *Gedichte* (Frankfurt, 1977), pp. 198–99.

13. *Die Aktion* 8, nos. 21–22 (1 June 1918): 278–79.

14. Notably in the poem, "Der Berliner Spartakusaufstand siegreich niedergeworfen," *Die Aktion* 9, nos. 2–5 (1 February 1919): 58; reprinted in Carl Zuckmayer, *Gedichte*, p. 156, and in the report, "Schlichter Bericht von einer verratenen Revolution," *Die Aktion* 9, nos. 47–48 (29 November 1919): 786–88.

15. Carl Zuckmayer, "Front der Unzerstörten," *Vossische Zeitung*, 20 December 1930.

16. Ibid.

17. Zuckmayer's drama *Bellman* was performed in Zurich in 1938 and revised after World War II. See chapter 3, section 2, pp. 66–70, and p. 148, n. 9.

18. Zuckmayer spoke at a memorial service for Mierendorff in New York on 10 March 1944. In his address, which was published several times, he pleaded eloquently for the "other," the non-Nazi Germany. The drama *The Devil's General* is dedicated to Haubach, among others.

19. Siegfried Jacobsohn, *Jahre der Bühne: Theaterkritische Schriften*, ed. Walter Karsch (Reinbek bei Hamburg, 1956), p. 198.

20. Review by Alfred Kerr, in *Theater für die Republik 1917–1933 im Spiegel der Kritik*, ed. Günther Rühle (Frankfurt, 1967), p. 275.

21. Review by Emil Faktor, in *Theater für die Republik*, ed. Rühle, p. 274.

22. Oskar Kanehl, "Bürgerliche Revolutionshelden," *Die Aktion* 10, nos. 51–52 (12 December 1920): 717.

23. Cf. Jacobsohn, *Jahre der Bühne*, p. 198, and Wilfried Adling, "Die Entwicklung des Dramatikers Carl Zuckmayer," in *Schriften zur Theaterwissenschaft*, vol. 1, ed. Theaterhochschule Leipzig (Berlin, 1959), p. 40.

24. Review by Herbert Ihering, in *Theater für die Republik*, ed. Rühle, p. 277. Also quoted by Zuckmayer in his preface to Ingeborg Engelsing-Malek, *"Amor Fati" in Zuckmayers Dramen* (Konstanz, 1960), p. viii.

25. Letter to Kurt Wolff, 20 February 1921. Cf. Kurt Wolff, *Briefwechsel eines Verlegers 1911–1963*, ed. Bernhard Zeller and Ellen Otten (Frankfurt, Scheffler, 1966), p. 373.

26. Cf. "Von Zirkus, Karussell und Jahrmarkt, von Schiffsschauklern, Gauklern und Vagabunden," *Die Weltbühne* 19, no. 13 (29 March 1923): 361–64. Cf. also *PoM*, 257.

27. The plot summary is based on the copy of a typescript obtained from the Bibliothek des Deutschen Literaturarchivs in Marbach. The play was published under the title "Pankraz erwacht. Stück aus dem fernen Westen in drei Akten" in a critical edition by Barbara Glauert, in *Carl Zuckmayer '78, Ein Jahrbuch* (Frankfurt, 1978), pp. 47–163.

28. Klaus Schuhmann, *Der Lyriker Bertolt Brecht* (Munich; dtv, 1971), p. 89. For a more detailed comparison of the two playwrights, see Siegfried Mews and Raymond English, "The *Jungle* Transcended: Brecht and Zuckmayer," in *Essays on Brecht: Theater and Politics*, ed. Siegfried Mews and Herbert Knust, University of North Carolina Studies in the Germanic Lan-

guages and Literatures, no. 79. (Chapel Hill, 1974), pp. 79–98. See also the revised version of this essay, "Im amerikanischen Dickicht: Brecht und Zuckmayer (*Pankraz erwacht—Im Dickicht der Städte*)," in *Carl Zuckmayer '78*, pp. 181–207.

29. See, e.g., the review by Felix Hollaender, in *Carl Zuckmayer '78*, pp. 168–71.

30. Herbert Ihering, *Von Reinhardt bis Brecht: Vier Jahrzehnte Theater und Film*, vol. 2 (Berlin, 1959), p. 97.

31. Cf. Siegfried Mews, "From Karl May to Horace A. W. Tabor: Carl Zuckmayer's View of America," *Mosaic* 6, no. 2 (Winter 1973): 125–142.

32. Ihering, *Von Reinhardt bis Brecht*, 2:96.

33. Cark Zuckmayer, *Gedichte 1918–1948* (Berlin, 1948). Further collections of the poems are those in *GW*, *WA*, and the most inclusive *Gedichte*.

34. The translation of the passage in question in *PoM* is incorrect. Instead of "I managed to find my own tone in a few poems, *though not* in my prose writings" read ". . . and *even more so* in my prose writings" (my italics).

35. Carl Zuckmayer, *Die langen Wege* (Frankfurt, 1952), pp. 68–70.

36. Bertolt Brecht, *Poems*, ed. John Willett and Ralph Manheim with the cooperation of Erich Fried (London: Eyre Methuen, 1976), p. 107.

37. Schuhmann, *Der Lyriker Bertolt Brecht*, p. 109.

38. Bertolt Brecht, *Gesammelte Werke*, Werkausgabe edition suhrkamp (Frankfurt: Suhrkamp, 1967), 8:85–86.

39. Bertolt Brecht, *Die Hauspostille: Manual of Piety*, A Bilingual Edition with English Text by Eric Bentley and Notes by Hugo Schmidt (New York: Grove Press, 1966), pp. 134–37. The version of the poem in *Manual of Piety* differs slightly from that in *Baal*.

40. Brecht, *Poems*, p. 74.

41. Cf. Knut Brynhildsvoll, "Leben und Weltverständnis in der frühen Lyrik Zuckmayers," *Blätter der Carl-Zuckmayer-Gesellschaft*, 2, no. 2 (1 November 1976): 55–56.

42. Adling, "Die Entwicklung des Dramatikers Carl Zuckmayer," pp. 46–47.

43. Raymond E. Barrick, "A Characterization of the Mystical Philosophy of Carl Zuckmayer as Revealed in His Life and Works" (Ph.D. diss., Tulane University, 1964), p. 94.

44. Although the short story is thematically related to Zuckmayer's prose narratives about World War I, it was not published until 1940 (under the title "Even in Hell . . .") as chapter 3 of *Second Wind*, trans. Elizabeth Reynolds Hapgood, intro. Dorothy Thompson (New York, 1940). The story was first published in German in volume 4 of *Gesammelte Werke in Einzelausgaben* (Frankfurt, 1952). In this edition as well as in later collections, including *WA*, Zuckmayer did not adhere to a strict chronological sequence based on the time of the stories' origin.

## Chapter Two

1. Review by Alfred Kerr, in *Theater für die Republik 1917–1933 im Spiegel der Kritik*, ed. Günther Rühle, p. 671.

2. See, e.g., the review by Bernhard Diebold, in *Theater für die Republik*, ed. Rühle, p. 673.

3. Citation by Paul Fechter, in *Carl Zuckmayer. Das Bühnenwerk im Spiegel der Kritik*, ed. Barbara Glauert (Frankfurt, 1977), p. 27.

4. Kerr, in *Theater für die Republik*, ed. Rühle, p. 670.

5. Erwin Rotermund, "Zur Erneuerung des Volksstücks in der Weimarer Republik: Zuckmayer und Horváth," in *Volkskultur und Geschichte. Festgabe für Josef Dünninger zum 65. Geburtstag*, ed. Dieter Harmening et al. (Berlin, 1970), p. 618.

6. Bertolt Brecht, "Notes on the Folk Play," in *Brecht on Theatre. The Development of an Aesthetic*, ed. and trans. John Willett (New York: Hill and Wang, 1964), p. 153.

7. For a brief comparison of the two plays, see Jost Hermand, "Herr Puntila und sein Knecht Matti. Brechts Volksstück," *Brecht Heute—Brecht Today* 1 (1971): 124–26. A summary of recent criticism of the play may be found in Siegfried Mews, *Bertolt Brecht: Herr Puntila und sein Knecht Matti* (Frankfurt: Moritz Diesterweg, 1975), pp. 47–72.

8. Quoted in Günther Rühle, *Zeit und Theater*, vol. 2, *Von der Republik zur Diktatur 1925–1933* (Berlin, n.d.), p. 773.

9. Elisabeth Frenzel, *Judengestalten auf der deutschen Bühne* (Munich, n.d.), p. 224. The 1953 film version avoided controversy by converting the two Jews into Swiss citizens.

10. Wilfried Adling, "Die Entwicklung des Dramatikers Carl Zuckmayer," in *Schriften zur Theaterwissenschaft*, vol. 1, ed. Theaterhochschule Leipzig (Berlin, 1959), p. 64.

11. Review by Friedrich Dürrenmatt in *Die Weltwoche*, 9 May 1952.

12. Günther Rühle, "Carl Zuckmayers versöhnende Weisheit," *Frankfurter Allgemeine Zeitung*, 20 January 1977.

13. Printed in *Fülle der Zeit: Carl Zuckmayer und sein Werk* (Frankfurt, 1956), pp. 137–45.

14. See chapter 1, section 3, pp. 26–27, and p. 142, n. 26.

15. See Carl Zuckmayer, "Der Schinderhannes," in *Carl Zuckmayer*, ed. Glauert, pp. 101–5.

16. See Carl Zuckmayer, "Franzosenzeit am Oberrhein," *Vossische Zeitung*, 29 June 1930; reprinted as "Franzosenzeit (1918 bis 1930)," *Blätter der Carl-Zuckmayer-Gesellschaft* 4, no. 1 (1 February 1978): 21–25.

17. E. Speidel, "The Stage as Metaphysical Institution: Zuckmayer's Dramas *Schinderhannes* and *Der Hauptmann von Köpenick*," *Modern Language Review* 63 (1968): 430.

18. Review of a 1977 performance by Lothar Orzechowski, in *Blätter der Carl-Zuckmayer-Gesellschaft*, 4, no. 1 (1 February 1978): 18.

19. Felix Hollaender, *Lebendiges Theater* (Berlin, 1932), p. 166.

20. Review by Kerr, in *Theater für die Republik*, ed. Rühle, p. 804.

21. Zuckmayer again experienced difficulties for inadvertently using a name—this time that of the owners of the Swiss National Circus. See *PoM*, 307–10.

22. Review of the London performance by Charles Morgan, *New York Times*, 1 May 1932, sec. 8, p. 2.

23. See the reviews in *Theater für die Republik*, ed. Rühle, pp. 910–16.

24. Carl Zuckmayer, "Ein deutsches Märchen," in *Carl Zuckmayer*, ed. Glauert, pp. 155–57.

25. Carl Zuckmayer," The Captain of Köpenick," trans. Carl Richard Mueller, in *German Drama between the Wars*, ed. George E. Wellwarth (New York, 1974), pp. 179–296. All references in the text are to this edition.

26. Review by Bernhard Diebold, in *Theater für die Republik*, ed. Rühle, p. 1080.

27. Inexplicably, this important sentence has been omitted from the translation cited above, n. 25.

28. Zuckmayer, "Ein deutsches Märchen," p. 156.

29. Review by Herbert Ihering, in *Theater für die Republik*, ed. Rühle, p. 1076.

30. Paul Rilla, "Zuckmayer und die Uniform," in *Literatur, Kritik und Polemik* (Berlin, 1950), pp. 7–10.

31. Adling, "Die Entwicklung des Dramatikers Carl Zuckmayer," pp. 114–16.

32. Review by F. Düsel, in *Das deutsche Drama in Geschichte und Gegenwart*, vol. 3, ed. Richard Elsner (Berlin, [1931]), pp. 265–66. See also Joseph Goebbels, in *Der Angriff*, 12 March 1931.

33. See Rudolf Koester, "The Ascent of the Criminal in German Comedy," *German Quarterly* 63 (1970): 376–93.

34. Speidel, "The Stage as Metaphysical Institution," p. 432.

35. Ibid.

36. John Mortimer, Intro., *The Captin of Köpenick*, by Carl Zuckmayer (London, 1971), p. [xv].

37. Ibid., p. [xvi].

38. See chapter 2, section 1, p. 40, and n. 12, above.

39. Mortimer, Intro., p. [xv].

40. Maxwell Anderson and Laurence Stallings, "What Price Glory," in *Three American Plays* (New York: Harcourt, Brace, 1926), pp. 1–89.

41. Carl Zuckmayer, "Meine 'Rivalen-Bearbeitung.' Aus einem Gespräch," in *Carl Zuckmayer*, ed. Glauert, pp. 131–32.

42. See chapter 1, section 5, pp. 32–33.

43. Zuckmayer, "Meine 'Rivalen-Bearbeitung,' " p. 131.

44. See *Theater für die Republik*, ed. Rühle, pp. 951–55.

45. Review by C. Hooper Trask, *New York Times*, 28 April 1929, sec. 9, p. 1.

46. Pauline Steiner and Horst Frenz, "Anderson and Stalling's [*sic*] *What Price Glory?* and Carl Zuckmayer's *Rivalen*," *German Quarterly* 20 (1947): 240. Zuckmayer's play was published as a typescript for the use of stages (*Bühnenmanuskript*): "Rivalen (What price glory?). Ein Stück in drei Akten (nach dem amerikanischen Schauspiel von Maxwell Anderson und Laurence Stallings)," frei bearbeitet von Carl Zuckmayer (Berlin, 1929).

47. Zuckmayer, "Meine 'Rivalen-Bearbeitung,' " p. 131.

48. Review by Stark Young, *New York Times*, 6 September 1924, p. 14.

49. Steiner and Frenz, "Anderson's and Stalling's *What Price Glory*," p. 241.

50. Review of the film by Mordaunt Hall, *New York Times*, 24 November 1926, p. 26.

51. See chapter 1, section 5, p. 33.

52. Herbert Ihering, *Von Reinhardt bis Brecht: Vier Jahrzehnte Theater und Film*, vol. 2 (Berlin, 1959), p. 390.

53. See chapter 1, section 2, pp. 18–20.

54. Carl Zuckmayer, "Front der Unzerstörten," *Vossische Zeitung*, 20 December 1930.

55. Letter of Carl Zuckmayer to the *Vossische Zeitung*, 25 August 1931; reprinted in *Carl Zuckmayer*, ed. Glauert, p. 175.

56. Ibid.

57. A fairly detailed account of the structural changes Zuckmayer and Hilpert undertook is provided by Wayne Kvam, "Zuckmayer, Hilpert, and Hemingway," *Publications of the Modern Language Association of America* 91 (1976): 202, 204, n. 17.

58. Review by Franz Köppen, in *Carl Zuckmayer*, ed. Glauert, p. 181.

59. Kvam, "Zuckmayer, Hilpert, and Hemingway," p. 202.

60. Ibid.

61. Letter of Zuckmayer, in *Carl Zuckmayer*, ed. Glauert, p. 175.

62. Review by Alfred Kerr, in *Carl Zuckmayer*, ed. Glauert, pp. 151–52.

63. This is the title of a 1944 American version based on the first English translation of Heinrich Mann's novel by an anonymous translator who, however, had adopted the title of the film for his translation (London: Jarrold, 1932).

64. *Heinrich Mann. Texte zu seiner Wirkungsgeschichte*, ed. Renate Werner (Tübingen: Max Niemeyer, 1977), p. 117.

65. See Josef von Sternberg, *Fun in a Chinese Laundry* (New York: Macmillan, 1965), pp. 136–38; 230.

66. Josef von Sternberg, introduction to *The Blue Angel* (New York: Simon and Schuster, 1968), p. 12. On p. 16, Zuckmayer, together with Karl Vollmoeller, is given only "courtesy credits."

67. For a detailed account of the controversy, see Ulrich Weisstein, "*Professor Unrat, Small Town Tyrant*, and *The Blue Angel*: Translations,

Versions, and Adaptations of Heinrich Mann's Novel in Two Media," *Film Journal*, 1, nos. 3–4 (1972): 53–61; reprinted in *Actes du VI<sup>e</sup> Congrès de l'Association Internationale de Littérature Comparée*, ed. Michel Cadot et al. (Stuttgart, 1975), pp. 251–57.

68. See chapter 6, p. 140.

69. See chapter 1, section 5, pp. 31–33.

70. "Sitting Bull. Ein Indianer-Roman, unvollendet (1924/25)," in *GW* 1:151–97.

71. See chapter 2, section 1, pp. 34–40.

72. For a more detailed discussion of Zuckmayer's view of America, see Siegfried Mews, "From Karl May to Horace A. W. Tabor: Carl Zuckmayer's View of America." *Mosaic*, no. 2 (1973): 125–42: reprinted in *Deutschlands literarisches Amerikabild. Neuere Forschungen zur Amerikarezeption der deutschen Literatur*, ed. Alexander Ritter (Hildesheim: Olms, 1977), pp. 476–94.

73. Translated under the title "Monkey Wedding" by F. A. Beaumont in the London magazine *Argosy*, March 1938, pp. 53–69. The American publisher Benjamin Huebsch had apparently declined publication as is evident from an unpublished letter by Zuckmayer to Huebsch (16 June 1932) in the Manuscript Division, Library of Congress, Washington, D.C.

74. See Hans-Albert Walter, *Deutsche Exilliteratur 1933–1950*, vol. 2, 2d ed. (Darmstadt, 1973), p. 54.

75. See *PoM*, 324, and *WA*, 4:270. Gottfried Bermann Fischer, *Bedroht-Bewahrt*. (Frankfurt, 1971), p. 53, explicitly states that it was Ullstein's handling of *A Love Story* that contributed to Zuckmayer's changing publishers. Subsequently, after the difficult exile period of both writer and publisher, Zuckmayer became one of the most successful authors of the S. Fischer firm.

76. See chapter 1, section 5, pp. 32–33.

### Chapter Three

1. See chapter 2, section 6, p. 61.

2. See Siegfried Mews, "Die unpolitischen Exildramen Carl Zuckmayers," in *Deutsches Exildrama und Exiltheater: Akten des Exilliteratur-Symposiums der University of South Carolina 1976*, ed. Wolfgang Elfe, James Hardin, and Günther Holst, *Jahrbuch für internationale Germanistik*, ser. A, vol. 3 (Berne, 1977), pp. 139–48.

3. Apart from the aforementioned *Deutsche Volkslegenden vom Niederrhein*, Zuckmayer lists (*WA*, 8:8) the *Novellen* by the nineteenth-century Austrian writer Julius von der Traun (Julius Alexander Schindler) and Rudolf Borchardt's adaptation of a minnesong.

4. See "*Der Schelm von Bergen*," in *Kindlers Literatur Lexikon* (Darmstadt, 1970–1974), 9:84–86.

5. See Ludwig Emanuel Reindl, *Zuckmayer: Eine Bildbiographie* (Munich, 1962), p. 55.

6. See the reviews, including that of the Berlin *Deutsche Allgemeine Zeitung*, in *Carl Zuckmayer: Das Bühnenwerk im Spiegel der Kritik*, ed. Barbara Glauert (Frankfurt, 1977), pp. 187–95.

7. Ingeborg Engelsing-Malek, *"Amor Fati" in Zuckmayers Dramen* (Konstanz, 1960), pp. 68–69.

8. Carl Zuckmayer, *Pro Domo* (Stockholm, 1938), pp. 79–80. See also Carl Zuckmayer, "Der Kaiser im 'Schelm von Bergen,' " in *Carl Zuckmayer*, ed. Glauert, p. 187.

9. The two versions were published as follows: *Bellman: Schauspiel in drei Akten* (Chur, 1938); *Ulla Winblad, oder Musik und Leben des Carl Michael Bellman* (Frankfurt, 1953). The now defunct A. G. für Verlagsrechte was one of the ventures of Gottfried Bermann Fischer, Zuckmayer's publisher, who was forced to leave first Berlin and then Vienna. Thus the publication history of the play itself is indicative of the exigencies of exile. All quotations in the text are from *WA*.

10. As to Zuckmayer's historical accuracy, see Ian C. Loram, "Ulla Winblad: Words and Music by Zuckmayer and Bellman," *Monatshefte* 47 (1955): 11–18.

11. Carl Zuckmayer, "Wie 'Ulla Winblad' entstand," in *Carl Zuckmayer*, ed. Glauert, p. 315. A similar criticism had been voiced in the review of the play by the *Neue Zürcher Zeitung*, 20 November 1938.

12. Zuckmayer, "Wie 'Ulla Winblad' entstand," pp. 313, 315.

13. Ibid., p. 315.

14. See chapter 3, section 4, pp. 77–79.

15. See chapter 4, section 1, p. 86–87.

16. Luise Rinser, "Porträtskizze," in *Fülle der Zeit: Carl Zuckmayer und sein Werk* (Frankfurt, 1956), p. 13.

17. J[ohannes] K[lein], "Ulla Winblad," in *Lexikon der Weltliteratur*, ed. Gero von Wilpert (Stuttgart, 1963–1968), 2:1074.

18. For a more detailed discussion of Zuckmayer's concepts of the people (*Volk*) and the masses, see Arnold John Jacobius, *Motive und Dramaturgie im Schauspiel Carl Zuckmayers* (Frankfurt, 1971), pp. 67–76.

19. Loram, "Ulla Winblad," p. 17, comments on Zuckmayer's use of Bellman's songs: "Out of the enormous reservoir of these songs Zuckmayer has carefully selected eleven. For some he has written new words, others are taken directly from the standard German translations. . . ."

20. Engelsing-Malek, *"Amor Fati" in Zuckmayers Dramen*, p. 152, makes the additional and slightly dubious point that Bellman comes close to repenting his previous carefree and unfettered existence.

21. K[laus] H[aberkamm], "Ulla Winblad," *Kindlers Literatur Lexikon*, 11:9710.

22. Bertolt Brecht, *Gesammelte Werke*, Werkausgabe edition suhrkamp (Frankfurt: Suhrkamp Verlag, 1967), 14:1383.

23. Carl Zuckmayer, "Die Magdalena von Bozen; Eingang des Romans," *Die Neue Rundschau*, 46, no. 2 (November 1935): 484–520. Although *Die Neue Rundschau* was a publication of the S. Fischer firm, the periodical continued to be published in Germany until 1944 by Peter Suhrkamp. In 1945 Bermann Fischer resumed publication of the periodical.

24. See *WA*, 5:239.

25. Gottfried Bermann Fischer, *Bedroht-Bewahrt* (Frankfurt, 1971), pp. 93–123.

26. Letter by Berman-Fischer Verlag, dated 21 September 1936, to Keyser'sche Buchhandlung in Erfurt. Jan Hans of the Arbeitsstelle für deutsche Exilliteratur of the University of Hamburg kindly made the letter available to me.

27. The British and American publications of the novel differ in their titles: *The Moon in the South*, trans. M[oray] Firth [pseud.] (London, 1937); *The Moons Ride Over*, trans. Moray Firth (New York, 1937). Zuckmayer had been in contact with Benjamin Huebsch of the Viking Press since at least 1932 (see chapter 2, section 6, p. 60, and p. 147, n. 73), but although the *New York Times* had reported fairly regularly about the Berlin performances of Zuckmayer's plays in the late twenties and early thirties, only "The Story of Bal, Governor of the Lapps," in *The Best Continental Short Stories of 1927*, ed. R. Eaton (New York, 1928), pp. 246–54, had been anonymously translated for the American market. *The Captain of Köpenick. A Modern Fairy Tale in Three Acts*, trans. David Portman (London, 1932), a translation, incidentally, about which Zuckmayer repeatedly expressed his dissatisfaction, was presumably not distributed in the United States.

28. Review by Alfred Kazin, *New York Times*, 7 February 1937, p. 4.

29. Ibid.

30. See Jacobius, *Motive und Dramaturgie im Schauspiel Carl Zuckmayers*, p. 14.

31. See *WA*, 5:134–37, 196–97.

32. Review by William Soskin, *New York Herald Tribune*, books sec., 14 February 1937, p. 4.

33. Review by Anon., *Saturday Review of Literature*, 20 May 1937, p. 6.

34. Carl Zuckmayer, *Ein Sommer in Österreich. Erzählung* (Vienna, 1937); not included in either *GW* or *WA*.

35. *Auf einem Weg im Frühling. Erzählung—Wiedersehen mit einer Stadt: Aus dem Stegreif erzählt* (Salzburg, 1970) is not included in *WA*. *Henndorfer Pastorale* (Salzburg, 1972) appears in *WA*, 4:57–104, among the short stories from the collection *A Farmer from the Taunus and Other Stories* (1927). Zuckmayer reminisces, from the vantage point of 1970, about his entire stay in Henndorf, i.e., from 1926 to 1938; hence it is justified to discuss the work in the context of the writer's Austrian exile.

36. See "1926–1934: A Moment in Paradise," *PoM*, 3–28, and chapter 8, "A Moment Lived in Paradise," of *Second Wind*, trans. Elizabeth Reynolds Hapgood, intro. Dorothy Thompson (New York, 1940). See also chapter 4, section 6, pp. 111–13.

37. Zuckmayer published eight poems under the title of the first poem, "Danksagung an den Bach," *Die Neue Rundschau*, 46, no. 2 (August 1935): 148–54.

38. The poem belongs to the "Svendborg Poems" and was apparently completed in 1938. See Bertolt Brecht, *Poems*, ed. John Willett and Ralph Manheim with the cooperation of Erich Fried (London: Eyre Methuen, 1976), pp. 318–20, 573–74.

39. The "Programme" (available at the New York Public Library at Lincoln Center) reads: "Sir Oswald Stoll Presents Ludwig Berger's Stage Production 'The Golden Toy.' A Romantic Play by Carl Zuckmayer (Based on some motives of the old Indian Play 'Vasantasena') in thirty-two scenes. Music by Schumann. English book and lyrics by Dion Titheradge. Additional lyrics by R. H. Elkin." Ludwig Berger had been the director of the premiere of *Crossroads* in 1920.

40. Review by D. C. F., *Theatre World* 21 (April 1934): 169.

41. See chapter 2, section 5, pp. 58–59.

42. For a survey of the film projects Zuckmayer was involved in, see Heinz Grothe, "Zwischen Berlin und Hollywood: Carl Zuckmayer und der Film," *Blätter der Carl-Zuckmayer-Gesellschaft* 3, no. 1 (1 March 1977): 27–29.

43. For example, all those films were reviewed in the *New York Times*.

44. Apart from the stories or scenarios for the films mentioned above, Zuckmayer also wrote the following film story: *Stroller's Fate: The Life of Edmund Kean* (London, [1936]). For other film projects, see the survey by Grothe, (n. 42) and Arnold John Jacobius, *Carl Zuckmayer: Eine Bibliographie 1917–1971* (Frankfurt, 1971), pp. 333–35.

45. See chapter 3, section 4, p. 76. His experiences in Hollywood did not deter Zuckmayer from further collaboration with the film industry, however, after World War II. In the fifties he wrote the German screenplays for *Decision Before Dawn*, *The Moon is Blue*, and *The Man with the Golden Arm*.

46. See Wolfgang Paulsen, "Carl Zuckmayer," in *Deutsche Literatur im 20. Jahrhundert*, 5th rev. ed., ed. Otto Mann and Wolfgang Rothe. (Berne, 1967), 2:343–44.

47. Both *Herr über Leben und Tod* and *Pro Domo* were published by Bermann Fischer Verlag in 1938. Bermann Fischer had, after the *Anschluss*, reestablished his firm in Stockholm. An English translation of an excerpt from *Pro Domo* (pp. 12–16) appeared in *Living Age*, March 1939, pp. 35–36.

48. In *PoM* six chapters precede the final chapter, "1939–1954: Departure and Return."

49. Zuckmayer, *Pro Domo*, pp. 79–80. See also chapter 2, section 1, pp. 34–40.

50. Zuckmayer, *Pro Domo*, p. 84.

51. Review by Alfred Polgar, *Das Neue Tage-Buch* 7 (4 February 1939): 141.

52. Lawrence Langner, "A Theatre Guild Director Writes of the Influx of Foreign Authors," *New York Times*, 4 May 1941, sec. 9, p. 1.

53. Carl Zuckmayer, "No More Summer in Austria," *Harper's Magazine*, July 1940, pp. 156–65.

54. *Second Wind* was published both in the United States (New York, 1940) and in Great Britain (London, 1941).

55. Review by Ursula Wasserman, *New York Herald Tribune*, book sec., 12 January 1941, p. 2.

56. Hans-Christof Wächter, *Theater im Exil: Sozialgeschichte des deutschen Exiltheaters 1933–1945* (Munich, 1973), p. 160.

57. Henry Marx, "Exiltheater in den USA 1933–1945," in *Schauspielwochen Hamburg 76. Arbeitsmaterialien zur Ausstellung "Deutsche Theaterleute im amerikanischen Exil,"* ed. Jan Hans (Hamburg, n.d.), pp. 9–10. The play has not been published, but the prompt script is available at the Fritz-Kortner-Archiv of the Akademie der Künste, Berlin. For a more detailed discussion of the play, see Siegfried Mews, *"Somewhere in France: Ein antifaschistisches Exildrama von Carl Zuckmayer und Fritz Kortner,"* in *Deutsche Exilliteratur—Literatur im Dritten Reich: Akten des II. Exilliteratur–Symposiums der University of South Carolina 1977*, ed. Wolfgang Elfe, James Hardin, and Günther Holst, *Jahrbuch für internationale Germanistik*, ser. A, vol. 6 (Berne, 1979), pp. 122–31.

58. Nelson B. Bell, "Guild Play Has Premiere at the National," *Washington Post*, 29 April 1941.

59. "Collapse of France Depicted in Play," *New York Times*, 29 April 1941, p. 16.

60. Bell, *Washington Post*, 29 April 1941.

61. *New York Times*, 29 April 1941.

62. See *PoM*, 355.

63. See chapter 2, section 5, pp. 55–56.

64. For an account of the years in Vermont, see Alice Herdan-Zuckmayer, *Die Farm in den grünen Bergen* (Frankfurt, 1956).

65. See Carl Zuckmayer, *Second Wind* (London, 1941), pp. 88–89.

66. See Zuckmayer's letter to Kesten of 10 May 1943, in *Deutsche Literatur im Exil: Briefe europäischer Autoren 1933-1949*, ed. Hermann Kesten (Frankfurt, 1973), pp. 183–85. Zuckmayer errs, however, in attributing the English translation to the British publisher of *The Captain of Köpenick*, G. Bles. Rather, David Portman is listed as translator.

67. *Heart of Europe: An Anthology of Creative Writing in Europe, 1920–1940*, ed. Klaus Mann and Hermann Kesten, intro. Dorothy Canfield Fisher (New York: L. B. Fischer, 1943), pp. 720–21; rpt. *The Best of*

*Modern European Literature (Heart of Europe)* (Philadelphia: Blakiston, 1945).

68. Carl Zuckmayer, "Neue Gedichte," in *Die Rappen: Jahrbuch 1937* (Wien, 1937), pp. 60–66.

69. Carl Zuckmayer, "The Swiss Pension; A Fragment of Middle-Class Anthropology," *Harper's Magazine*, February 1942, pp. 277–85.

70. Carl Zuckmayer, "Don't Give Your Animals a Name," *Ladies' Home Journal*, January 1945, pp. 4–5, 84, 112–13.

71. Carl Zuckmayer, "A Tiger's Heart," *Esquire*, June 1947, pp. 82, 176, 181–84.

72. Zuckmayer sent "Aufruf zum Leben" to friends and then published it in the New York German-language publication *Aufbau* 8, no. 8 (20 March 1942): 3. An English translation, "Appeal to the Living," by Gerard Willem van Loon appeared in the monthly *Free World*, June 1942, pp. 40–41.

73. Carl Zuckmayer, "Appeal to the Living," p. 40.

74. Carl Zuckmayer, *Aufruf zum Leben: Porträts und Zeugnisse aus bewegten Zeiten* (Frankfurt, 1976), pp. 7–14. "Aufruf zum Leben" has repeatedly been included in anthologies of exile literature.

75. See Zuckmayer, *Aufruf zum Leben*, p. 10.

76. Erika Mann, "Eine Ablehnung," *Aufbau*, 10, no. 16 (21 April 1944): 7.

77. Carl Zuckmayer, "Offener Brief an Erika Mann," *Aufbau* 10, no. 19 (12 May 1944): 7–8. Erika Mann's reply to Zuckmayer appears in the same issue of *Aufbau*. For Zuckmayer's attitude concerning Germany, see also *PoM*, 383–84.

78. See Herbert Lehnert, "Bert Brecht und Thomas Mann im Streit über Deutschland," in *Deutsche Exilliteratur seit 1933*, ed. John M. Spalek and Joseph Strelka, vol. 1, *Kalifornien* (Berne: Francke, 1976), pp. 62–88.

79. Zuckmayer, "Offener Brief," p. 8.

80. See chapter 4, section 1, pp. 82–90.

81. See Hans Steinitz, "Aufbau, Neubau, Brückenbau," in *Aufbau. Reconstruction*, ed. Will Schaber (New York: Overlook Press: 1972), pp. 11–20.

82. Zuckmayer published between 1942 and 1945 in *Aufbau* (five contributions), *German American* (New York; two contributions), *Demokratische Post* (Mexico; one contribution), *Deutsche Blätter* (Santiago de Chile; two contributions). Most of these contributions are not included in Jacobius, *Carl Zuckmayer: Eine Bibliographie*, but are listed in Lieselotte Maas, *Handbuch der deutschen Exilpresse 1933–1945*, 2 vols. (Munich, 1976–1978).

*Chapter Four*

1. *PoM*, 381–82.

2. The third act of *Des Teufels General* was published in *Die Neue Rundschau* (October 1945): 85–108. The first book publication appeared in the following year (Stockholm, 1946).

3. According to *Der Spiegel*, 7 September 1955, p. 39, there were more than five thousand performances of *The Devil's General*—a number not reached by any other serious drama in the postwar period.

4. Parenthetical references in the text and notes are to "The Devil's General," trans. Ingrid G. and William F. Gilbert, in *Masters of Modern Drama*, ed. H. M. Block and R. G. Shedd (New York, 1962), pp. 911–58.

5. Dr. Schmidt-Lausitz is a functionary (*Kulturleiter*) in the ministry of culture (*Propagandaministerium*) but not the "Minister of Culture" (p. 911), as the English translation has it.

6. Murray B. Peppard, "Moment of Moral Decision: Carl Zuckmayer's Latest Plays," *Monatshefte* 44 (1952): 359, draws attention to the extraordinarily long exposition that is designed to evoke "a well-rounded picture of Nazi Germany." Ingeborg Engelsing-Malek, *"Amor Fati" in Zuckmayers Dramen* (Konstanz, 1960), p. 88, divides the large cast of male and female characters into four groups according to their view of Nazism. Roy C. Cowen, "Type-Casting in Carl Zuckmayer's *The Devil's General*," *University of Dayton Review* 13 (1976): 81–94, discusses the characters in terms of their geographical area of origin, social rank, age, and related factors.

7. See Peppard, "Moment of Moral Decision," p. 351.

8. My translation. The English rendering of the passage in question (p. 958) is inadequate.

9. For summaries and documentation of both critics' and theater reviewers' reactions to the play, see Siegfried Mews, *Carl Zuckmayer: Des Teufels General*, 2d, enl. ed. (Frankfurt, 1979), pp. 42–73. Additional reviews are to be found in *Carl Zuckmayer: Das Bühnenwerk im Spiegel der Kritik*, ed. Barbara Glauert (Frankfurt, 1977) pp. 213–71.

10. Erich Müller-Gangloff, "Faust als Fliegergeneral," *Berliner Hefte für geistiges Leben* 4 (1949): 90–93.

11. Wilfried Adling, "Die Entwicklung des Dramatikers Carl Zuckmayer," in *Schriften zur Theaterwissenschaft*, vol. 1, ed. Theaterhochschule Leipzig (Berlin, 1959), pp. 206–9.

12. See J. Vandenrath, "Drama und Theater in Zuckmayers Bühnendichtung" (Ph. D. diss., Liège, 1960), pp. 173–76.

13. See Luise Rinser, "Porträtskizze," in *Fülle der Zeit: Carl Zuckmayer und sein Werk* (Frankfurt, 1956), pp. 21–23.

14. See Henry Glade, "Carl Zuckmayer's *The Devil's General* as Autobiography," *Modern Drama* 9 (1966–1967): 54–61.

15. See Paul Rilla, "Carl Zuckmayer. Des Teufels General," in *Das deutsche Drama vom Expressionismus bis zur Gegenwart*, ed. Manfred Brauneck (Bamberg, 1970), pp. 99–107.

16. See Hanns Braun, "Glosse zu 'Des Teufels General,' " in *Carl Zuckmayer*, ed. Glauert, pp. 246–49.

17. J. A. "Dolchstoss durch Oderbruch? Carl Zuckmayer zur Diskussion über 'Des Teufels General,' " *Die Welt*, 28 February 1948.

18. Carl Zuckmayer, "Persönliche Notizen zu meinem Stück Des Teufels General,' " in *Carl Zuckmayer*, ed. Glauert, p. 214.

19. *GW*, vol. 3, prints the old version on which the American translation (cf. n. 4, above) is based. *WA*, vol. 8, prints the 1966 version. The two versions have been published in Mews, *Zuckmayer: Des Teufels General*, pp. 16–19.

20. See chapter 3, section 4, pp. 80–81.

21. Carl Zuckmayer, *Momento zum 20. Juli 1969* (Frankfurt, 1969). The dedication of *The Devil's General* (omitted in the English translation) to Theodor Haubach, Wilhelm Leuschner, and Count Hellmuth von Moltke, members of an opposition group who were hanged, as well as his frequently published tribute to the German socialist Carlo Mierendorff shows Zuckmayer's awareness of the resistance movement.

22. For example, *The Devil's General* was the first play of a "trilogy" (the other two dramas were Bertolt Brecht's *Fear and Misery of the Third Reich* and Wolfgang Borchert's *The Man Outside)* with which the Städtische Bühnen Mainz wished to explore the Nazi past as depicted in drama. See Dietrich Taube, "Konzeptionelle Überlegungen zur Inszenierung von Carl Zuckmayers 'Des Teufels General,' " *Blätter der Carl-Zuckmayer-Gesellschaft* 4, no. 4 (1 November 1978): 129–32.

23. Walther Killy, "Ein Zeitgenosse, kein Prophet. Eine Würdigung des grossen alten Mannes der deutschen Literatur," *Die Zeit* (Overseas ed.), 31 December 1976, p. 12; reprinted in *Blätter der Carl-Zuckmayer-Gesellschaft* 4, no. 2 (1 May 1978): 4–9.

24. See, for example, Volker Wehdeking, "Mythologisches Ungewitter: Carl Zuckmayers problematisches Exildrama 'Des Teufels General,' " in *Die deutsche Exilliteratur 1933–1945*, ed. Manfred Durzak (Stuttgart, 1973), pp. 509–17.

25. See Henning Rischbieter and Ernst Wendt, *Deutsche Dramatik in West und Ost* (Velber, 1965), p. 42.

26. See Taube, "Konzeptionelle Überlegungen," p. 130.

27. See chapter 3, section 1, pp. 63–66.

28. See Alice Herdan-Zuckmayer, *Die Farm in den grünen Bergen* (Frankfurt, 1956), p. 170.

29. See Engelsing-Malek, *"Amor Fati" in Zuckmayers Dramen*, p. 105.

30. See Rudolf Lange, *Carl Zuckmayer* (Velber, 1969), p.74.

31. Carl Zuckmayer, "Zu 'Barbara Blomberg,' " in *Carl Zuckmayer*, ed. Glauert, p. 275.

32. See Adling, "Die Entwicklung des Dramatikers Carl Zuckmayer," pp. 229–34.

33. Ibid.

34. Carl Zuckmayer, "Oder ist sie doch buckelig? Unerboste, aber unbekehrte Anmerkungen zur Berliner Kritik meiner 'Barbara Blomberg,' " in *Blätter der Carl-Zuckmayer-Gesellschaft*, 2, no. 1 (1 June 1976): 2.

35. Paul Bäcker, "Notizen zu Blomberg," *Blätter der Carl-Zuckmayer-Gesellschaft*, 2, no. 1 (1 June 1976): 14.

36. See the review by Horst Köpke in *Blätter der Carl-Zuckmayer-Gesellschaft*, 2, no. 1 (1 June 1976): 18.

37. Henry Glade, "*Der Gesang im Feuerofen:* Quintessential Zuckmayer," in *Views and Reviews of Modern German Literature. Festschrift for Adolf D. Klarmann*, ed. Karl S. Weimar (Munich, 1974), p. 164, perhaps unnecessarily complicates matters by speaking of three (i.e., the realistic, allegorical, and surrealistic) levels.

38. See the review by K. H. Ruppel, in *Carl Zuckmayer*, ed. Glauert, p. 302.

39. See Carl Zuckmayer, "Zeichen für Klage und Lust. Zur Hamburger Fassung meines Dramas 'Der Gesang im Feuerofen,' " in *Carl Zuckmayer*, ed. Glauert, pp. 291–93.

40. Ibid., p. 291.

41. Glade, "*Der Gesang im Feuerofen*," p. 167.

42. This part of the prologue (i.e., act 1, scene 1) was placed at the end of the play in the revised Hamburg version. See Carl Zuckmayer, *Meisterdramen* (New York, 1966), pp. 578–79. However, the WA of 1976 reverts to the text of the first edition of the play (1950) that also appears in *GW*.

43. See Glade, "*Der Gesang im Feuerofen*," p. 165.

44. See Engelsing-Makek, "*Amor Fati*" *in Zuckmayers Dramen*, pp. 133–34.

45. The text is printed in *WA*, 9:140.

46. See chapter 4, section 1, pp. 88–89.

47. Glade, "*Der Gesang im Feuerofen*," p. 165.

48. Adling, "Die Entwicklung des Dramatikers Carl Zuckmayer," pp. 242–43.

49. The expressionist elements of the play, notably the introduction of surrealist elements that are reminiscent of the early play *Crossroads* (chapter 4, section 3, pp. 20–25), do, of course, counteract any "documentary" tendency. The insufficient fusion of realistic and nonrealistic elements, by the way, is decidedly an artistic weakness.

50. Engelsing-Malek, "*Amor Fati*" *in Zuckmayers Dramen*, p. 154.

51. Murray B. Peppard, "Carl Zuckmayer: Cold Light in a Divided World," *Monatshefte* 49 (1957): 125.

52. Apparently the play has not been produced in the United States.

53. See Peppard, "Carl Zuckmayer," p. 128.

54. Ibid., p. 129.

55. See the review by Friedrich Torberg, *Das fünfte Rad am Thespis-karren: Theaterkritiken* (Munich, 1966), pp. 116–18.

56. Bertolt Brecht, "Life of Galileo," trans. Wolfgang Sauerlander and Ralph Manheim, in *Collected Plays*, vol. 5 (New York: Vintage Books, 1972), p. 94.

57. Gerty Agoston, " 'Das Kalte Licht' und der Verräter: Carl Zuck-mayers Appell an das Weltgewissen," *Sonntagsblatt. Staats-Zeitung und Herold*, 6 November 1955, p. 6C.

58. Fritz Erpenbeck in his 1955 review of the play; quoted from Otto F. Riewoldt, *Von Zuckmayer bis Kroetz: Die Rezeption westdeutscher Thea-terstücke durch Kritik und Wissenschaft in der DDR* (Berlin, 1977), p. 85.

59. Adling, "Die Entwicklung des Dramatikers Carl Zuckmayer," p. 259.

60. Heinz Geiger, *Widerstand und Mitschuld: Zum deutschen Drama von Brecht bis Weiss* (Düsseldorf, 1973), pp. 68–98, gives a survey of those dramas.

61. See Geiger, *Widerstand und Mitschuld*, p. 82.

62. Heinar Kipphardt, *In the Matter of J. Robert Oppenheimer: A Play Freely Adapted on the Basis of the Documents*, trans. Ruth Spiers (New York: Hill and Wang, 1969), p. 126.

63. See Geiger, *Widerstand und Mitschuld*, p. 84. The other pertinent secondary literature is briefly discussed by Siegfried Mews, "Die Zuck-mayerforschung 1961–1977," in *Carl Zuckmayer '78. Ein Jahrbuch* (Frank-furt, 1978), p. 259.

64. See chapter 5, section 2, pp. 123–29.

65. See chapter 1, section 4, pp. 27–29.

66. See chapter 2, section 5, pp. 53–57.

67. See chapter 1, section 5, pp. 32–33.

68. Arnold John Jacobius. *Carl Zuckmayer: Eine Bibliographie* (Frank-furt, 1971), p. 71, gives the publication information of Zuckmayer's adap-tation as follows: *Die Unvergessliche* [*I Remember Mama*]; *ein Stück in zwei Akten, von John von Druten; deutsche Bearbeitung von Carl Zuckmayer*. (Als Sonderdruck veröffentlicht: "Property of the Director of Information Control, Theater and Music Branch, APO 742, U.S. Army.") 1947. The information suggests that the adaptation was commissioned by the U.S. Army while Zuckmayer was a civilian employee of the U.S. Government.

69. Zuckmayer's remarks in the program of the Zurich performance are quoted by Adling, "Die Entwicklung des Dramatikers Carl Zuckmayer," p. 223.

70. The essay was first published in *Neue Schweizer Rundschau*, n.s. 16, no. 8 (December 1948): 451–74.

71. See Peter Demetz, "Geh ins Kino, deutscher Geist!" *Die Zeit* (Overseas ed.), 16 April 1976.

72. See, for example, the following collections of essays that explore the views of America held by German men of letters: *Amerika in der deutschen Literatur. Neue Welt-Nordamerika-USA*, ed. Sigrid Bauschinger, Horst Denkler, and Wilfried Malsch (Stuttgart: Reclam, 1975); *Deutschlands literarisches Amerikabild. Neuere Forschungen zur Amerikarezeption der deutschen Literatur*, ed. Alexander Ritter (Hildesheim: Olms, 1977); *Die USA und Deutschland. Wechselseitige Spiegelungen in der Literatur der Gegenwart*, ed. Wolfgang Paulsen (Berne: Francke, 1976).

73. Anon., "John van Druten: 'Die Unvergessliche,' " *Neue Zürcher Zeitung*, 20 September 1947.

74. See chapter 1, section 3, p. 25, and p. 142, n. 23.

75. The most detailed account of the relationship between Zuckmayer and Hauptmann is provided by Marvin R. Maddox, "Carl Zuckmayer's Relation to Gerhart Hauptmann: 'Meisterschaft, Vorbild, Verpflichtung' " (Ph.D. diss., University of North Carolina, 1975).

76. Carl Zuckmayer, *Ein voller Erdentag: Zu Gerhart Hauptmanns hundertstem Geburtstag* (Frankfurt, 1962), p. 39.

77. See C. F. W. Behl, "Zuckmayers Hauptmann-Drama," *Deutsche Rundschau* 78 (June 1952): 609–10.

78. *Herbert Engelmann: Drama in vier Akten*, Aus dem Nachlass von Gerhart Hauptmann, ausgeführt von Carl Zuckmayer. Beide Fassungen (Munich, 1952). The adaptation is not included in either *GW* or *WA*. All references in the text are to this edition.

79. Engelsing-Malek, *"Amor Fati" in Zuckmayers Dramen*, p. 207, n. 13, mentions that Hauptmann had based his drama on an actual murder of a mailman in Berlin.

80. Maddox, "Carl Zuckmayer's Relation to Gerhart Hauptmann," pp. 170–72, points out the analogy between Herbert Engelmann and Fuhrmann Henschel in the drama by the same name, Johannes Vockerat in *Einsame Menschen*, Arnold Kramer in *Michael Kramer,* and Gabriel Schilling in *Gabriel Schillings Flucht.*

81. A further, although more superficial point of comparison between *Herbert Engelmann* and *Cold Light* is the fact that Zuckmayer turned Hauptmann's *writer* Engelmann into a *nuclear physicist*. Although Hauptmann had contemplated in 1941 to have Engelmann appear as a bacteriologist, he abandoned his plan. Zuckmayer's change occasionally strains plausibility and is called "cheap" striving for topicality by C. F. W. Behl, "Zuckmayers Hauptmann–Drama," p. 611.

82. See Engelsing-Malek, *"Amor Fati" in Zuckmayers Dramen*, p. 143.

83. See Maddox, "Carl Zuckmayer's Relation to Gerhart Hauptmann," pp. 160–61.

84. Blake Lee Spahr, "A Note on Herbert Engelmann," *Monatshefte* 46 (1954): 343, contends that Hauptmann's Engelmann prepared for the court trial with "great care and cunning." Engelmann's protestation of his innocence before his arrest and trial could then be construed as part of his

preparation. J. Vandenrath, "Zuckmayers Bearbeitung von Gerhart Hauptmanns 'Herbert Engelmann,' " *Revue des Langues Vivantes* 27 (1961): 220, n. 8, points out correctly that Engelmann is definitely not a cold-blooded murderer and hence is unlikely to plan for his defence in court like a cunning criminal.

85. Engelsing-Malek, *"Amor Fati" in Zuckmayers Dramen*, p. 142.

86. East German critics like Bruno Fischer, " 'Herbert Engelmann.' Ein nachgelassenes Dramenfragment von Gerhart Hauptmann," *Neue Deutsche Literatur*, no. 4 (April 1957): 157, see in Hauptmann's play a "condemnation of imperialism and imperialist wars."

87. Although Siegfried H. Muller, "Another Note on 'Herbert Engelmann,' " *Monatshefte* 54 (1962): 293, credits Zuckmayer with "having brought order into the chronology of events" of Hauptmann's version, Zuckmayer does not adhere to an historically accurate chronology either. Thus, in the passage referred to above *(Herbert Engelmann*, p. 219), he has Hitler still imprisoned after the Treaty of Locarno had been signed. Actually, Hitler was released at the end of 1924, almost a year before the Treaty of Locarno.

88. Vandenrath, "Zuckmayers Bearbeitung von Gerhart Hauptmanns 'Herbert Engelmann,' " p. 225, considers Zuckmayer's accumulation of comical effects, of which the scene in question is one instance, a serious flaw.

89. Spahr, "A Note on 'Herbert Engelmann,' " p. 345.

90. Vandenrath, "Zuckmayers Bearbeitung von Gerhart Hauptmanns 'Herbert Engelmann,' " p. 231.

91. Zuckmayer, *Ein voller Erdentag*, p. 9, rejected this classification as too narrow.

92. See chapter 3, section 2, pp. 66–70.

93. See *WA*, 2:553. The passage is not included in *PoM*.

94. Julius Bab, "Zwei deutsche Novellen," *Sonntagsblatt. Staats-Zeitung und Herold*, 26 May 1946.

95. Carl Zuckmayer, *Der Seelenbräu* (Stockholm, 1945).

96. See *WA*, 2:584. The passage is not included in *PoM*.

97. Carl Zuckmayer, "Die wandernden Hütten. Erzählung," *Die Neue Rundschau*, December 1948, pp. 369–89.

98. Carl Zuckmayer, *Die Brüder Grimm. Ein Beitrag zur deutschen Humanität* (Frankfurt, 1948). According to *WA*, 2:553, the essay was written simultaneously with *Der Seelenbräu* (n. 95) in early 1945. The reference is not included in *PoM*.

99. See Werner Imseng, *Carl Zuckmayer in Saas-Fee: Ein Album* (Frankfurt, 1976), p. 23.

100. Raymond E. Barrick, "A Characterization of the Mystical Philosophy of Carl Zuckmayer as Revealed in His Life and Works" (Ph.D. diss., Tulane University, 1964) pp. 114–15, sees in Lucas a "Judas figure."

101. Derrick Barlow, Intro., *Three Stories*, by Carl Zuckmayer (London, 1963), p. 32.

102. Cf. also Zuckmayer, *Die Brüder Grimm*, (n. 98); reprinted in Carl Zuckmayer, *Aufruf zum Leben. Porträts und Zeugnisse aus bewegten Zeiten* (Frankfurt, 1976), p. 276.

103. Carl Zuckmayer, *Die Fastnachtsbeichte* (Frankfurt, 1959).

104. See chapter 1, section 5, p. 33, and p. 143, n. 44.

105. See Mews, "Die Zuckmayerforschung 1961–1977," pp. 266–67.

106. Review of *A Part of Myself* by J. P. Bauke, *New York Times Book Review*, 17 December 1970, p. 4.

107. Carl Zuckmayer, *Die langen Wege* (Frankfurt, 1952).

108. See chapter 3, section 3, pp. 74–75.

109. See chapter 3, section 3, p. 72, and p. 149, n. 35.

110. In the ten-volume *WA* the prose narratives comprise three volumes.

111. Alexander Lernet-Holenia, "Die schöne Disharmonie. Anmerkungen zu Carl Zuckmayers 'Die Fastnachtsbeichte,'" *Forum* 7 (February 1960): 67, speaks of the mingling of the human, the animalistic, and the demonic in the narrative.

112. Derrick Barlow, Intro., *Die Fastnachtsbeichte*, by Carl Zuckmayer (Oxford, 1966), p. xxvi.

### Chapter Five

1. Letter of Carl Zuckmayer to Paula Wessely, dated Corpus Christi 1961, in *Blätter der Carl-Zuckmayer-Gesellschaft* 4, no. 4 (1 November 1978): 124. See also Horst Bienek, *Werkstattgespräche mit Schriftstellern* (Munich, 1962), p. 171.

2. See Carl Zuckmayer and Heinz Rosenthal, "Gespräch über das Stück," in *Carl Zuckmayer. Das Bühnenwerk in Spiegel der Kritik*, ed. Barbara Glauert (Frankfurt, 1977), p. 345.

3. See Rudolf Lange, *Carl Zuckmayer* (Velber, 1969), p. 84.

4. See Zuckmayer and Rosenthal, "Gespräch," p. 346.

5. Helen Swediuk-Cheyne, Intro., *Die Uhr schlägt eins. Ein historisches Drama aus der Gegenwart*, by Carl Zuckmayer (Berne, Peter Lang, 1977), p. 17.

6. See the reviews by Otto F. Beer, Oskar Maurus Fontana, and Piero Rismondo in *Carl Zuckmayer*, ed. Glauert, pp. 348–57.

7. Anon., "Zuckmayer: Schlägt dreizehn," *Der Spiegel*, 25 October 1961, pp. 86, 88–89.

8. Carl Zuckmayer, "Kranichtanz," *Die Neue Rundschau* 72, no. 4 (1961): 794–811.

9. See the interview with Zuckmayer, in *Carl Zuckmayer*, ed. Glauert, p. 346. See also Zuckmayer's letter to Günther Fleckenstein of 29 April 1976, in *Blätter der Carl-Zuckmayer-Gesellschaft* 3, no. 1 (1 March 1977): 20.

10. See the review of W. v. O., in *Carl Zuckmayer*, ed. Glauert, p. 380.

11. See the review by Thomas Terry; quoted by Lange, *Carl Zuckmayer*, p. 122.

12. See Carl Zuckmayer, "Epilog for the Reader," *WA*, 10:259.

13. See the jacket of the opera recording, MCM Academy Series, n.p., n.d.

14. See chapter 3, section 4, pp. 77–79.

15. See chapter 4, section 1, pp. 83–90.

16. It should be noted that it is characteristic of Zuckmayer to gain "productive distance" from his subject matter. See Wolfgang Paulsen, "Carl Zuckmayer," in *Deutsche Literatur im 20. Jahrhundert: Strukturen und Gestalten*. 5th rev. ed., ed. Otto Mann and Wolfgang Rothe (Berne, 1967), 2:355.

17. See the reviews listed in Arnold John Jacobius, *Carl Zuckmayer: Eine Bibliographie 1917–1971* (Frankfurt, 1971), pp. 267–77. For a more detailed interpretation of the play, see Siegfried Mews, "Von Karl May zu Karl Marx: Zuckmayers Bonanza-Millionär Tabor," in *Die USA und Deutschland. Wechselseitige Spiegelungen in der Literatur der Gegenwart*, ed. Wolfgang Paulsen (Berne, 1976), pp. 84–91.

18. See chapter 1, section 4, pp. 27–29.

19. Carl Zuckmayer, "Anmerkungen zu einem Theaterstück," in *Carl Zuckmayer*, ed. Glauert, p. 361, draws attention to the "epic" tendency of his drama. At the same time, however, he disclaims the use of Brechtian "epic theater" devices.

20. Marianne Kesting, "Carl Zuckmayer—Zwischen Volksstück und Kolportage," in *Panorama des zeitgenössischen Theaters*. Rev. and enl. ed. (Munich, 1969), p. 283.

21. See Urs Helmensdorfer, Intro., *Das Mädchen aus der Feenwelt oder Der Bauer als Millionär. Romantisches Original–Zaubermärchen mit Gesang in drei Aufzügen*, by Ferdinand Raimund (Berlin: de Gruyter, 1966), p. 92.

22. Anon., "Zuckmayer-Premiere," *Der Spiegel*, 25 November 1964, p. 142.

23. See the review by Petra Kipphoff, in *Carl Zuckmayer*, ed. Glauert, pp. 369–73.

24. Carl Zuckmayer, *Der Rattenfänger: Eine Fabel* (Frankfurt, 1975).

25. *Rattenfänger* simply means "rat catcher."

26. See the review by I. V., *Neue Zürcher Zeitung*, 24 February 1975.

27. See Carl Zuckmayer, "Stoff und Quellen," in *Carl Zuckmayer*, ed. Glauert, pp. 386–87.

28. See the review by Georg Hensel, in *Carl Zuckmayer*, ed. Glauert, pp. 390–94.

29. See the review by Kurt Heinz, in *Carl Zuckmayer*, ed. Glauert, p. 388.

30. See chapter 1, section 4, pp. 27–29.

31. Georg Büchner, *Complete Plays and Prose*, trans. Carl Richard Mueller (New York: Hill and Wang, 1963), p. 44.

## Chapter Six

1. For some of the official honors Zuckmayer received, see chronology, p. 11. See also Thomas Ayck, *Carl Zuckmayer in Selbstzeugnissen und Bilddokumenten* (Reinbek bei Hamburg, 1977), pp. 129–30.

2. See *Geständnisse: Heine im Bewusstsein heutiger Autoren*, ed. Wilhelm Gössmann (Düsseldorf, 1972), p. 20.

3. Carl Zuckmayer, *Heinrich Heine und der liebe Gott und ich* (Düsseldorf, 1972); reprinted in Carl Zuckmayer, *Aufruf zum Leben. Porträts und Zeugnisse aus bewegten Zeiten* (Frankfurt, 1976), pp. 309–22.

4. See the brief accounts in Jost Hermand, *Streitobjekt Heine: Ein Forschungsbericht 1945–1975* (Frankfurt: Athenäum Fischer Taschenbuch Verlag, 1975), pp. 31–32, and Ayck, *Carl Zuckmayer*, pp. 7–8.

5. See Walter Killy, "Ein Zeitgenosse, kein Prophet. Eine Würdigung des grossen alten Mannes der deutschen Literatur," *Die Zeit* (Overseas ed.), 31 December 1976, p. 12; reprinted in *Blätter der Carl-Zuckmayer-Gesellschaft* 4, no. 2 (1 May 1978): 4–9.

6. Ibid.

7. Dorothy Thompson, Intro., *Second Wind*, by Carl Zuckmayer, trans. Elizabeth Reynolds Hapgood (London, 1941), pp. 10, 11.

8. See Günther Rühle, "Carl Zuckmayers versöhnende Weisheit," *Frankfurter Allgemeine Zeitung*, 20 January 1977.

9. Carl Zuckmayer, "The Story of Bal, Governor of the Lapps," in *The Best Continental Short Stories of 1927*, ed. R. Eaton (New York, 1928), pp. 246–54. "Bal" was first published in 1927, then omitted from *GW* and other anthologies of prose fiction, but included in *WA*, 4:123–34. See also chapter 1, section 5, p. 32.

10. See chapter 3, section 3, pp. 70–72.

11. See chapter 3, section 4, pp. 76–77.

12. See chapter 3, section 4, pp. 80–82.

13. The following Berlin premieres were reviewed in the *New York Times*: *Katharina Knie* (10 March 1929), the adaptation of *What Price Glory* (28 April 1929), the adaptation of *A Farewell to Arms* (4 October 1931), *The Captain of Köpenick* (26 April 1931), and the London premiere of *Katharina Knie* under the title *Caravan* (1 May 1932).

14. See chapter 3, section 3, p. 74.

15. Carl Zuckmayer, *The Captain of Köpenick. A Modern Fairy Tale in Three Acts*, trans. David Portman (London, 1932). According to Arnold John Jacobius, *Motive und Dramaturgie im Schauspiel Carl Zuckmayers* (Frankfurt, 1971), p. 129, the BBC broadcast *The Captain of Köpenick* in 1933.

16. The translation cited above (p. 145, n. 25) was first published in 1972.

17. See p. 145, n. 36.

18. See p. 153, n. 4.

19. See the review of the London performance of *The Devil's General* by W. A. Darlington, *New York Times*, 11 October 1953. Although there was no English-language performance in New York, the Schiller Theater Berlin produced *The Captain of Köpenick* in German. See the review by Richard F. Shepard, *New York Times*, 3 December 1964.

20. See chapter 3, section 4, pp. 77–79.

21. Ulrich Weisstein, "The Reception of Twentieth Century German Literature in the United States," in *Comparative Literature. Proceedings of the Second Congress of the ICLA*, ed. Werner P. Friederich (Chapel Hill: University of North Carolina Press, 1959), p. 552, n. 8, does not mention Zuckmayer among the German dramatists whose plays were performed from 1918 through 1959.

22. Mrs. Elizabeth Morton of New York City, representative of the S. Fischer company in the United States, kindly informed me that there have been performances of *The Devil's General* in Sarasota, Florida (1970) and Dallas, Texas (1979). Significantly, *Samuel French's Basic Catalog of Plays* (1977) and the *1979 Supplement* do not list any plays by Zuckmayer.

23. See chapter 3, section 4, pp. 80–81.

24. Weisstein, "The Reception of Twentieth Century German Literature," p. 557.

25. P. Beaumont Wadsworth, "The Young Writers of Germany," *Bookman* 75 (June–July 1932): p. 268.

26. Carl Zuckmayer, "Germany's Lost Youth," *Life*, 15 September 1947, pp. 125–38.

27. "Carl Zuckmayer, 80, Satiric Playwright," *New York Times*, 20 January 1977.

28. See chapter 2, section 5, pp. 58–59.

29. For details, see J. Vandenrath, "Der Stand der Zuckmayerforschung. Beitrag zu einer kritischen Bibliographie," *Modern Language Notes* 76 (1961): 829–39, and Siegfried Mews, "Die Zuckmayerforschung 1961–1977," in *Carl Zuckmayer '78. Ein Jahrbuch* (Frankfurt, 1978), pp. 228–72.

30. See, for example, the two introductory essays by Ian C. Loram, "Carl Zuckmayer: An Introduction," *German Quarterly* 27 (1954): 137–49, and "Carl Zuckmayer—German Playwright in America," *Educational Theatre Journal* 9 (1957): 177–83.

# Selected Bibliography

PRIMARY SOURCES

1. **German editions**
a. Most complete editions
*Gesammelte Werke.* 4 vols. Frankfurt: S. Fischer, 1960.
*Werkausgabe in zehn Bänden 1920–1975.* 10 vols. Frankfurt: Fischer Taschenbuch Verlag, 1976.

b. Other useful collections
*Gedichte.* Frankfurt: S. Fischer, 1977. So far, the most complete collection of Zuckmayer's poetry.
*Meisterdramen.* Frankfurt: G. B. Fischer, 1966.
*Meistererzählungen.* Frankfurt: G. B. Fischer, 1967.
*Zuckmayer Lesebuch.* Frankfurt: S. Fischer, 1976.

c. Works (adaptations, dramas, prose narratives) not included in either *GW* or *WA*
*Auf einem Weg im Frühling. Erzählung—Wiedersehen mit einer Stadt: Aus dem Stegreif erzählt.* Salzburg: Residenz Verlag, 1970.
*Bellman: Schauspiel in drei Akten.* Chur: A. G. für Verlagsrechte, 1938.
*Herbert Engelmann. Drama in vier Akten.* Aus dem Nachlass von Gerhart Hauptmann. Ausgeführt von Carl Zuckmayer. Beide Fassungen. Munich: Beck, 1952.
*Kakadu, Kakada: Ein Kinderstück.* Berlin: Propyläen–Verlag, 1929.
"*Kat:* Schauspiel nach Ernest Hemingway von Carl Zuckmayer und Heinz Hilpert." Hamburg: Georg Marton, n.d.
"*Pankraz erwacht.* Stück aus dem fernen Westen in drei Akten." Edited by Barbara Glauert. In *Carl Zuckmayer '78. Ein Jahrbuch.* Frankfurt: S. Fischer, 1978. Pp. 47–163.
"*Rivalen* (What Price Glory?). Ein Stück in drei Akten (nach dem amerikanischen Schauspiel von Maxwell Anderson und Lawrence Stallings)." Berlin: Arcadia–Verlag, 1929.
*Ein Sommer in Österreich: Erzählung.* Vienna: Bermann-Fischer, 1937.
*Die Unvergessliche* [I Remember Mama]. Ein Stück in zwei Akten von John van Druten. Deutsche Bearbeitung von Carl Zuckmayer. N.p.: Property of the Director of Information Control, Theater and Music Branch, APO 742, U.S. Army, 1947.

d. Essays, short pieces, and anthologies
"Amerika ist anders." *Neue Schweizer Rundschau,* N.S. 16, no. 8 (December 1948): 451–74. Repeatedly reprinted.

*Aufruf zum Leben: Porträts und Zeugnisse aus bewegten Zeiten.* Frankfurt: S. Fischer, 1976. Includes the following essays: "Die Brüder Grimm. Ein Beitrag zur deutschen Humanität" (1948); "Carlo Mierendorff. Porträt eines deutschen Sozialisten" (1944); "Festrede für Gerhart Hauptmann" (1932); "Heinrich Heine und der liebe Gott und ich" (1972); "Memento zum 20. Juli 1969" (1969).

*Carl Zuckmayer. Das Bühnenwerk im Spiegel der Kritik.* Edited by Barbara Glauert. Frankfurt: S. Fischer, 1977. Includes the following shorter pieces by Zuckmayer: "Ein Brief [*Kat*]" (1931); "Ein deutsches Märchen" (1931); "Gespräch über das Stück [*Die Uhr schlägt eins*]" (1961); "Der Kaiser im 'Schelm von Bergen' " (1934); "Das Leben des Horace A. W. Tabor. Anmerkungen zu einem Theaterstück" (1965); "Persönliche Notizen zu meinem Stück 'Des Teufels General' " (1948); "Meine 'Rivalen-Bearbeitung' " (n.d.); "Der Schinderhannes" (1927); "Stoff und Quellen [Der Rattenfänger]" (1975); "Wie 'Ulla Winblad' entstand"(1965).

"Franzosenzeit am Oberrhein." *Vossische Zeitung,* 29 June 1930. Reprint. "Franzosenzeit (1918 bis 1930)." *Blätter der Carl-Zuckmayer-Gesellschaft* 4, no. 1 (1 February 1978): 21–25.

"Front der Unzerstörten." *Vossische Zeitung,* 20 December 1930.

*Die langen Wege.* Frankfurt: S. Fischer, 1952.

"Oder ist sie doch buckelig? Unerboste, aber unbekehrte Anmerkungen zur Berliner Kritik meiner 'Barbara Blomberg' " [1949]. *Blätter der Carl-Zuckmayer-Gesellschaft* 2, no. 1 (1 June 1976): 2.

"Offener Brief an Erika Mann." *Aufbau* 10, no. 19 (12 May 1944): 7–8.

*Pro Domo.* Stockholm: Bermann-Fischer, 1938.

*Über die musische Bestimmung des Menschen.* Salzburg: Festungsverlag, 1970.

*Ein voller Erdentag: Zu Gerhart Hauptmanns hundertstem Geburtstag.* Frankfurt: S. Fischer, 1962.

"Von Zirkus, Karussell und Jahrmarkt, von Schiffsschauklern, Gauklern und Vagabunden." *Die Weltbühne* 19, no. 13 (29 March 1923): 361–64.

*Ein Weg zu Schiller.* Frankfurt: S. Fischer, 1959.

e. Letters

"Aus einem Briefwechsel: Carl Zuckmayer und Gustav Gründgens." Edited by Rolf Badenhausen. *Blätter der Carl-Zuckmayer-Gesellschaft* 5, no. 4 (1 November 1979): 214–43.

"Carl Zuckmayer und sein Bibliograph: Aus dem Briefwechsel mit Arnold J. Jacobius (1953–1976)." Edited by Gerald P. R. Martin. *Blätter der Carl-Zuckmayer-Gesellschaft* 6, no. 3 (1 August 1980): 117–57.

*Späte Freundschaft: Carl Zuckmayer/Karl Barth in Briefen.* Zurich: Theologischer Verlag, 1977.

**2. English editions**

"Appeal to the Living." Translated by Gerard Willem van Loon. *Free World*, June 1942, pp. 40–41.

*The Captain of Köpenick: A Modern Fairy Tale in Three Acts*. Translated by David Portman. London: G. Bles, 1932.

*The Captain of Köpenick*. An Adaptation for the National Theatre London by John Mortimer. London: Methuen, 1971.

"The Captain of Köpenick." Translated by Carl Richard Mueller. In *German Drama between the Wars*, edited by George E. Wellwarth. New York: Dutton, 1974. Pp. 179–296.

"The Devil's General." Translated by Ingrid G. and William F. Gilbert. In *Masters of Modern Drama*, edited by H. M. Block and R. G. Shedd. New York: Random House, 1962. Pp. 911–58.

*Carnival Confession*. Translated by John and Necke Mander. London: Methuen, 1961.

"Don't Give Your Animals a Name." *Ladies' Home Journal*, January 1945, pp. 4–5, 84, 112–13.

"Germany's Lost Youth." *Life*, 15 September 1947, pp. 125–38.

"I Like it Here." *Senior Scholastic*, 22 March 1950, pp. 16, 18. Reprint. *Scholastic*, 6 January 1954, p. 24; *Senior Scholastic*, 28 February 1958, p. 20.

"Monkey Wedding." Translated by F. A. Beaumont. *Argosy*, March 1938, pp. 53–69.

*The Moon in the South*. Translated by M[oray] Firth. London: Secker and Warburg, 1937.

*The Moons Ride Over*. Translated by Moray Firth. New York: Viking Press, 1937.

"My Death. A Pious Wish." Translated by E. B. Ashton. In *Heart of Europe: An Anthology of Creative Writing in Europe, 1920–1940*, edited by Klaus Mann and Hermann Kesten, introduction by Dorothy Canfield Fisher (New York: L. B. Fischer, 1943), pp. 720–21. Reprint. *The Best of Modern European Literature (Heart of Europe)*. Philadelphia: Blakiston, 1945.

"No More Summer in Austria." *Harper's Magazine*, July 1940, pp. 156–65.

"A Non-Aryan without a Complex." *Living Age*, March 1939, pp. 35–36.

*A Part of Myself: Portrait of an Epoch*. Translated by Richard and Clara Winston. New York: Harcourt Brace Jovanovich, 1970.

*Second Wind*. Translated by Elizabeth Reynolds Hapgood, introduction by Dorothy Thompson. New York: Doubleday Doran, 1940.

"The Story of Bal, Governor of the Lapps." In *The Best Continental Short Stories of 1927*, edited by R. Eaton. New York: Dodd, Mead, 1928. Pp. 246–54.

*Stroller's Fate: The Life of Edmund Kean*. London: British Cine-Alliance, [1936].

"The Swiss Pension; A Fragment of Middle-Class Anthropology." *Harper's Magazine*, February 1942, pp. 277–85.
"A Tiger's Heart." *Esquire*, June 1947, pp. 82, 176, 181–84.

## 3. Film

STERNBERG, JOSEF VON. *The Blue Angel. A Film.* An Authorized Translation of the German Continuity. New York: Simon and Schuster, 1968.

### SECONDARY SOURCES

1. Bibliographies and review essays

GLAUERT, BARBARA. "Carl Zuckmayer 1971–1977. Eine Bibliographie." In *Carl Zuckmayer '78. Ein Jahrbuch*. Frankfurt: S. Fischer, 1978. Pp. 305–83.

JACOBIUS, ARNOLD JOHN. *Carl Zuckmayer. Eine Bibliographie 1917–1971*. Ab 1955 fortgeführt und auf den jüngsten Stand gebracht von Harro Kieser. Frankfurt: S. Fischer, 1971.

MEWS, SIEGFRIED. "Carl Zuckmayer (27 December 1896–18 January 1977)." *German Quarterly* 50 (1977): 298–308.

————. "Die Zuckmayerforschung 1961–1977." In *Carl Zuckmayer '78. Ein Jahrbuch*. Frankfurt: S. Fischer, 1978. Pp. 228–72. Revised and expanded from "Die Zuckmayerforschung der sechziger Jahre," *Modern Language Notes* 87 (1972): 465–93.

VANDENRATH, J. "Der Stand der Zuckmayerforschung. Beitrag zu einer kritischen Bibliographie." *Modern Language Notes* 76 (1961): 829–39.


2. Critical Works in German

*Abschied von Carl Zuckmayer: Ehrung, Dank und Freundschaft*. Edited by Landeshauptstadt Mainz and Landesregierung Rheinland-Pfalz. Mainz: Dr. Hanns Krach, 1977.

ADLING, WILFRIED. "Die Entwicklung des Dramatikers Carl Zuckmayer." *Schriften zur Theaterwissenschaft*. Vol. 1. Edited by Theaterhochschule Leipzig. Berlin: Henschelverlag, 1959, pp. 9–286.

AYCK, THOMAS. *Carl Zuckmayer in Selbstzeugnissen und Bilddokumenten*. Reinbek bei Hamburg: Rowohlt Taschenbuch, 1977.

BÄCKER, PAUL. "Notizen zu *Blomberg*." *Blätter der Carl-Zuckmayer-Gesellschaft* 2, no. 1 (1 June 1976): 8–16.

BAUER, ARNOLD. *Carl Zuckmayer*. Berlin: Colloquium, 1970.

BEHL, C. F. W. "Zuckmayers Hauptmann-Drama." *Deutsche Rundschau* 78 (June 1952): 609–11.

BERMANN FISCHER, GOTTFRIED. *Bedroht—Bewahrt: Der Weg eines Verlegers*. Frankfurt: Fischer Bücherei, 1971.

BIENEK, HORST. "Carl Zuckmayer." In *Werkstattgespräche mit Schriftstellern*. Munich: Hanser, 1962. Pp. 164–78, 224.

*Blätter der Carl-Zuckmayer-Gesellschaft*. Mainz, 1975–.

BRYNHILDSVOLL, KNUT. "Leben und Weltverständnis in der frühen Lyrik Zuckmayers." *Blätter der Carl-Zuckmayer-Gesellschaft* 2, no. 2 (1 November 1976): 45–75.

*Carl Zuckmayer '78. Ein Jahrbuch.* Frankfurt: Fischer, 1978.

ELSNER, RICHARD, ed. *Das deutsche Drama in Geschichte und Gegenwart.* Vol. 3. Berlin: Wolf Heyer, 1931.

ENGELSING-MALEK, INGEBORG. *"Amor Fati" in Zuckmayers Dramen.* Konstanz: Rosgarten, 1960.

*Festschrift für Carl Zuckmayer: Zu seinem 80. Geburtstag am 27. Dezember 1976.* Edited by Landeshauptstadt Mainz and Carl-Zuckmayer-Gesellschaft. Mainz: Dr. Hanns Krach, 1976.

FISCHER, BRUNO. *"Herbert Engelmann:* Ein nachgelassenes Dramenfragment von Gerhart Hauptmann." *Neue Deutsche Literatur* 5, no. 4 (April 1957): 155–58.

FRENZEL, ELISABETH. *Judengestalten auf der deutschen Bühne: Ein notwendiger Querschnitt durch 700 Jahre Rollengeschichte.* Munich: Deutscher Volksverlag, n.d.

*Fülle der Zeit: Carl Zuckmayer und sein Werk.* Frankfurt: S. Fischer, 1956.

GLAUERT, BARBARA, ed. *Carl Zuckmayer: Das Bühnenwerk im Spiegel der Kritik.* Frankfurt: S. Fischer, 1977.

GEIGER, HEINZ. *Widerstand und Mitschuld: Zum deutschen Drama von Brecht bis Weiss.* Düsseldorf: Bertelsmann Universitätsverlag, 1973.

GLADE, HENRY. "Das Begegnungsmotiv in Carl Zuckmayers Dramen." *Blätter der Carl-Zuckmayer-Gesellschaft* 4, no. 4 (1 November 1978): 153–60.

GÖSSMANN, WILHELM, ed. *Heine im Bewusstsein heutiger Autoren.* Düsseldorf: Droste, 1972.

GROTHE, HEINZ. "Zwischen Berlin und Hollywood. Carl Zuckmayer und der Film." *Blätter der Carl-Zuckmayer-Gesellschaft* 3, no. 1 (1 March 1977): 27–29.

H[ABERKAMM], K[LAUS]. "Ulla Winblad." In *Kindlers Literatur Lexikon.* Darmstadt: Wissenschaftliche Buchgesellschaft, 1970–1974. 11: 9710.

HEIN, JÜRGEN. "Zuckmayer. *Der Hauptmann von Köpenick.*" In *Die deutsche Komödie—Vom Mittelalter bis zur Gegenwart,* edited by Walter Hinck. Düsseldorf: August Bagel, 1977. Pp. 269–86, 399–401.

HERDAN-ZUCKMAYER, ALICE. *Die Farm in den grünen Bergen.* Frankfurt: Fischer Bücherei, 1956.

HERMAND, JOST. "Herr Puntila und sein Knecht Matti. Brechts Volksstück." *Brecht Heute—Brecht Today* 1 (1971): 114–36. Reprint. *Die deutsche Komödie—Vom Mittelalter bis zur Gegenwart,* edited by Walter Hinck. Düsseldorf: August Bagel, 1977. Pp. 287–304, 401–4.

HOLLAENDER, FELIX. *Lebendiges Theater.* Berlin: S. Fischer, 1932.

IHERING, HERBERT. *Von Reinhardt bis Brecht: Vier Jahrzehnte Theater und Film.* Vol. 2. Berlin: Aufbau Verlag, 1959.

IMSENG, WERNER. *Carl Zuckmayer in Saas-Fee: Ein Album*. Frankfurt: S. Fischer, 1976.

JACOBIUS, ARNOLD JOHN. *Motive und Dramaturgie im Schauspiel Carl Zuckmayers*. Frankfurt: Athenäum, 1971.

JACOBSOHN, SIEGFRIED. *Jahre der Bühne: Theaterkritische Schriften*. Edited by Walter Karsch. Reinbek bei Hamburg: Rowohlt, 1956.

KANEHL, OSKAR. "Bürgerliche Revolutionshelden." *Die Aktion* 10, nos. 51–52 (12 December 1920): 717.

KELLER, BERNHARD. "Die Auseinandersetzung mit dem Nationalsozialismus im Drama: Vergleichende Analyse von Zuckmayers *Des Teufels General* und Brechts *Arturo Ui*." *Sammlung: Jahrbuch für antifaschistische Literatur und Kunst* 1 (1978): 147–58.

KESTEN, HERMANN, ed. *Deutsche Literatur im Exil: Briefe europäischer Autoren 1933–1949*. Frankfurt: Fischer Taschenbuch Verlag, 1973.

KESTING, MARIANNE. "Carl Zuckmayer—Zwischen Volksstück und Kolportage." *Panorama des zeitgenössischen Theaters*. Rev. and enl. ed. Munich: Piper, 1969. Pp. 278–83.

KILLY, WALTER. "Ein Zeitgenosse, kein Prophet. Eine Würdigung des grossen alten Mannes der deutschen Literatur." *Die Zeit* (Overseas ed.), 31 October 1976, p. 12. Reprint. *Blätter der Carl-Zuckmayer-Gesellschaft*, 4, no. 2 (1 May 1978): 4–9.

K[LEIN], J[OHANNES], "Ulla Winblad." In *Lexikon der Weltliteratur*, edited by Gero von Wilpert. Stuttgart: Kröner, 1963–1968. 2: 1074.

LANGE, RUDOLF. *Carl Zuckmayer*. Velber: Friedrich, 1969.

LERNET-HOLENIA, ALEXANDER. "Die schöne Disharmonie. Anmerkungen zu Carl Zuckmayers *Die Fastnachtsbeichte*." *Forum* 7 (February 1960): 66–67.

MANN, ERIKA. "Eine Ablehnung." *Aufbau* 10, no. 16 (21 April 1944): 7.

———. "Offene Antwort an Carl Zuckmayer." *Aufbau* 10, no. 19 (12 May 1944): 7–8.

MARX, HENRY. "Exiltheater in den USA 1933–1945." In *Schauspielwochen Hamburg 76. Arbeitsmaterialien zur Ausstellung "Deutsche Theaterleute im amerikanischen Exil,"* edited by Jan Hans. Hamburg, n.d. Pp. 1–16.

MAAS, LIESELOTTE. *Handbuch der deutschen Exilpresse 1933–1945*. 2 vols. Munich: Hanser, 1976–1978.

MEWS, SIEGFRIED and ENGLISH, RAYMOND. "Im amerikanischen Dickicht: Brecht und Zuckmayer (*Pankraz erwacht—Im Dickicht der Städte*)." In *Carl Zuckmayer '78. Ein Jahrbuch*. Frankfurt: S. Fischer, 1978. Pp. 181–207.

MEWS, SIEGFRIED. *Carl Zuckmayer: Der Hauptmann von Köpenick*. 2d ed. Frankfurt: Diesterweg, 1978.

———. "*Somewhere in France*: Ein antifaschistisches Exildrama von Carl

Zuckmayer und Fritz Kortner." In *Deutsche Exilliteratur—Literatur im Dritten Reich. Akten des II. Exilliteratur-Symposiums der University of South Carolina 1977*, edited by Wolfgang Elfe, James Hardin, and Günther Holst. In *Jahrbuch für internationale Germanistik.* Ser. A, vol. 6. Berne: Peter Lang, 1979. Pp. 122–31.

———. "Die unpolitischen Exildramen Carl Zuckmayers." In *Deutsches Exildrama und Exiltheater. Akten des Exilliteratur-Symposiums der University of South Carolina 1976*, edited by Wolfgang Elfe, James Hardin, and Günther Holst. In *Jahrbuch für internationale Germanistik.* Ser. A, vol. 3. Berne: Peter Lang, 1977. Pp. 139–48.

———. "Von Karl May zu Karl Marx: Zuckmayers Bonanza-Millionär Tabor." In *Die USA und Deutschland. Wechselseitige Spiegelungen in der Literatur der Gegenwart*, edited by Wolfgang Paulsen. Berne: Francke, 1976, pp. 84–91.

———. *Carl Zuckmayer. Des Teufels General.* 2d, enl. ed. Frankfurt: Diesterweg, 1979.

PAULSEN, WOLFGANG. "Carl Zuckmayer." In *Deutsche Literatur im 20. Jahrhundert: Strukturen und Gestalten.* 5th rev. ed. Edited by Otto Mann and Wolfgang Rothe. Berne: Francke, 1967. 2: 332–61, 441–42.

REINDL, LUDWIG EMANUEL. *Zuckmayer: Eine Bildbiographie.* Munich: Kindler, 1962.

RIEGEL, PAUL. "Carl Zuckmayer. *Der Hauptmann von Köpenick.*" In *Das europäische Drama von Ibsen bis Zuckmayer*, edited by Ludwig Büttner. Frankfurt: Diesterweg, 1960. Pp. 195–208.

RIEWOLDT, OTTO F. *Von Zuckmayer bis Kroetz: Die Rezeption westdeutscher Theaterstücke durch Kritik und Wissenschaft in der DDR.* Berlin: Erich Schmidt, 1977.

RILLA, PAUL. "Zuckmayer und die Uniform." In *Literatur, Kritik und Polemik.* Berlin: Henschel, 1950. Pp. 7–27. Reprint. *Vom bürgerlichen zum sozialistischen Realismus.* Leipzig: Reclam, 1967. Pp. 83–102. Reprint. "Carl Zuckmayer. *Des Teufels General.*" In *Das deutsche Drama vom Expressionismus bis zur Gegenwart*, edited by Manfred Brauneck. Bamberg: Buchner, 1970. Pp. 99–107.

RINSER, LUISE. "Porträtskizze." In *Fülle der Zeit: Carl Zuckmayer und sein Werk.* Frankfurt: S. Fischer, 1956. Pp. 13–30.

RISCHBIETER, HENNING, and WENDT, ERNST. *Deutsche Dramatik in West und Ost.* Velber: Friedrich, 1965.

ROTERMUND, ERWIN. "Zur Erneuerung des Volksstücks in der Weimarer Republik: Zuckmayer und Horváth." In *Volkskultur und Geschichte. Festgabe für Josef Dünninger zum 65. Geburtstag*, edited by Dieter Harmening et al. Berlin: Erich Schmidt, 1970. Pp. 612–30. Reprint. *Über Ödön von Horváth*, edited by Dieter Hildebrandt and Traugott Krischke. Frankfurt: Suhrkamp, 1972. Pp. 18–45.

————. "Zur Vergangenheitsbewältigung im deutschen Nachkriegsdrama: Zuckmayer, Borchert, Frisch." *Blätter der Carl-Zuckmayer-Gesellschaft* 2, no. 2 (1 November 1976): 76–85.

RÜHLE, GÜNTHER. "Carl Zuckmayers versöhnende Weisheit." *Frankfurter Allgemeine Zeitung*, 20 January 1977.

————, ed. *Theater für die Republik 1917–1933 im Spiegel der Kritik*. Frankfurt: S. Fischer, 1967.

————. *Zeit und Theater*. Vol. 2. *Von der Republik zur Diktatur 1925–1933*. Berlin: Propyläen, n.d.

SCHEIBLE, HARTMUT, ed. *Carl Zuckmayer: Der Hauptmann von Köpenick*. Erläuterungen und Dokumente. Stuttgart: Reclam, 1977.

"Der Schelm von Bergen. In *Kindlers Literatur Lexikon*. Darmstadt: Wissenschaftliche Buchgesellschaft, 1970–1974. 9: 8686.

SUDHOF, SIEGFRIED. "Carl Zuckmayer." *Deutsche Dichter der Gegenwart: Ihr Leben und Werk*, edited by Benno von Wiese. Berlin: Erich Schmidt, 1973. Pp. 64–82.

TAUBE, DIETRICH. "Konzeptionelle Überlegungen zur Inszenierung von Carl Zuckmayers *Des Teufels General*." *Blätter der Carl-Zuckmayer-Gesellschaft* 4, no. 4 (1 November 1978): 129–32.

TORBERG, FRIEDRICH. *Das fünfte Rad am Thespiskarren: Theaterkritiken*. Munich: Langen Müller, 1966.

VANDENRATH, J. "Drama und Theater in Zuckmayers Bühnendichtung." Ph.D. dissertation, Liège, 1960.

————. "Carl Zuckmayers expressionistischer Erstling *Kreuzweg*." *Revue des Langues Vivantes* 23 (1957): 37–59.

————. "Zuckmayers Bearbeitung von Gerhart Hauptmanns *Herbert Engelmann*." *Revue des Langes Vivantes* 27 (1961): 216–31.

WÄCHTER, HANS-CHRISTOF. *Theater im Exil: Sozialgeschichte des deutschen Exiltheaters 1933–1945*. Munich: Hanser, 1973.

WALTER, HANS-ALBERT. *Deutsche Exilliteratur 1933–1950*. Vol. 1. 2d ed. Darmstadt: Luchterhand, 1973.

WEHDEKING, VOLKER. "Mythologisches Ungewitter: Carl Zuckmayers problematisches Exildrama *Des Teufels General*." In *Die deutsche Exilliteratur 1933–1945*, edited by Manfred Durzak. Stuttgart: Reclam, 1973. Pp. 509–17.

WOLFF, KURT. *Briefwechsel eines Verlegers*. Edited by Bernhard Zeller and Ellen Otten. Frankfurt: Scheffler, 1966.

"Zuckmayer. Der fröhliche Wanderer." *Der Spiegel*, 7 September 1955, pp. 38–46.

3. Critical Works in English

BALINKIN, AUSMA. *The Central Women Figures in Carl Zuckmayer's Dramas*. Berne: Peter Lang, 1978.

BARLOW, DERRICK. Introduction to *Die Fastnachtsbeichte*, by Carl Zuckmayer. Oxford: Blackwell, 1966.

————. Introduction to *Three Stories*, by Carl Zuckmayer. London: Oxford University Press, 1963.

BARRICK, RAYMOND E. "A Characterization of the Mystical Philosophy of Carl Zuckmayer as Revealed in His Life and Works." Ph.D. dissertation, Tulane University, 1964. *Dissertation Abstracts* 25, no. 10 (1965): 5924–25.

BAUER, ARNOLD. *Carl Zuckmayer*. Translated by Edith Simmons. New York: Frederick Ungar, 1976.

COWEN, ROY C. "Type-Casting in Carl Zuckmayer's *The Devil's General.*" *University of Dayton Review* 13 (1976): 81–94.

GLADE, HENRY. "Carl Zuckmayer's *The Devil's General* as Autobiography." *Modern Drama* 9 (1966–1967): 54–61.

————. "Carl Zuckmayer's Theory of Aesthetics." *Monatshefte* 52 (1960): 163–70.

————. "*Der Gesang im Feuerofen:* Quintessential Zuckmayer." In *Views and Reviews of Modern German Literature. Festschrift for Adolf D. Klarmann*, edited by Karl S. Weimar. Munich: Delp, 1974. Pp. 163–70.

————. "The Motif of Encounter in Zuckmayer's Dramas." *Kentucky Foreign Language Quarterly* 10, no. 4 (1963): 183–90.

KOESTER, RUDOLF. "The Ascent of the Criminal in German Comedy." *German Quarterly* 63 (1970): 376–93.

KVAM, WAYNE. "Zuckmayer, Hilpert, and Hemingway." *PMLA* 91 (1976): 194–205.

LANGNER, LAWRENCE. "A Theatre Guild Director Writes of the Influx of Foreign Authors." *New York Times*, 4 May 1941, sec. 9, p. 1.

LORAM, IAN C. "Carl Zuckmayer—German Playwright in America." *Educational Theatre Journal* 9 (1957): 177–83.

————. "Carl Zuckmayer: An Introduction." *German Quarterly* 21 (1954): 137–49.

————. "*Ulla Winblad:* Words and Music by Zuckmayer and Bellman." *Monatshefte* 47 (1955): 11–18.

MADDOX, MARVIN R. "Carl Zuckmayer's Relation to Gerhart Hauptmann: 'Meisterschaft, Vorbild, Verpflichtung.' " Ph.D. dissertation, University of North Carolina, 1975. *Dissertation Abstracts* 37, no. 3 (1976): 1577A–78A.

MEWS, SIEGFRIED. "From Karl May to Horace A. W. Tabor: Carl Zuckmayer's View of America." *Mosaic* 6, no. 2 (1973): 125–42. Reprint. *Deutschlands literarisches Amerikabild. Neuere Forschungen zur Amerikarezeption der deutschen Literatur*, edited by Alexander Ritter. Hildesheim: Olms, 1977. Pp. 476–94.

MEWS, SIEGFRIED and ENGLISH, RAYMOND. "The Jungle Transcended: Brecht and Zuckmayer." In *Essays on Brecht: Theater and Politics*, edited by Siegfried Mews and Herbert Knust. Chapel Hill: University of North Carolina Press, 1974. Pp. 79–98. Reprint. New York, AMS Press, 1979.

MULLER, SIEGFRIED H. "Another Note on *Herbert Engelmann*." *Monatshefte* 54 (1962): 291–96.

PEPPARD, MURRAY B. "Carl Zuckmayer: Cold Light in a Divided World." *Monatshefte* 49 (1957): 121–29.

———. "Moment of Moral Decision: Carl Zuckmayer's Latest Plays." *Monatshefte* 44 (1952): 349–56.

ROOKE, SHEILA. "Carl Zuckmayer." In *German Men of Letters*, edited by Alex Natan. Vol. 3. London: Oswald Wolff, 1964. Pp. 209–33.

SPAHR, BLAKE LEE. "A Note on *Herbert Engelmann*." *Monatshefte* 46 (1954): 339–45.

SPEIDEL, E. "The Stage as Metaphysical Institution: Zuckmayer's Dramas *Schinderhannes* and *Der Hauptmann von Köpenick*." *Modern Language Review* 63 (1968): 425–36.

STEINER, PAULINE, and FRENZ, HORST. "Anderson's and Stalling's [*sic*] *What Price Glory?* and Carl Zuckmayer's *Rivalen*." *German Quarterly* 20 (1947): 239–51.

SWEDIUK-CHEYNE, HELEN. Introduction to *Die Uhr schlägt eins: Ein historisches Drama aus der Gegenwart*, by Carl Zuckmayer. Berne: Lang, 1977.

WADSWORTH, BEAUMONT F. "The Young Writers of Germany." *Bookman* 75 (June–July 1932): 260–68.

WEIMAR, KARL S. "The Scientist and Society. A Study of Three Modern Plays." *Modern Language Quarterly* 27 (1966): 431–38.

WEISSTEIN, ULRICH. "*Professor Unrat, Small Town Tyrant*, and *The Blue Angel*: Translations, Versions, and Adaptations of Heinrich Mann's Novel in Two Media." *Film Journal* 1, nos. 3–4 (1972): 53–61. Reprint. *Actes du VIᵉ Congrès de l' Association Internationale de Littérature Comparée*, edited by Michel Cadot et al. Stuttgart: Bieber, 1975. Pp. 251–57.

———. "The Reception of Twentieth Century German Literature in the United States." In *Comparative Literature: Proceedings of the Second Congress of the ICLA*, edited by Werner P. Friederich. chapel Hill: University of North Carolina Press, 1959. Pp. 458–57.

# Index